BEGINNING OPENGL® GAME PROGRAMMING, SECOND EDITION

LUKE BENSTEAD

WITH

DAVE ASTLE AND KEVIN HAWKINS

Course Technology PTR

A part of Cengage Learning

COURSE TECHNOLOGY
CENGAGE Learning™

Australia • Brazil • Japan • Korea • Mexico • Singapore • Spain • United Kingdom • United States

COURSE TECHNOLOGY
CENGAGE Learning

Beginning OpenGL® Game Programming, Second Edition
Luke Benstead
with Dave Astle and Kevin Hawkins

Publisher and General Manager, Course Technology PTR: Stacy L. Hiquet

Associate Director of Marketing: Sarah Panella

Manager of Editorial Services: Heather Talbot

Marketing Manager: Jordan Casey

Acquisitions Editor: Heather Hurley

Project Editor: Jenny Davidson

Technical Reviewer: Carsten Haubold

PTR Editorial Services Coordinator: Jen Blaney

Interior Layout Tech: Macmillan Publishing Solutions

Cover Designer: Mike Tanamachi

CD-ROM Producer: Brandon Penticuff

Indexer: Kelly Henthorne

Proofreader: Sara Gullion

For product information and technology assistance, contact us at **Cengage Learning Customer & Sales Support, 1-800-354-9706**

For permission to use material from this text or product, submit all requests online at **www.cengage.com/permissions**
Further permissions questions can be emailed to **permissionrequest@cengage.com**

OpenGL is a registered trademark of SGI.

GLee © 2009 Ben Woodhouse, ben@elf-stone.com, with parts copyright by SGI.

Code::Blocks – the open source, cross platform IDE, Copyright © 2002-2009, Yiannis Mandravelos and The Code::Blocks Team.

FreeType Copyright 1996-2002, 2006-2009 by David Turner, Robert Wilhelm, and Werner Lemberg

SDL – Simple DirectMedia Layer Copyright © 1997-2009 Sam Lantinga

All other trademarks are the property of their respective owners.

Library of Congress Control Number: 2008929236

ISBN-13: 978-1-59863-528-7

ISBN-10: 1-59863-528-X

Course Technology, a part of Cengage Learning
20 Channel Center Street
Boston, MA 02210
USA

Cengage Learning is a leading provider of customized learning solutions with office locations around the globe, including Singapore, the United Kingdom, Australia, Mexico, Brazil, and Japan. Locate your local office at: **international.cengage.com/region**

Cengage Learning products are represented in Canada by Nelson Education, Ltd.

For your lifelong learning solutions, visit **courseptr.com**

Visit our corporate website at **cengage.com**

Printed in the United States of America
1 2 3 4 5 6 7 11 10 09

For Alison.

ACKNOWLEDGMENTS

First, I'd like to thank my girlfriend Alison, who supported me while I was writing this book and provided me with endless cups of tea throughout. I promise I'll spend less time on the computer now. . . for a little while anyway.

I would also like to thank Carsten Haubold for being an excellent technical editor, and especially for his help with the sample applications; without him, they would not look as good, be as stable, or be so numerous. It's been great working with you, Carsten. Thanks also to Jenny, Heather, and Brandon, and everyone who has been involved in producing this book; you're all great!

Jeff Molofee deserves a special mention. If he didn't start the NeHe website I would never have become interested in OpenGL and programming in general.

I'd like to thank my family: Gayna and Nigel, Stephen and Terry, Josh, Lee, Abigail, and George and the many others I don't have room to mention! And lastly, I'd like to thank my friends: Sean, Jayne, Rob, Hayley, and Natalie and Wayne. Thanks for the much deserved distractions.

About the Authors

Luke Benstead is a co-maintainer of http://nehe.gamedev.net/ and has been programming in OpenGL and C++ for 7 years. He is currently a software developer in London, England. He has a bachelor's degree in Multimedia Programming from the University of Portsmouth.

Kevin Hawkins received a bachelor's degree in Computer Science and master's degree in Software Engineering from Embry-Riddle University. He is currently the Technical Director of Software Engineering at Raydon Corporation. Along with Dave, Kevin is co-founder of GameDev.net and co-author of the first edition of *Beginning OpenGL Game Programming* and *More OpenGL Game Programming*.

Dave Astle has been involved in the world of game development for over a decade. Currently, he's a staff engineer and technology evangelist in the Advanced Content Group at QUALCOMM, Inc. He cofounded GameDev.net, where he currently serves as CEO and Executive Director. He co-authored the first edition of *Beginning OpenGL Game Programming*, *OpenGL Game Programming*, *More OpenGL Game Programming*, and *OpenGL ES Game Development*, contributed to several other game development books, and speaks regularly at industry conferences, including the Game Developers Conference. He has a bachelor's degree in Computer Science from the University of Utah.

CONTENTS

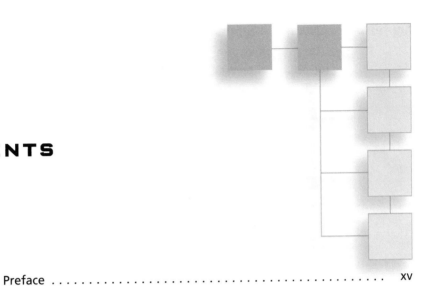

PREFACE

The book you are reading has quite a history to it. In 2001 Dave Astle and Kevin Hawkins, cofounders of GameDev.net, wrote *OpenGL Game Programming*—an excellent book covering OpenGL 1.2 and spanning no fewer than 780 pages. It covered a whole range of topics from curved surfaces to game physics and from simulating shadows to providing sound using the DirectX API. It was the first OpenGL book I purchased, and my copy has been thumbed through so many times the cover is being held together with sticky tape! At the time, it was *the* book to buy if you wanted to learn OpenGL.

By 2004, OpenGL 1.5 had been released and the rapidly advancing graphics industry had moved on. Kevin and Dave joined forces once again to not only bring the book up to date, but also to extend it to cover new, more advanced features. The decision was made to create two volumes. The first took a revised core of the book (with some material removed) to create the first edition of *Beginning OpenGL Game Programming*, while the more advanced topics became a second volume: *More OpenGL Game Programming*.

In late 2007, I was approached to update *Beginning OpenGL Game Programming* for this, its second edition. At the time, OpenGL 2.1 was the most recent release, but an upcoming OpenGL 3.0 had been announced. The original changes proposed for OpenGL 3.0 would quickly make any book on OpenGL 2.1 out of date, so the decision was made to wait. OpenGL 3.0 was eventually released in August 2008 and production of the book started soon after.

I hope you enjoy this second edition of *Beginning OpenGL Game Programming*; let the learning begin!

—Luke Benstead

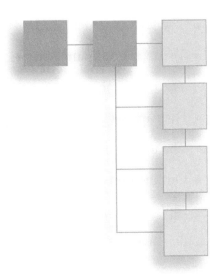

INTRODUCTION

Changes from the First Edition

Generally, the idea of this edition is to teach the future-proof, *fast path,* of rendering. The traditional methods of rendering with OpenGL that you may be familiar with, such as immediate mode, vertex arrays, and display lists are marked for removal (deprecated) from a future version of OpenGL. These methods are still briefly covered in this edition, but only as a stepping-stone to get you started before moving on to the faster, slightly more complex method of rendering with vertex buffer objects and the OpenGL Shading Language (GLSL).

The major change from the first edition is probably the inclusion of GLSL, which wasn't featured at all in the first edition. Shading languages are now commonplace and rendering without them (using the fixed-function pipeline) is now deprecated in the OpenGL 3.0 specification. This does (unfortunately) make the learning curve a lot steeper than it used to be, but, it is generally a good idea to learn the best practice from the outset.

The following items no longer feature (or only feature briefly) in this edition because they have been marked as deprecated:

- Stipple patterns

- Quads and polygons

- Secondary color

- Resident textures and texture priority

- The texture matrix stack

- Texture coordinate generation

- Texture combiners

- Display lists

- The accumulation buffer

- Outline fonts and bitmap fonts using "wgl"

- Alpha testing

- OpenGL fog

The following new subjects are covered in this edition:

- The OpenGL Shading Language (GLSL 1.30)

- The deprecation model

- MD2 model loading and animation

- Point sprites

- Fonts using FreeType

- OpenGL 3.0 context creation

- Vertex buffer objects

- Alpha testing with GLSL

- Fog with GLSL

Who Should Read This Book?

This book is intended for programmers who are just getting started in 3D graphics programming or are migrating from another 3D API (such as Direct3D). You should have some experience programming in C++ and at least a basic understanding of 3D graphics and mathematics. By the end of the book, you should be able to apply your newfound knowledge of OpenGL to create your own games.

What Will and Won't Be Covered?

The focus of this book is to get you started programming 3D graphics using OpenGL. To keep the book concise, some assumptions of basic knowledge have to be made.

The first assumption is you know how to program C++ on your platform of choice. C++ is a massive language that takes years to master; you aren't expected to be a guru, but you should have a basic knowledge of the following:

- Compiling programs and linking to external libraries

- Classes, inheritance, and virtual functions

- Arrays and pointers

- The standard template library containers (vector, list, etc.)

There is a list of excellent C++ references in Appendix B, "Further Reading." Even if you do have a good knowledge of C++, they are worth a look anyway!

The second assumption is that you have some understanding of 3D math. 3D mathematics is only covered in this book in relation to OpenGL, and then only very briefly. Not so long ago you could use OpenGL for quite a while before needing any solid 3D math skills. However, with the move to shader-based rendering, at least a basic understanding of matrices is required straight out of the gate.

Finally, this book will only cover game development topics directly related to graphics. Subjects like game architecture, physics, AI, and audio are required in most games, but they are such big topics that they all deserve a book of their own!

About the Target Platform

The key advantage to OpenGL over other graphics APIs is that it works on many, many platforms. Although the OpenGL API works on all platforms, the source code needed to create an OpenGL-capable window and handle input and system events is very much platform specific. It would be an unrealistic goal to plan to write code for every platform. For this reason, a decision was made to primarily target the most commonly used operating system, Microsoft Windows. But, to show how easy it is to port OpenGL code to another OS, on the CD there are also versions of all the examples written for GNU/Linux. The Linux versions of the source were written, tested, and compiled under Ubuntu 8.10. The Windows versions of the source code were tested under Windows Vista and Windows XP.

For users of Linux and other alternative operating systems (such as OSX), you will be glad to hear that the majority of the book applies to all platforms; the exception to this rule is Chapter 2, "Creating a Simple OpenGL Application," which targets the Microsoft Windows platform.

OpenGL 2.1 and OpenGL 3.0

This book primarily targets OpenGL 3.0, as it is the most recent release of OpenGL. OpenGL 3.0 differs from previous versions in that it sets a minimum level of support from the graphics card to create a context. For this reason, the text assumes both OpenGL 3.0-capable hardware *and* OpenGL 3.0-capable graphics drivers.

OpenGL 3.0 is still a very new release, and at the time of this writing, not all graphics vendors have released full, OpenGL 3.0-capable drivers. Obviously, it would be a shame if many people could not use the book's source code because they were waiting for their graphics vendors to release new drivers. So, on the CD there are two versions of the code for each platform; one version is designed for OpenGL 3.0 (and its corresponding shading language GLSL 1.30) and the other version is designed for OpenGL 2.1 (and GLSL 1.20).

The differences between these two versions of the code are minimal:

- **Chapters 1-4**—The source code is the same for both versions except for the OpenGL context creation that falls back to an OpenGL 2.1 context in the 2.1 version.

- **Chapter 5**—The code is the same except for the *manual extensions* example, which uses glGetString() under 2.1 rather than glGetStringi(), which is only supported under OpenGL 3.0.

- **Chapters 6-12**—The C++ source code is the same, but the GLSL shaders differ.

- **Chapter 13**—The only source code for this chapter is the final game. There is only one version of the game that falls back to OpenGL 2.1 and GLSL 1.20 if OpenGL 3.0 is unsupported.

Of course, this still assumes graphics driver support for OpenGL 2.1. If you have trouble running any of the samples, upgrading your graphics drivers will likely solve the problem.

Using This Book

The CD

The CD contains the source code for all of the sample applications that accompany the book. You'll want to have access to these source files to use in conjunction with the text.

Extensions

Extensions are discussed in detail in Chapter 5, "OpenGL Extensions." Extensions are required to access all features above OpenGL 1.1 on the Windows platform. Rather than listing all of the required extensions, driver support for at least OpenGL 2.1 core functionality is assumed.

Language and Tools

To compile the examples on the CD, you are first going to need to acquire a C++ IDE/compiler. The Windows version of the source code is compiled using the free to use Visual C++ 2008 Express Edition, whereas the GNU/Linux version of the code is compiled using Code::Blocks and the GNU G++ Compiler.

The CD includes the Code::Blocks IDE for the Windows, Linux, and Mac OSX platforms, which should get you started. If you are using Code::Blocks on the Windows platform, a Visual C++ Project import function will convert the Visual C++ project to Code::Blocks.

Headers and Libraries

When compiling OpenGL applications, several libraries need to be linked and header files included. The header files are conventionally stored in an include directory called GL. The following header files may be included in a project depending on the platform and features required:

- **gl.h** This is the primary header file that defines most of the OpenGL functions.

- **glu.h** The header for the OpenGL Utility library.

- **glext.h** The OpenGL extensions header file. This header file is regularly updated and available on opengl.org. It includes constants and definitions for the most recent OpenGL extensions.

- **wglext.h** The Windows extensions header file. The same as glext.h but for Windows-only extensions.

- **glxext.h** The GLX extensions header file; contains constants for GLX extensions.

All OpenGL applications must link to at least `opengl32.lib` on Windows, or `libGL.a` on Linux. If the application makes use of the OpenGL Utility library, then `glu32.lib` (on Windows) or `libGLU.a` (on Linux) must also be linked.

C++ Usage

Throughout the source code, we have made use of a limited subset of the Standard Template Library. Using the STL containers and algorithms is good practice. Their usage makes the code more concise, safer, simpler, and normally faster. If you do not have any knowledge of the STL, look through the C++ resources in Appendix B. In the source code, the following STL members have been used:

- `std::vector`—A dynamically resizable array. The vector manages its own memory and stores its elements consecutively in memory in the same way as a C-style array. For this reason, vectors can be passed into C functions (e.g., OpenGL) by passing a pointer to the first element (e.g., `&myArray[0]`).

- `std::string`—A string class. `string` replaces the use of character arrays pretty much completely. The `string` class has many useful built-in methods. Strings can be passed to C functions by using the `c_str()` method, which returns a `const char*`.

- `std::ifstream`—A file input stream. `ifstream` is used in the book to read data from files. It is used to load shaders from text files, textures from TGA images, and models from MD2 files. `ifstream` replaces the C `FILE` and its associated functions.

- `std::map`—An associative container. A `map` stores an ordered set of key-value pairs.

- **std::list**—A container that behaves like a doubly linked list. This container is only used in the final game to store a list of entities.

All of these classes are explained in detail in any C++ reference book, and in the references listed in Appendix B.

Support Website

The website that accompanies the book can be found at http://glbook.gamedev. net/. Here we will post program updates and errata as needed. Please check this site if you experience any problems.

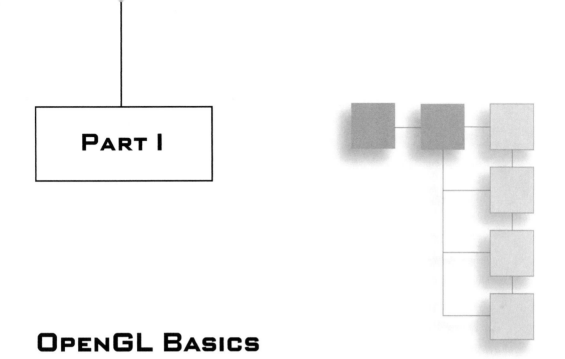

PART I

OpenGL Basics

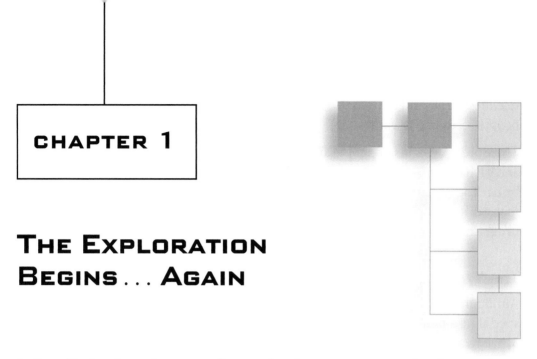

CHAPTER 1

THE EXPLORATION BEGINS... AGAIN

Before digging into the meat of game development, you need to have a foundational understanding of the medium in which you'll be working. You'll be using the OpenGL API for graphics, so we'll look at OpenGL's origins, design, and evolution. We'll also provide an overview of the game industry, as well as a look at the core elements involved in a game.

In this chapter, you will learn:

- What a game is

- About OpenGL and its history

- About the future of OpenGL

- About libraries that can be used to expand OpenGL's functionality

Why Make Games?

Interactive entertainment has grown by leaps and bounds in the last decade. Computer games, which used to be a niche market, have now grown in to a multibillion-dollar industry. Recent years have shown a trend of accelerating growth, and the end is not in sight. The interactive entertainment industry is an explosive market that pushes the latest computer technologies to the edge and helps drive research in areas such as graphics and artificial intelligence. It is this relentless drive and growth that attracts many people to this industry, but why do people really make games?

There are thousands of people around the world who are learning to write games, and each one of them is being driven by one thing alone: fun. Game development brings together many different skills, which is the reason it is so appealing to so many different people. Artists and musicians can apply their creative talents and programmers can use their problem-solving skills!

The World of 3D Games

Although many companies have contributed to the growth of 3D gaming, a special nod must be given to id Software, which was a major catalyst in the rise of 3D games. More than 15 years ago, John Carmack and company unleashed a little game called *Wolfenstein 3D* upon the world. *Wolf3D* brought the gaming world to its knees with realtime ray-casting 3D graphics and an immersive world that left gamers sitting at their computers for hours upon hours. The game was a new beginning for the industry, and it never looked back. In 1993, the world of *Doom* went on a rampage and pushed 3D graphics technology past yet another limit with its 2.5D engine. The gaming world reveled in the technical achievement brought by id in their game *Doom*, but it did not stop there. Several years later, *Quake* changed 3D gaming for good. No longer were enemies "fake 3D," but rather full 3D entities that could move around in a fully polygonal 3D. The possibilities were now limited only by how many polygons the CPU (and eventually, the GPU) could process and display on the screen. *Quake* also brought multiplayer gaming over a network to reality as hordes of Internet users joined in the fun of death matches with 30 other people.

Since the release of *Quake*, the industry has been blessed by new technological advancements nearly every few months. The 3D gaming sector has brought on 3D accelerator hardware that performs the 3D math right in silicon. Now, new hardware is released every six months that seems to double its predecessor in raw power, speed, and flexibility. With all these advancements, there could not be a more exciting time than now for 3D game development.

The Elements of a Game

You may now be asking, "How is a game made?" Before we can answer this question, you must understand that games are, at their lowest level, software. Today's software is developed in teams, where each member of a team works on his or her specialty until everyone's work is integrated to create a single, coherent work of art. Games are developed in much the same way, except programming is not the only area of expertise. Artists are required to generate the images and beautiful scenery that is prevalent in so many of today's games. Level designers bring the virtual world to life and use the art provided to them by the artists to create worlds beyond belief.

Programmers piece together each element and make sure everything works as a whole. Sound techs and musicians create the audio necessary to provide the gamer with a rich, multimedia, believable, and virtual experience. Designers come up with the game concept, and producers coordinate everyone's efforts.

With each person working on different areas of expertise, the game must be divided into various elements that will be pieced together in the end. In general, games are divided into these areas:

- Graphics

- Input

- Music and sound

- Game logic and artificial intelligence

- Networking

- User interface and menuing system

Each of these areas can be further divided into more specific systems. For example, game logic would consist of physics and particle systems, while graphics might have a 2D and/or 3D renderer. Figure 1.1 shows an example of a simplistic game architecture.

As you can see, each element of a game is divided into its own separate piece and communicates with other elements of the game. The game logic element tends to be the hub of the game, where decisions are made for processing input and sending output. The architecture shown in Figure 1.1 is very simplistic, however; Figure 1.2 shows what a more advanced game's architecture might look like.

As you can see in Figure 1.2, a more complex game requires a more complex architectural design. More detailed components are developed and used to implement specific features or functionality that the game software needs to operate smoothly. One thing to keep in mind is that games feature some of the

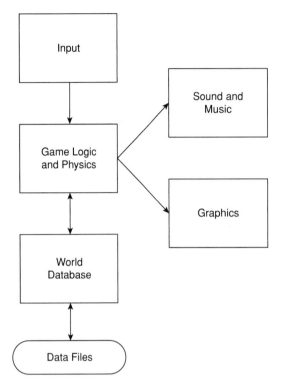

Figure 1.1
A game is composed of various subsystems.

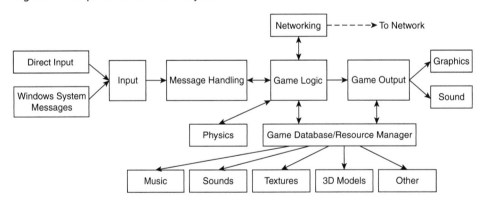

Figure 1.2
A more advanced game architectural design.

most complex blends of technology and software designs, and as such, game development requires abstract thinking and implementation on a higher level than traditional software development. When you are developing a game, you are developing a work of art, and it needs to be treated as such. Be ready to try new things on your own and redesign existing technologies to suit your needs. There is no set way to develop games, much as there is no set way to paint a painting. Strive to be innovative and set new standards!

What Is OpenGL?

OpenGL is a low-level API (Application Programming Interface), which allows you the programmer, an interface to graphics hardware. OpenGL doesn't provide higher-level functionality such as math functions or an interface to any other hardware. OpenGL only deals with graphics.

The key advantage that OpenGL has over other graphics APIs is that it runs on many different platforms. OpenGL can run on Windows, Linux, Mac OSX, and portable devices such as the open Pandora project. Its cut down sibling OpenGL ES runs on many portable devices.

OpenGL is used in many kinds of applications, from CAD programs to games such as *Doom 3*, and from scientific simulations to 3D modeling applications.

Tip

OpenGL stands for "Open Graphics Library." "Open" is used because OpenGL is an open standard, meaning that many companies are able to contribute to the development. It does not mean that OpenGL is open source.

OpenGL History

OpenGL was originally developed by Silicon Graphics, Inc. (SGI) as a multipurpose, platform-independent graphics API. From 1992, the development of OpenGL was overseen by the OpenGL Architecture Review Board (ARB), which was made up of major graphics vendors and other industry leaders, consisting of 3DLabs, ATI, Dell, Evans & Sutherland, Hewlett-Packard, IBM, Intel, Matrox, NVIDIA, SGI, Sun Microsystems, Silicon Graphics, and until 2003, Microsoft. The role of the ARB was to establish and maintain the OpenGL specification, which dictates which features must be included when one is developing an OpenGL distribution.

In 2006, control of the OpenGL specification was passed on to the Khronos group. The Khronos group maintains open media standards and is also made up of most of the same members of the original ARB. This meant the move to the new group went very smoothly. The OpenGL working group at Khronos is still known as the ARB for historical reasons. Khronos has continued to develop the

OpenGL specification, releasing OpenGL 3.0 in late 2008, and pledging the prompt release of OpenGL 3.1.

The designers of OpenGL knew that hardware vendors would want to add features that may not be exposed by core OpenGL interfaces. To address this, they included a method for extending OpenGL. These extensions are sometimes adopted by other hardware vendors, and if support for an extension becomes wide enough—or the extension is deemed important enough by the ARB—the extension may be promoted to the core OpenGL specification. Almost all of the most recent additions to OpenGL started out as extensions—many of them directly pertaining to video games. Extensions are covered in detail in Chapter 5, "OpenGL Extensions."

OpenGL Architecture

The original architecture of OpenGL was based on an internal state machine. The programmer would use an OpenGL function to change a particular state and OpenGL would render using this state until it was changed again. For example, if you wanted to draw in red, you would set the color state to red, draw some objects, and then perhaps change it to white. In fixed-function OpenGL these states could affect lighting, colors, culling, etc.

In OpenGL 3.0, we began to see a move to a less state-oriented API. State functions for color, normals, lighting, and others have been deprecated because they don't make sense in a programmable pipeline. When using shaders, it is up to the programmer to not only pass in the correct information (for example the color of the vertex) but also apply this information to the vertex in the shader.

Fixed-Function vs. Programmability

When OpenGL was first invented, available computer processing power was obviously far less than it is today. A PC would normally have a single processor (CPU), which performed all system and graphics processing. The fixed-function pipeline was designed to make the most of the hardware by using a single path of rendering. In the late '90s, 3D graphics cards started appearing on the market. These cards contained dedicated graphics processors that would perform rendering separately from the main CPU. PCs suddenly had the power to render far more complicated scenes in realtime. It soon became apparent to graphics vendors that being able to run custom compiled programs on the graphics processor (GPU) would provide programmers far more control, flexibility, and power than using the standard fixed function model.

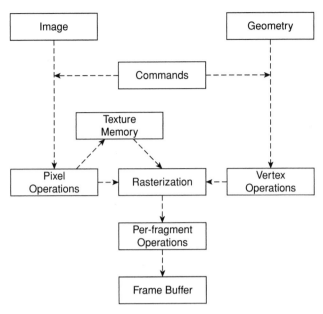

Figure 1.3
The OpenGL rendering pipeline.

Over the last few years, the use of these GPU shader programs has taken over as the preferred method of rendering. In the programmable pipeline, shaders take over different parts of the rendering process. At the time of writing, you can provide three kinds of shaders in OpenGL. *Vertex shaders*, which operate on every vertex sent to the pipeline, *Fragment shaders*, which operate on every pixel that is rendered to the screen after culling, and most recently, *Geometry shaders*, which actually allow the programmer to generate vertices on the graphics card. Currently Geometry shaders are not part of the OpenGL core but are provided as vendor-specific extensions. This will likely change in the next OpenGL release with Geometry shaders being moved into the core API. Vertex and Fragment shaders are already part of the core of OpenGL.

The Deprecation Model

In 2007, the Khronos group announced that the OpenGL API would undergo a major cleanup. This was originally to be done in two stages. The first, codenamed "Longs Peak," aimed to trim down the API, breaking backwards-compatibility for the first time in OpenGL's history and introducing a new object model. A little later, Longs Peak was to be followed by Mt. Evans. This would introduce advanced, modern functionality (including Geometry shaders) into the core of OpenGL.

Unfortunately, things didn't go entirely to plan. After a year of delays, Khronos announced OpenGL 3.0. Although it didn't contain everything that Longs Peak originally promised, it did have one brand new feature that paved the way for a new, clean, slim API: the deprecation model.

The deprecation model was introduced to provide a process for removing parts of the API. The removal of a feature from OpenGL can follow several stages. First, a function or token is marked as deprecated. A deprecated feature should not be used in any new code. Then, in some future version, the deprecated feature will be removed from the core. The removed feature may then be implemented as an extension so that legacy code can continue using the feature with only minor changes. Eventually the feature will no longer be supported.

Each implementation can provide a method for creating a *forward-compatible* context during initialization. Using a deprecated feature in this type of context will result in an INVALID_OPERATION error.

Deprecated Features in This Book

We will not be covering any of the deprecated functionality in this book except where it aids learning. Any deprecated functionality mentioned will be labeled as such. At the time of writing not all OpenGL 3.0 drivers support the forward-compatible context so all source code will use a backwards-compatible context but will not use deprecated features. In Chapter 2, "Creating a Simple OpenGL Application," you will learn how to create a forward-compatible context on the Windows platform.

Related Libraries

There are many libraries available that build upon and around OpenGL to add support and functionality beyond the low-level rendering support that it excels at. We don't have space to cover all of the OpenGL-related libraries, and new ones are cropping up all the time, so we'll limit our coverage here to two of the most important: GLUT and SDL. We'll cover an additional library, GLee, when we discuss extensions a little later.

GLUT

GLUT, short for OpenGL Utility Toolkit, is a set of support libraries available on every major platform. OpenGL does not directly support any form of win-dowing, menus, or input. That's where GLUT comes in. It provides basic functionality in all of those areas, while remaining platform independent, so that you can easily move GLUT-based applications from, for example, Windows to UNIX with few, if any, changes.

GLUT is easy to use and learn, and although it does not provide you with all the functionality the operating system offers, it works quite well for demos and simple applications.

Because your ultimate goal is going to be to create a fairly complex game, you're going to need more flexibility than GLUT offers. For this reason, it is not used in the code in the book. However, if you'd like to know more, visit the official GLUT webpage at http://www.opengl.org/resources/libraries/glut.html.

SDL

The Simple Direct Media Layer (SDL) is a cross-platform multimedia library, including support for audio, input, 2D graphics, and many other things. It also provides direct support for 3D graphics through OpenGL, so it's a popular choice for cross-platform game development. More information on SDL can be found at www.libsdl.org.

A Sneak Peek

Let's jump ahead and take a look at a section of OpenGL code. It won't make much sense now, but in a few chapters you will understand it all. On the CD, open up the project called "Simple," which is stored in the Chapter 1 folder. This example program displays two overlapping polygons.

Caution

In the following example we will be using the now deprecated matrix functions (`glMatrixMode()`, `gluLookAt()`, `glLoadIdentity()`, and `gluPerspective`) as well as the deprecated immediate mode renderings that the code isn't too complicated. In Chapter 6, you will learn how to handle your own matrices instead.

Note that this code uses SDL for the operating system specific stuff. This keeps the code simple so that you can focus on the OpenGL calls. This example uses the original, old-style way of rendering called *immediate mode*. In immediate mode, primitives are formed by sending OpenGL a series of vertices one at a time. Later, we will cover other, more efficient methods of rendering. First, let's take a look at the `initialize()` method, which is called after we have an OpenGL context.

```
bool SimpleApp::initialize()
{
    //Enable depth testing
    glEnable(GL_DEPTH_TEST);
    //Set up the projection matrix
    resize(WINDOW_WIDTH, WINDOW_HEIGHT);
    return true;
}
```

It's not particularly exciting (yet!). The first OpenGL command enables z-buffering, which ensures that objects closer to the viewer get drawn over objects that are farther away. The final line in initialization() calls the resize() method. This method sets up what is known as the *projection matrix*. This is required to make the primitives display correctly and show objects further from the camera appear smaller. The resize() method is automatically called each time the window is resized. Let's take a look at it now:

```
void SimpleApp::resize(int w, int h)
{
    //Prevent a divide by zero error
    if (h <= 0)
    {
        h = 1;
    }

    //When we resize the window, we tell OpenGL about the new viewport size
    glViewport(0, 0, (GLsizei)w, (GLsizei)h);

    glMatrixMode(GL_PROJECTION); //deprecated
    glLoadIdentity();
    //Then we set up our projection matrix with the correct aspect ratio
    gluPerspective(60.0f, float(w) / float(h), 1.0f, 100.0f); //deprecated

    glMatrixMode(GL_MODELVIEW); //deprecated
    glLoadIdentity(); //deprecated
}
```

This sets up the way in which objects in the world are transformed into pixels on the screen.

Finally, let's take a look at code that actually does the rendering in the unsurprisingly named render() method. This method is called every frame to update the screen.

```
glClear(GL_COLOR_BUFFER_BIT | GL_DEPTH_BUFFER_BIT);
glLoadIdentity();

gluLookAt(0.0, 1.0, 6.0, //Position
          0.0, 0.0, 0.0, //Where we are looking
          0.0, 1.0, 0.0); //Up vector
```

These first few lines clear the screen and reset the view. `gluLookAt()` sets up a camera looking down the z-axis towards our polygons.

```
glBegin(GL_TRIANGLES);
    //Send the vertices and colors for the triangle
    glColor4f(1.0f, 0.0f, 0.0f, 1.0f);
    glVertex3f(2.0f, 2.5f, -1.0f);
    glColor4f(0.0f, 1.0f, 0.0f, 1.0f);
    glVertex3f(-3.5f, -2.5f, -1.0f);
    glColor4f(0.0f, 0.0f, 1.0f, 1.0f);
    glVertex3f(2.0f, -4.0f, -1.0f);
glEnd();
```

These lines render a triangle by passing a list of *vertices* (points in 3D space) to OpenGL. The first line tells OpenGL that we are about to render a triangle. Before each vertex declaration, we change the current color.

```
glBegin(GL_TRIANGLE_FAN);
    //Send the vertices and colors for the pentagon
    glColor4f(1.0f, 1.0f, 1.0f, 1.0f);
    glVertex3f(-1.0f, 2.0f, 0.0f);
    glColor4f(1.0f, 1.0f, 0.0f, 1.0f);
    glVertex3f(-3.0f, -0.5f, 0.0f);
    glColor4f(0.0f, 1.0f, 1.0f, 1.0f);
    glVertex3f(-1.5f, -3.0f, 0.0f);
    glColor4f(0.0f, 0.0f, 0.0f, 1.0f);
    glVertex3f(1.0f, -2.0f, 0.0f);
    glColor4f(1.0f, 0.0f, 1.0f, 1.0f);
    glVertex3f(1.0f, 1.0f, 0.0f);
glEnd();
```

Here we do almost exactly the same with the pentagon, except this time, we render a *triangle fan*. A triangle fan is a series of triangles that all share a single vertex. A first triangle is specified using three vertices, and then for every other vertex sent to OpenGL, another triangle is formed by combining it with the previous vertex and the first vertex in the set. If that sounds complicated, don't worry, triangle fans will be explained in detail in the next chapter.

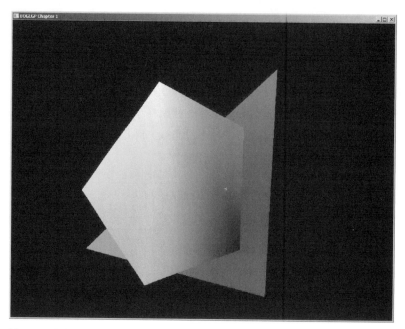

Figure 1.4
A simple OpenGL example.

Summary

In this chapter, you took a first look at OpenGL, which you'll be using throughout the remainder of this book for graphics demos and games. Now that you have an overview of the API you will be using, you can get into the fun part of actual development!

What You Have Learned

- 3D gaming is a rapidly growing and exciting field.

- OpenGL is a graphics library used in many applications.

- OpenGL has been around for over 16 years. Its development is overseen by the Khronos group.

- OpenGL has undergone some radical changes in its most recent release.

- Libraries such as SDL can be used in conjunction with OpenGL for faster development and added functionality.

Review Questions

1. When was OpenGL introduced?

2. What is the most recent version of OpenGL?

3. Who decides what changes are made to OpenGL?

On Your Own

1. Modify the example program so that the pentagon is red, and the triangle is blue.

2. Add another triangle to the program.

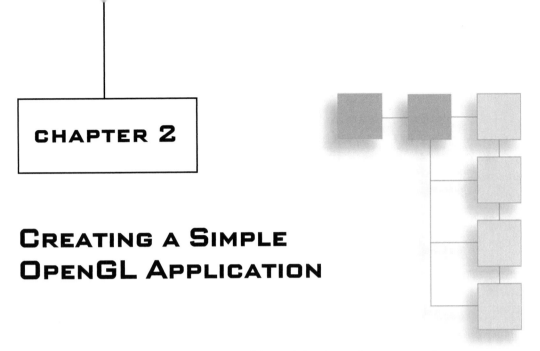

CHAPTER 2

CREATING A SIMPLE OPENGL APPLICATION

Before we can start rendering graphics with OpenGL, we need to create an OpenGL-enabled window.

In this chapter, you will learn about:

- The WGL and related Windows functions that support OpenGL

- Pixel formats

- Using OpenGL with Windows

- Full-screen OpenGL

About the Platform

Before we begin implementing our first OpenGL application, there are some platform issues that need to be discussed. Although OpenGL is a cross-platform API, there are many other factors in developing a game that depend on the platform that the program will run on. Each operating system has a different way of creating a window, generating an OpenGL context, and processing events.

There are of course methods to create cross-platform applications (you saw one in the last chapter by using the SDL library), but libraries such as SDL (and there are many others!) introduce dependencies to the program and might not support the functionality you require on your chosen platform.

Obviously, we can't cover every platform in detail in this book, so a compromise is in order. Because Windows is the most widespread platform (especially when it comes to games development), this chapter will demonstrate how to create an OpenGL window class using the Win32 API. For those of you using GNU/Linux, on the CD, you'll find an equivalent class written using GLX, which is a drop-in replacement for the Win32 version.

This is the only chapter of the book that is specific to the Windows platform. Everything else will run absolutely fine on any platform with a capable OpenGL context.

Introduction to WGL

The set of APIs used to set up OpenGL on Windows is collectively known as WGL, sometimes pronounced, "wiggle." Some of the things WGL allows you to do include:

- Creating and selecting a rendering context

- Using Windows font support in OpenGL applications

- Loading OpenGL extensions

We'll cover fonts and extensions in Chapter 11, "Displaying Text," and Chapter 5, "OpenGL Extensions," respectively. Rendering contexts are covered here.

Note

WGL provides considerable functionality in addition to what's been listed here. However, the additional features are either rather advanced (and require extensions) or very specialized, so we won't be covering them in this volume.

The Rendering Context

For an operating system to be able to work with OpenGL, it needs a means of connecting OpenGL to a window. If it allows multiple applications to be running at once, it also needs a way to prevent multiple OpenGL applications from interfering with each other. This is done through the use of a *rendering context*. In Windows, the Graphics Device Interface (or GDI) uses a device context to remember settings about drawing modes and commands. The rendering context serves the same purpose for OpenGL. Keep in mind, however, that a rendering context does not replace a device context on Windows. The two interact to ensure that your application behaves properly. In fact, you need to set up the device context first and then create the rendering context with a matching pixel format. We'll get into the details of this shortly.

You can actually create multiple rendering contexts for a single application. This is useful for applications such as 3D modelers, where you have multiple windows or viewports, and each needs to keep track of its settings independently. You could also use it to have one rendering context manage your primary display while another manages user interface components. The only catch is that there can be only one active rendering context per thread at any given time, though you can have multiple threads—each with its own context—rendering to a single window at once.

Let's take a look at the most important WGL functions for managing contexts.

wglCreateContext

Before you can use a rendering context, you need to create one. You do this through:

```
HGLRC wglCreateContext(HDC hDC);
```

hDC is the handle for the device context that you previously created for your Windows application. You should call this function only after the pixel format for the device context has been set, so that the pixel formats match. (We'll cover pixel formats shortly.) Rather than returning the actual rendering context, a handle is returned, which you can use to pass the rendering context to other functions. It is not possible to use wglCreateContext() to create a context for version 3.0 or later; to do this, you must use wglCreateContextAttribsARB(), which I will discuss in a moment.

wglDeleteContext

When you are finished with your rendering context, you should let the system know that it can deallocate the resources attached to it. You can do this by using:

```
BOOL wglDeleteContext(HGLRC hRC);
```

wglMakeCurrent

To call any OpenGL functions, you must have a currently active rendering context. This makes sense because a context contains all of the state needed by

OpenGL to operate. The function you need to use to make a context current in the active thread is:

```
BOOL wglMakeCurrent(HDC hDC, HGLRC hRC);
```

The hDC and the hRC must share the same pixel format for the function to work. If you want to deselect the current context, you pass NULL for the second parameter.

wglCreateContext() and wglMakeCurrent() must be called during the initialization stage of your application for OpenGL to work correctly. You can do this by calling them when the WM_CREATE message is handled. Similarly, you can call the wglDestroyContext() when your application handles the WM_DESTROY message. It's a good idea to deselect the current rendering context before calling wglDestroyContext().

Here's a small snippet of code to demonstrate the initialization and destruction of an OpenGL context using the Windows message handling:

```
LRESULT CALLBACK WndProc(HWND hWnd, UINT uMsg, WPARAM wParam, LPARAM lParam)
{
    static HRC hRC;
    static HDC hDC;

    switch(uMsg)
    {
        case WM_CREATE:             //On the create message
            hDC = GetDC(hWnd);          //Get the device context for the window
            hRC = wglCreateContext(hDC); //Create a new rendering context
            wglMakeCurrent(hDC, hRC); //Make it current for the active thread
        break;
        case WM_DESTROY: //On the destroy message
            wglMakeCurrent(hDC, NULL); //Deselect the current context
            wglDeleteContext(hRC); //Delete the rendering context
            PostQuitMessage(0); //Send the WM_QUIT message
        break;
    }
}
```

wglCreateContextAttribsARB

Before OpenGL 3.0, that would have been all you needed to know about creating and managing rendering contexts. But as I mentioned in the previous chapter, version 3.0 introduced a special forward-compatible context that only allows non-deprecated functionality. There is no way to pass any extra information into wglCreateContext to specify that you want a forward-compatible context, or to choose for which version of OpenGL you want to create the forward-compatible context (OpenGL 3.1 for example may deprecate more functionality than 3.0). So OpenGL 3.0 introduced a new function called wglCreateContextAttribsARB. Currently, wglCreateContextAttribsARB is provided as an extension and must be accessed using the extension mechanism that is described in detail in Chapter 5.

The definition of the function is as follows:

```
HGLRC wglCreateContextAttribsARB(HDC hDC, HGLRC hShareContext, const int
*attribList)
```

The same as wglCreateContext(), the function takes the device context as a parameter, but with the addition of two new parameters. The first, hShared Context, is a previously created OpenGL context with which you want to share data (textures, buffers, etc.). Normally, you would pass NULL for this parameter if you do not want to share resources. The last parameter takes a series of key-value pairs of data in an array that sets options for the new context. In this array you can specify the OpenGL version you want (WGL_CONTEXT_MAJOR_VERSION_ARB and WGL_CONTEXT_MINOR_VERSION_ARB) and also special context flags using WGL_CONTEXT_FLAGS_ARB. This item in the array is a bit mask that can be used to specify whether you want to enable a forward-compatible context (WGL_CONTEXT_FORWARD_COMPATIBLE_BIT_ARB) and/or a debug context (WGL_CONTEXT_DEBUG_BIT_ARB).

Interestingly, because this function is an OpenGL extension, you must have an OpenGL context to access it...to use it to create the OpenGL context. This seems to be impossible, but the key is to use the old-style wglCreateContext() to create a temporary context, and then while that context is current, grab a pointer to the new function, create the new context using the function pointer, and then destroy the temporary one. A section of code speaks a thousand words:

```
//Set the version that we want, in this case 3.0
int attribs[] = {
    WGL_CONTEXT_MAJOR_VERSION_ARB, 3,
    WGL_CONTEXT_MINOR_VERSION_ARB, 0,
    WGL_CONTEXT_FLAGS_ARB,
0}; //zero indicates the end of the array

//Create temporary context so we can get a pointer to the function
```

```
HGLRC tmpContext = wglCreateContext(m_hdc);
//Make it current
wglMakeCurrent(m_hdc, tmpContext);

//Get the function pointer
wglCreateContextAttribsARB = (PFNWGLCREATECONTEXTATTRIBSARBPROC)
wglGetProcAddress("wglCreateContextAttribsARB");

//If this is NULL then OpenGL 3.0 is not supported
if (!wglCreateContextAttribsARB)
{
    MessageBox(NULL, "OpenGL 3.0 is not supported", "An error occurred",
MB_ICONERROR | MB_OK);
    DestroyWindow(hWnd);
    Return 0;
}

// Create an OpenGL 3.0 context using the new function and the attribs array
m_hglrc = wglCreateContextAttribsARB(m_hdc, 0, attribs);

//Delete the temporary context
wglDeleteContext(tmpContext);

//Make the GL3 context current
wglMakeCurrent(m_hdc, m_hglrc);
```

Getting the Current Context

Most of the time you will store the handle to your rendering context in a global or member variable, but at times you don't have that information available. This is often the case when you're using multiple rendering contexts in a multithreaded application. To get the handle to the current context, you can use the following:

```
HGLRC wglGetCurrentContext();
```

If there is no current rendering context, this will return NULL. You can acquire a handle to the current device context in a similar manner:

```
HDC wglGetCurrentDC();
```

Now that you know the basics of dealing with rendering contexts, we need to discuss pixel formats and the PIXELFORMATDESCRIPTOR structure and how you use them to set up your window.

Pixel Formats

OpenGL provides a finite number of *pixel formats* that include such properties as the color mode, depth buffer, bits per pixel, and whether the window is double buffered. The pixel format is associated with your rendering window and device context, describing what types of data they support. Before creating a rendering context, you must select an appropriate pixel format to use.

The first thing you need to do is use the PIXELFORMATDESCRIPTOR structure to define the characteristics and behavior you desire for the window. This structure is defined as:

```
typedef struct tagPIXELFORMATDESCRIPTOR {
    WORD  nSize;              // size of the structure
    WORD  nVersion;          // always set to 1
    DWORD dwFlags;           // flags for pixel buffer properties
    BYTE  iPixelType;        // type of pixel data
    BYTE  cColorBits;        // number of bits per pixel
    BYTE  cRedBits;          // number of red bits
    BYTE  cRedShift;         // shift count for red bits
    BYTE  cGreenBits;        // number of green bits
    BYTE  cGreenShift;       // shift count for green bits
    BYTE  cBlueBits;         // number of blue bits
    BYTE  cBlueShift;        // shift count for blue bits
    BYTE  cAlphaBits;        // number of alpha bits
    BYTE  cAlphaShift;       // shift count for alpha bits
    BYTE  cAccumBits;        // number of accumulation buffer bits
    BYTE  cAccumRedBits;     // number of red accumulation bits
    BYTE  cAccumGreenBits;   // number of green accumulation bits
    BYTE  cAccumBlueBits;    // number of blue accumulation bits
    BYTE  cAccumAlphaBits;   // number of alpha accumulation bits
    BYTE  cDepthBits;        // number of depth buffer bits
    BYTE  cStencilBits;      // number of stencil buffer bits
    BYTE  cAuxBuffers;       // number of auxiliary buffer. Not supported.
    BYTE  iLayerType;        // no longer used
    BYTE  bReserved;         // number of overlay and underlay planes
    DWORD dwLayerMask;       // no longer used
    DWORD dwVisibleMask;     // transparent underlay plane color
    DWORD dwDamageMask;      // no longer used
} PIXELFORMATDESCRIPTOR;
```

Let's look at the more important fields in this structure.

Table 2.1 Pixel Format Flags

Value	Meaning
PFD_DRAW_TO_WINDOW	The buffer can draw to a window or device surface.
PFD_SUPPORT_OPENGL	The buffer supports OpenGL drawing.
PFD_DOUBLEBUFFER	Double buffering is supported. This flag and PFD_SUPPORT_GDI are mutually exclusive.
PFD_DEPTH_DONTCARE	The requested pixel format can either have or not have a depth buffer. To select a pixel format without a depth buffer, you must specify this flag. Otherwise, only pixel formats with a depth buffer are considered.
PFD_DOUBLEBUFFER_DONTCARE	The requested pixel format can be either single or double buffered.
PFD_GENERIC_ACCELERATED	The requested pixel format is accelerated by the device driver.
PFD_GENERIC_FORMAT	The requested pixel format is supported only in software. (Check for this flag if your application is running slower than expected.)

nSize

The first of the more important fields in the structure is nSize. This field should always be set equal to the size of the structure, like this:

```
pfd.nSize = sizeof(PIXELFORMATDESCRIPTOR);
```

This is straightforward and is a common requirement for data structures that are passed as pointers. Often, a structure needs to know its size and how much memory has been allocated for it when performing various operations. A size field allows easy and accurate access to this information.

dwFlags

The next field, dwFlags, specifies the pixel buffer properties. Table 2.1 shows the more common values that you need for dwFlags.

iPixelType

The iPixelType field specifies the type of pixel data. You can set this field to one of the following values:

- PFD_TYPE_RGBA. RGBA pixels. Each pixel has four components in this order: red, green, blue, and alpha.

- PFD_TYPE_COLORINDEX. Paletted mode. Each pixel uses a color-index value.

For our purposes, the iPixelType field will always be set to PFD_TYPE_RGBA. This allows you to use the standard RGB color model with an alpha component for effects such as transparency.

cColorBits

The cColorBits field specifies the bits per pixel available in each color buffer. At the present time, this value can be set to 8, 16, 24, or 32. If the requested color bits are not available on the hardware present in the machine, the highest setting closest to the one you choose will be used. For example, if you set cColorBits to 24 and the graphics hardware does not support 24-bit rendering, but it does support 16-bit rendering, the device context that is created will be 16 bit.

Setting the Pixel Format

After you have the fields of the PIXELFORMATDESCRIPTOR structure set to your desired values, the next step is to pass the structure to the ChoosePixelFormat() function:

```
int ChoosePixelFormat(HDC hdc, CONST PIXELFORMATDESCRIPTOR *ppfd);
```

This function attempts to find a predefined pixel format that matches the one specified by your PIXELFORMATDESCRIPTOR. If it can't find an exact match, it will find the closest one it can and change the fields of the pixel format descriptor to match what it actually gave you. The pixel format itself is returned as an integer representing an ID. You can use this value with the SetPixelFormat() function:

```
BOOL SetPixelFormat(HDC hdc, int pixelFormat, const PIXELFORMATDESCRIPTOR *ppfd);
```

This sets the pixel format for the device context and window associated with it. Note that the pixel format can be set only once for a window, so if you decide to change it, you must destroy and re-create your window.

The following listing shows an example of setting up a pixel format:

```
PIXELFORMATDESCRIPTOR pfd;
memset(&pfd, 0, sizeof(PIXELFORMATDESCRIPTOR));
pfd.nSize = sizeof(PIXELFORMATDESCRIPTOR); // size
pfd.dwFlags = PFD_DRAW_TO_WINDOW | PFD_SUPPORT_OPENGL | PFD_DOUBLEBUFFER;
pfd.nVersion = 1; // version
pfd.iPixelType = PFD_TYPE_RGBA; // color type
```

```
pfd.cColorBits = 32; // preferred color depth
pfd.cDepthBits = 24; // depth buffer
pfd.iLayerType = PFD_MAIN_PLANE; // main layer

// choose best matching pixel format, return index
int pixelFormat = ChoosePixelFormat(hDC, &pfd);

// set pixel format to device context
SetPixelFormat(hDC, pixelFormat, &pfd);
```

One of the first things you might notice about that snippet is that the pixel format descriptor is first initialized to zero, and only a few of the fields are set. This simply means that there are several fields that you don't even need in order to set the pixel format. At times, you may need these other fields, but for now, you can just set them equal to zero.

An OpenGL Application

You have the tools, so now let's apply them. In this section of the chapter, you will piece together the previous sections to create an OpenGL-enabled window. The code has been designed to give you a basic framework that you can build on for your OpenGL applications.

The source code is divided into two classes: GLWindow and Example. GLWindow handles the creation and destruction of the window, and also the processing of events. It also holds all the platform-specific code. The Example class encapsulates all the platform-independent OpenGL code for each book sample, making it totally portable.

Before we dive into the specifics of window creation, let's take a look at the WinMain method—the entry point of the application—to get a general overview of how the program works:

```
#define WIN32_LEAN_AND_MEAN
#define WIN32_EXTRA_LEAN

#include <windows.h>
#include "glwindow.h"
#include "example.h"
```

```
int WINAPI WinMain(HINSTANCE hInstance,
                              HINSTANCE hPrevInstance,
                              LPSTR cmdLine,
                              int cmdShow)
{
    //Set our window settings
    const int windowWidth = 1024;
    const int windowHeight = 768;
    const int windowBPP = 32;
    const int windowFullscreen = false;

    //This is our window
    GLWindow programWindow(hInstance);

    //The example OpenGL code
    Example example;

    //Attach our example to our window
    programWindow.attachExample(&example);
```

The above code defines our #includes and sets our window attributes (size, color depth, and whether we want a fullscreen window or not). The programWindow variable is initialized by passing in the hInstance argument from WinMain; this is required later during window creation. The example variable handles our OpenGL scene and must be attached to the window before entering the main loop.

```
    //Attempt to create the window
    if (!programWindow.create(windowWidth, windowHeight, windowBPP,
windowFullscreen))
    {
        MessageBox(NULL, "Unable to create the OpenGL Window", "An error
occurred", MB_ICONERROR | MB_OK);
        programWindow.destroy();
        return 1;
    }

    if (!example.init()) //Initialize our example
    {
        MessageBox(NULL, "Could not initialize the application", "An error
occurred", MB_ICONERROR | MB_OK);
```

```
        programWindow.destroy();
        return 1;
    }
```

The window is created using the settings that were defined earlier; if window creation fails for some reason then an error message is displayed before destroying the window. Once the window has been created, the example must be initialized. If init() returns false, the program will exit.

```
    //This is the mainloop, we render frames until isRunning returns false
    while(programWindow.isRunning())
    {
        programWindow.processEvents(); //Process any window events

        //We get the time that passed since the last frame
        float elapsedTime = programWindow.getElapsedSeconds();

        example.prepare(elapsedTime); //Do any pre-rendering logic
        example.render(); //Render the scene

        programWindow.swapBuffers();
    }

    example.shutdown(); //Free any resources
    programWindow.destroy(); //Destroy the program window

    return 0; //Return success
}
```

This is where all the action happens! Until a WM_DESTROY message is received by the event-handling system, the program loops, each time generating a single frame. processEvents() handles Windows messages such as resize events and then performs the appropriate action. Next, getElapsedSeconds() returns the number of seconds that have passed since the last time it was called, so in this case it returns the time taken to render a single frame. This information is sent to the prepare() method. prepare is used to perform any actions needed before rendering. If you were writing a game, this is where you would handle key presses or process player movement. Next up is render(), which, as you probably guessed, is where the OpenGL calls for drawing to the screen are. The swapBuffers() method is just a wrapper around the Windows SwapBuffers function that swaps the front buffer (which is what is drawn to the screen) with the back buffer (which is where the rendering is done); this process is called double buffering.

Once a `WM_DESTROY` message is received by the `processEvents()` method the running flag will be set to false and will end the game loop. At this point, the `example` will be shut down, freeing any allocated resources, and then the `destroy()` method is called, resetting the display settings if we were full-screen.

So, those are stages of the running application. Now, let's take a closer look at the code that creates the window:

```
bool GLWindow::create(int width, int height, int bpp, bool fullscreen)
{
    DWORD       dwExStyle;        // Window Extended Style
    DWORD       dwStyle;          // Window Style

    m_isFullscreen = fullscreen; //Store the fullscreen flag

    m_windowRect.left = (long)0; // Set Left Value To 0
    m_windowRect.right = (long)width; // Set Right Value To Requested Width
    m_windowRect.top = (long)0;   // Set Top Value To 0
    m_windowRect.bottom = (long)height; // Set Bottom Value To Requested Height

        // fill out the window class structure
    m_windowClass.cbSize          = sizeof(WNDCLASSEX);
    m_windowClass.style           = CS_HREDRAW | CS_VREDRAW;
    m_windowClass.lpfnWndProc     = GLWindow::StaticWndProc; //We set our
    static method as the event handler
    m_windowClass.cbClsExtra      = 0;
    m_windowClass.cbWndExtra      = 0;
    m_windowClass.hInstance       = m_hinstance;
    m_windowClass.hIcon           = LoadIcon(NULL, IDI_APPLICATION); // default
    icon
    m_windowClass.hCursor         = LoadCursor(NULL, IDC_ARROW); // default
    arrow
    m_windowClass.hbrBackground   = NULL;              // don't need background
    m_windowClass.lpszMenuName    = NULL;              // no menu
    m_windowClass.lpszClassName   = "GLClass";
    m_windowClass.hIconSm         = LoadIcon(NULL, IDI_WINLOGO); // windows
    logo small icon

    // register the windows class
    if (!RegisterClassEx(&m_windowClass))
    {
        MessageBox(NULL, "Failed to register window class", NULL, MB_OK);
        return false;
```

```
        }

    if (m_isFullscreen) //If we are fullscreen, we need to change the display
mode
    {
        DEVMODE dmScreenSettings;                         // device mode

        memset(&dmScreenSettings, 0, sizeof(dmScreenSettings));
        dmScreenSettings.dmSize = sizeof(dmScreenSettings);

        dmScreenSettings.dmPelsWidth = width;             // screen width
        dmScreenSettings.dmPelsHeight = height;           // screen height
        dmScreenSettings.dmBitsPerPel = bpp;              // bits per pixel
        dmScreenSettings.dmFields = DM_BITSPERPEL | DM_PELSWIDTH | DM_PELSHEIGHT;

        if
        (ChangeDisplaySettings(&dmScreenSettings, CDS_FULLSCREEN) !=
DISP_ CHANGE_SUCCESSFUL)
        {
            // setting display mode failed, switch to windowed
            MessageBox(NULL, "Display mode failed", NULL, MB_OK);
            m_isFullscreen = false;
        }
    }

    if (m_isFullscreen)                         // Are We Still In Fullscreen Mode?
    {
        dwExStyle = WS_EX_APPWINDOW;            // Window Extended Style
        dwStyle = WS_POPUP;                     // Windows Style
        ShowCursor(false);                      // Hide Mouse Pointer
    }
    else
    {
        dwExStyle = WS_EX_APPWINDOW | WS_EX_WINDOWEDGE;    // Window Extended
Style
        dwStyle = WS_OVERLAPPEDWINDOW;                     // Windows Style
    }

    AdjustWindowRectEx(&m_windowRect, dwStyle, false, dwExStyle);
    // Adjust Window To True Requested Size

    // class registered, so now create our window
    m_hwnd = CreateWindowEx(NULL,                          // extended style
```

```
            "GLClass",                      // class name
            "BOGLGP - Chapter 2 - OpenGL Application",      // app name
            dwStyle | WS_CLIPCHILDREN |
            WS_CLIPSIBLINGS,
            0, 0,                           // x,y coordinate
            m_windowRect.right - m_windowRect.left,
            m_windowRect.bottom - m_windowRect.top, // width, height
            NULL,                           // handle to parent
            NULL,                           // handle to menu
            m_hinstance,                    // application instance
            this);                          // we pass a pointer to the GLWindow here

    // check if window creation failed (hwnd would equal NULL)
    if (!m_hwnd)
        return 0;

    m_hdc = GetDC(m_hwnd);

    ShowWindow(m_hwnd, SW_SHOW);            // display the window
    UpdateWindow(m_hwnd);                   // update the window

    m_lastTime = GetTickCount() / 1000.0f;  //Initialize the timer
    return true;
}
```

The major points in this function are the creation and registration of the window class and the call to the CreateWindowEx() function to create the window. Pay attention to the last parameter of CreateWindowEx(). This parameter allows you to attach some additional data to a window. In our case, the this pointer is stored as the additional data so that a clever trick can be performed! On Windows, the message handling is performed by a function passed as the lpfnWndProc member of the window class. Unfortunately, you can't pass a member function for this parameter; you must use a global non-member function or a static method of a class. The drawback of this is that you can't access member variables or member functions from the message handling procedure. Notice in the above code we pass GLWindow::StaticWndProc as the lpfnWndProc member that is a static method. Let's look at that method now:

```
LRESULT CALLBACK GLWindow::StaticWndProc(HWND hWnd, UINT uMsg, WPARAM wParam,
LPARAM lParam)
{
    GLWindow* window = NULL;
```

```
//If this is the create message
if(uMsg == WM_CREATE)
{
  //Get the pointer we stored during create
    window = (GLWindow*)((LPCREATESTRUCT)lParam)->lpCreateParams;

  //Associate the window pointer with the hwnd for the other events to access
    SetWindowLongPtr(hWnd, GWL_USERDATA, (LONG_PTR)window);
  }
  else
  {
    //If this is not a creation event, then we should have stored a pointer to the
window
        window = (GLWindow*)GetWindowLongPtr(hWnd, GWL_USERDATA);

        if(!window)
        {
            //Do the default event handling
            return DefWindowProc(hWnd, uMsg, wParam, lParam);
        }
    }

    //Call our window's member WndProc (allows us to access member variables)
    return window->WndProc(hWnd, uMsg, wParam, lParam);
}
```

When a window is created using CreateWindowEx(), a WM_CREATE message is sent by Windows. Messages are processed by the StaticWndProc() method and as you can see, the WM_CREATE message is treated as a special case. When a WM_CREATE message is received, the pointer that was stored by the CreateWindowEx() call is passed into SetWindowLongPtr() to be stored permanently for other messages to use. The next time a message comes in (e.g., WM_SIZE) the code in the else statement will handle it. This will retrieve the stored pointer, and then call the non-static WndProc for the window. In the WndProc method, we are free to access member variables. The code is entirely wrapped in the GLWindow class so there is no need for any global functions, and it makes replacing the Win32 window (with say, an SDL one) very easy.

Now let's look at the WndProc method:

```
LRESULT GLWindow::WndProc(HWND hWnd, UINT uMsg, WPARAM wParam, LPARAM lParam)
{
```

```
    switch(uMsg)
    {
    case WM_CREATE:            // window creation
    {
        m_hdc = GetDC(hWnd);
        setupPixelFormat();

        //Set the version that we want, in this case 3.0
        int attribs[] = {
            WGL_CONTEXT_MAJOR_VERSION_ARB, 3,
            WGL_CONTEXT_MINOR_VERSION_ARB, 0,
        0}; //zero indicates the end of the array

        //Create temporary context so we can get a pointer to the function
        HGLRC tmpContext = wglCreateContext(m_hdc);
        //Make it current
        wglMakeCurrent(m_hdc, tmpContext);

        //Get the function pointer
        wglCreateContextAttribsARB = (PFNWGLCREATECONTEXTATTRIBSARBPROC)
wglGetProcAddress("wglCreateContextAttribsARB");

        //If this is NULL then OpenGL 3.0 is not supported
        if (!wglCreateContextAttribsARB)
        {
            MessageBox(NULL, "OpenGL 3.0 is not supported", "An error occurred",
MB_ICONERROR | MB_OK);
            DestroyWindow(hWnd);
            return 0;
        }

        // Create an OpenGL 3.0 context using the new function
        m_hglrc = wglCreateContextAttribsARB(m_hdc, 0, attribs);
        //Delete the temporary context
        wglDeleteContext(tmpContext);
        //Make the GL3 context current
        wglMakeCurrent(m_hdc, m_hglrc);

        m_isRunning = true; //Mark our window as running
    }
    break;
    case WM_DESTROY: // window destroy
    case WM_CLOSE: // windows is closing
```

```
            wglMakeCurrent(m_hdc, NULL);
            wglDeleteContext(m_hglrc);
            m_isRunning = false; //Stop the main loop
            PostQuitMessage(0); //Send a WM_QUIT message
            return 0;
        break;
        case WM_SIZE:
        {
            int height = HIWORD(lParam);          // retrieve width and height
            int width = LOWORD(lParam);
            getAttachedExample()->onResize(width, height); //Call the example's
resize method
        }
        break;
        case WM_KEYDOWN:
            if (wParam == VK_ESCAPE) //If the escape key was pressed
            {
                DestroyWindow(m_hwnd); //Send a WM_DESTROY message
            }
        break;
        default:
            break;
    }

    return DefWindowProc(hWnd, uMsg, wParam, lParam);
}
```

This method is called by Windows whenever it receives a Windows message. I'm not going to go into detail about the Windows messaging system, as any good Windows book will do for you, but generally, you only need to concern yourself with the message handling during creation, destruction, and window resizing operations. We listen for the following messages:

- WM_CREATE: This message is sent when the window is created. We set up the pixel format here, retrieve the window's device context, and create the OpenGL rendering context.

- WM_DESTROY, WM_CLOSE: These messages are sent when the window is destroyed or the user closes the window. We destroy the rendering context here and then send the WM_QUIT message to Windows with the PostQuitMessage() function.

- WM_SIZE: This message is sent whenever the window size is being changed. It is also sent during part of the window creation sequence, as the operating system resizes and adjusts the window according to the parameters defined in the CreateWindowEx() function. We call our example's onResize method here so that we can set up the OpenGL viewport and projection settings.

- WM_KEYDOWN: This message is sent whenever a key on the keyboard is pressed. In this particular message code, we are interested only in retrieving the keycode and seeing if it is equal to the ESC virtual key code, VK_ESCAPE. If it is, we quit the application by calling the DestroyWindow() function.

The processEvents() method is responsible for adding these messages to the queue ready for processing:

```
void GLWindow::processEvents()
{
    MSG msg;

    //While there are messages in the queue, store them in msg
    while(PeekMessage(&msg, NULL, 0, 0, PM_REMOVE))
    {
        //Process the messages one-by-one
        TranslateMessage(&msg);
        DispatchMessage(&msg);
    }
}
```

The loop goes through all the messages in the queue and performs some basic processing on each message in the TranslateMessage() call. The call to DispatchMessage() is what triggers the StaticWndProc function.

You can learn more about Windows messages and how to handle them through the Microsoft Developer Network, MSDN; you can visit the MSDN website at http://msdn.microsoft.com.

Full-Screen OpenGL

In the create method described earlier, you will probably have noticed a section of code that enables a full-screen mode for our application if the m_isFullscreen variable is true. It's time to now explain that in detail.

Table 2.2 Important DEVMODE fields

Field	Description
dmSize	Size of the structure in bytes, used for versioning.
dmBitsPerPixel	The number of bits per pixel.
dmPelsWidth	Width of the screen.
dmPelsHeight	Height of the screen.
dmFields	Set of bit flags that indicate which fields are valid. The flags for the fields in this table are DM_BITSPERPIXEL, DM_PELSWIDTH, and DM_PELSHEIGHT.

In order to switch into full-screen mode, you must use the DEVMODE data structure, which contains information about a display device. The structure is actually fairly big, but fortunately, there are only a few members that you need to worry about. These are listed in Table 2.2.

After you have initialized the DEVMODE structure, you need to pass it to Change-DisplaySettings():

```
LONG ChangeDisplaySettings(LPDEVMODE pDevMode, DWORD dwFlags);
```

This takes a pointer to a DEVMODE structure as the first parameter and a set of flags describing exactly what you want to do. In this case, you'll be passing CDS_FULLSCREEN to remove the taskbar from the screen and force Windows to leave the rest of the screen alone when resizing and moving windows around in the new display mode. If the function is successful, it returns DISP_CHANGE_ SUCCESSFUL. You can change the display mode back to the default state by passing NULL and 0 as the pDevMode and dwFlags parameters.

There are a few things you need to keep in mind when switching to full-screen mode. The first is that you need to make sure that the width and height specified in the DEVMODE structure match the width and height you use to create the window. The simplest way to ensure this is to use the same width and height variables for both operations. Also, you need to be sure to change the display settings *before* creating the window.

The style settings for full-screen mode differ from those of regular windows, so you need to be able to handle both cases. If you are not in full-screen mode, you will use the same style settings as described in the sample program for the regular window. If you are in full-screen mode, you need to use the WS_EX_APPWINDOW flag for the extended style and the WS_POPUP flag for the normal window style. The WS_EX_APPWINDOW flag forces a top-level window down to the taskbar once your own window is visible. The WS_POPUP flag creates a window without a border, which is exactly what you want with a full-screen application. Another thing you'll probably want to do for full-screen is remove the mouse cursor from the screen, which you can do by using the following function:

```
int ShowCursor(BOOL bShow);
```

The Example Class

Now that you understand how to create an OpenGL window, let's look at the definition of the Example class:

```
class Example
{
public:
    Example();

    bool init();
    void prepare(float dt);
    void render();
    void shutdown();

    void onResize(int width, int height);

private:
    float m_rotationAngle;
};
```

I should mention that the Example class is by no means the only way to design your OpenGL application, but for the purposes of this book it provides a very neat and flexible way of isolating the code that will change for each sample in a cross-platform friendly way.

You will notice that besides the five public methods, there is also a private attribute called m_rotationAngle; this is for this chapter's example only and will be replaced by other variables in other chapters, depending on what it is we want to render.

Here's the implementation of the Example class for this chapter, which displays a multi-colored rotating triangle:

```
#ifdef _WIN32
#include <windows.h>
#endif
```

```cpp
#include <GL/gl.h>
#include <GL/glu.h>
#include "example.h"

Example::Example()
{
    m_rotationAngle = 0.0f;
}

bool Example::init()
{
    glEnable(GL_DEPTH_TEST);
    glClearColor(0.5f, 0.5f, 0.5f, 0.5f);

    //Return success
    return true;
}

void Example::prepare(float dt)
{
    const float SPEED = 15.0f;
    m_rotationAngle += SPEED * dt;
    if (m_rotationAngle > 360.0f)
    {
        m_rotationAngle -= 360.0f;
    }
}

void Example::render()
{
    glClear(GL_COLOR_BUFFER_BIT | GL_DEPTH_BUFFER_BIT);
    glLoadIdentity();

    glRotatef(m_rotationAngle, 0.0f, 0.0f, 1.0f);

    glBegin(GL_TRIANGLES);
        glColor3f(1.0f, 0.0f, 0.0f);
        glVertex3f(-0.5f, -0.5f, -2.0f);
        glColor3f(1.0f, 1.0f, 0.0f);
        glVertex3f( 0.5f, -0.5f, -2.0f);
        glColor3f(0.0f, 0.0f, 1.0f);
        glVertex3f( 0.0f, 0.5f, -2.0f);
    glEnd();
```

```
}

void Example::shutdown()
{
    //Nothing to do here yet
}

void Example::onResize(int width, int height)
{
    glViewport(0, 0, width, height);

    glMatrixMode(GL_PROJECTION);
    glLoadIdentity();

    gluPerspective(45.0f, float(width) / float(height), 1.0f, 100.0f);

    glMatrixMode(GL_MODELVIEW);
    glLoadIdentity();
}
```

The `init()` method enables depth testing and uses `glClearColor()` to clear the background color to gray. The `prepare()` method increments the rotation angle based on the frame time render to be used by `glRotatef()` in the render method. In this example, the `onResize` method sets up the viewport for perspective projection, which is described in detail in Chapter 4, "Transformations and Matrices."

The `render()` method is where we put all the OpenGL rendering calls. In this method, we first clear the color and depth buffers, both of which are described in Chapter 12, "OpenGL Buffers." Next, we reset the model matrix by loading the identity matrix with `glLoadIdentity()`, described in Chapter 4.

Next, the triangle is rendered with the `glBegin()`, `glVertex3f()`, and `glEnd()` functions. Before each vertex we change to a different color using `glColor3f()`, which takes a value between 0.0 and 1.0 for the red, green, and blue parameters. The first vertex is drawn in red, the second in yellow, and the third in blue.

N o t e

The method we have used for sending colors and vertices to OpenGL is called *immediate mode*. Immediate mode is the slowest method of rendering with OpenGL and is deprecated in OpenGL 3.0. It is however, the most easily understandable way of drawing, which is why I have chosen to use it in this chapter. In the next chapter, you will learn about Vertex Buffer Objects (or VBOs), which are the preferred and only non-deprecated method of sending primitive data in OpenGL 3.0.

Time-based Updates

Earlier, I glossed over the fact that we pass a time value into the `prepare()` method. This value is used to keep any movement updates independent of frame rate. Let's use an example; say in your classic first-person shooter, your character fires a rocket. If the rocket's position was updated every frame, it would travel faster on a PC with a high frame rate than one with a lower frame rate.

To prevent this, you need to multiply the constant speed by the elapsed seconds per frame. That keeps everything running at the same speed no matter how fast or slow the PC. That's what we do with the rotation angle in this chapter's example.

That's it. Everything you need to know about creating an OpenGL window on the Windows platform. Now, let's look at the exciting screenshot:

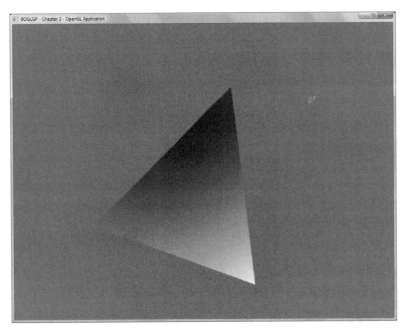

Figure 2.1
A spinning triangle!

Summary

In this chapter, you learned how to create a simple OpenGL application on the Windows platform. You learned about the rendering context and how it corresponds with the "wiggle" functions, `wglCreateContext()`, `wglDeleteContext()`, `wglMakeCurrent()`, `wglGetCurrentContext()`, and the new `wglCreateContextAttribsARB()`.

Pixel formats were also covered, and you learned how to set them up for OpenGL in the Windows operating system. Finally, we provided the full source code for a basic OpenGL application and discussed how to set up the window for full-screen mode in OpenGL.

What You Have Learned

- The WGL, or *wiggle*, functions are a set of extensions to the Win32 API that were created specifically for OpenGL. Several of the main functions involve the rendering context, which is used to remember OpenGL settings and commands. You can use several rendering contexts at once.

- The `PIXELFORMATDESCRIPTOR` is the structure that is used to describe a device context that will be used to render with OpenGL. This structure must be specified and defined before any OpenGL code will work on a window.

- Full-screen OpenGL is used by most 3D games that are being developed. You looked at how you can implement full-screen mode into your OpenGL applications and learned how to achieve frame-rate independent updates.

Review Questions

1. What is the rendering context?

2. How do you retrieve the current rendering context?

3. What is a `PIXELFORMATDESCRIPTOR`?

4. What does the `glClearColor()` OpenGL function do?

5. What struct is required to set up an application for full-screen?

On Your Own

1. Alter the application to show another triangle, this time in red, and clear the background color to white.

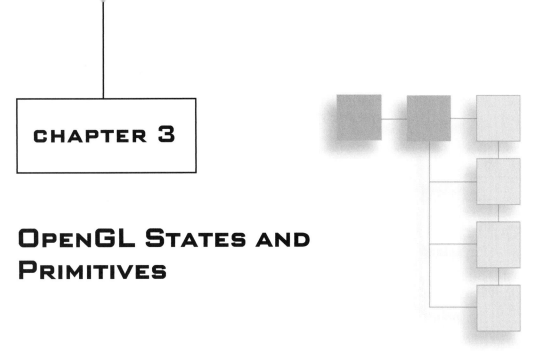

CHAPTER 3

OpenGL States and Primitives

Now it's time to finally get to the meat of OpenGL! To unlock the power of OpenGL, you need to start with the basics, and that means understanding primitives. Before we start, I need to discuss something that is going to come up during our discussion of primitives and pretty much everything else from this point on: the OpenGL state machine.

As you read this chapter, you will learn the following:

- How to access values in the OpenGL state machine

- The types of primitives available to OpenGL

- How immediate mode and vertex arrays work

- How to render primitives using vertex buffer objects

State Functions

The OpenGL state machine consists of hundreds of settings, which have a finite number of possible values (states). These settings are things like the current rendering color, or whether texturing is enabled. Each setting can be individually changed and queried using the OpenGL API. OpenGL provides a number of functions that allow you to query the state machine for a particular setting, and most of these functions begin with glGet. The most generic versions of these functions will be covered in this section, and the more specific ones will be covered with the features they're related to throughout the book.

Note

All the functions in this section require that you have a valid rendering context. Otherwise, the values they return are undefined.

Querying Numeric States

Four general-purpose functions allow you to retrieve numeric (or Boolean) values stored in OpenGL states. They are as follows:

```
void glGetBooleanv(GLenum pname, GLboolean *params);
void glGetDoublev(GLenum pname, GLdouble *params);
void glGetFloatv(GLenum pname, GLfloat *params);
void glGetIntegerv(GLenum pname, GLint *params);
```

In each of these prototypes, the parameter `pname` specifies the state setting you are querying, and `params` is an array that is large enough to hold all the values associated with the setting in question. The number of possible states is large, so instead of listing all of the states in this chapter, I will discuss the specific meaning of many of the `pname` values accepted by these functions as they come up. Most of them won't make much sense yet anyway (unless you are already an OpenGL guru, in which case, what are you doing reading this?).

Of course, determining the current state machine settings is interesting, but not nearly as interesting as being able to change the settings. Contrary to what you might expect, there is no `glSet()` or similar generic function for setting state machine values. Instead, there is a variety of more specific functions, which we will discuss as they become more relevant.

Enabling and Disabling States

You now know how to find out the states in the OpenGL state machine, so how do you turn the states on and off? Enter the `glEnable()` and `glDisable()` functions:

```
void glEnable(GLenum cap);
void glDisable(GLenum cap);
```

The `cap` parameter represents the OpenGL capability you want to enable or disable. `glEnable()` turns it on, and `glDisable()` turns it off. Easy! OpenGL includes over 40 capabilities that you can enable and disable. Some of these include GL_BLEND (for blending operations), GL_TEXTURE_2D (for 2D texturing), and as you have seen in previous examples, GL_DEPTH_TEST (for z-buffer depth sorting). As you progress throughout this book, you will learn more capabilities that you can turn on and off with these functions.

glIsEnabled()

Sometimes, you just want to find out whether a particular OpenGL capability is on or off. Although this can be done with glGetBooleanv(), it's easier to use glIsEnabled(), which has the following prototype:

```
GLboolean glIsEnabled(GLenum cap);
```

glIsEnabled() can be called with any of the values accepted by glEnable()/ glDisable(). It returns GL_TRUE if the capability is enabled and GL_FALSE otherwise. Again, we'll wait to explain the meaning of the various values as they come up.

Querying String Values

You can find out the details of the OpenGL implementation being used, at runtime, via the following function:

```
const GLubyte *glGetString(GLenum name);
```

The null-terminated string that is returned depends on the value passed as name, which can be any of the values in Table 3.1.

Table 3.1 glGetString() Parameters

Parameter	Definition
GL_VENDOR	The string that is returned indicates the name of the company whose OpenGL implementation you are using. For example, the vendor string for ATI drivers is ATI Technologies Inc. This value will typically always be the same for any given company.
GL_RENDERER	The string contains information that usually reflects the hardware being used. For example, mine returns GeForce 8400M GS/PCI/SSE2. Again, this value will not change from version to version.
GL_VERSION	The string contains a version number in the form of either major_number.minor_number or major_number.minor_number.release_number, possibly followed by additional information provided by the vendor. My current drivers return 3.0 NVIDIA 177.89.
GL_EXTENSIONS	The string returned contains a space-delimited list of all of the available OpenGL extensions. This will be covered in greater detail in Chapter 5, "OpenGL Extensions." This parameter has been deprecated in favor of using glGetStringi() discussed next.

Tip

---

glGetString() provides handy information about the OpenGL implementation, but be careful how you use it. Some new programmers use it to make decisions about which rendering options to use. For example, if they know that a feature is supported in hardware on Nvidia GeForce cards, but only in software on earlier cards, they may check the renderer string for geforce and, if it's not there, disable that functionality. This is a bad idea. The best way to determine which features are fast enough to use is to do some profiling the first time your game is run and profile again whenever you detect a change in hardware.

---

glGetStringi()

glGetStringi() was added in OpenGL 3.0 and allows you to grab strings from OpenGL using an index instead of returning all the strings joined together with spaces. At the time of this writing, the only valid parameter is GL_EXTENSIONS. The format of the call is:

```
GLubyte *glGetStringi(GLenum name, GLuint index);
```

index can be any value from zero to NUM_EXTENSIONS - 1. glGetStringi() will be covered in more detail in Chapter 5, "OpenGL Extensions."

Finding Errors

Passing incorrect values to OpenGL functions causes an error flag to be set. When this happens, the function returns without doing anything, so if you're not getting the results you expect, querying the error flag can help you to more easily track down problems in your code. You can do this through the following:

```
GLenum glGetError();
```

This returns one of the values in Table 3.2. The value that is returned indicates the first error that occurred since startup or since the last call to glGetError(). In other words, once an error is generated, the error flag is not modified until a call to glGetError() is made; after the call is made, the error flag will be reset to GL_NO_ERROR.

Colors in OpenGL

Before we go into details about rendering primitives, we will briefly discuss color. In OpenGL (and computer graphics generally), a color is formed from a combination of the three primary colors of light; red, green, and blue. Different colors can be created by varying the intensity of each color component. Besides the

Table 3.2 OpenGL Error Codes

Value	Meaning
GL_NO_ERROR	Self-explanatory. This is what you want it to be all the time.
GL_INVALID_ENUM	This error is generated when you pass an enumerated OpenGL value that the function doesn't normally accept.
GL_INVALID_VALUE	This error is generated when you use a numeric value that is outside of the accepted range.
GL_INVALID_OPERATION	This error can be harder to track down than the previous two. It happens when the combination of values you passed to a function either doesn't work together or doesn't work with the existing state configuration.
GL_INVALID_FRAMEBUF-FER_OPERATION	Framebuffer object is not complete in some way (i.e., there is a missing required attachment).
GL_STACK_OVERFLOW	OpenGL contains several stacks that you can directly manipulate, the most common being the matrix stack. This error happens when the function call would have caused the stack to overflow.
GL_STACK_UNDERFLOW	This is like the previous error, except that it happens when the function would have caused an underflow. This usually only happens when you have more pops than pushes.
GL_OUT_OF_MEMORY	This error is generated when the operation causes the system to run out of memory. Unlike the other error conditions, when this error occurs, the current OpenGL state may be modified. In fact, the entire OpenGL state, other than the error flag itself, becomes undefined. If you encounter this error, your application should try to exit as gracefully as possible.
GL_TABLE_TOO_LARGE	This error is uncommon, since it can only be generated by functions in OpenGL's imaging subset, which isn't used frequently in games. It happens as a result of using a table that is too large for the implementation to handle.

three visible color components, OpenGL also keeps track of another component called alpha. The alpha channel is used as a contribution factor in transparency and other effects.

Each color component is usually expressed as a floating-point value between 0.0 and 1.0, with 1.0 representing full intensity, and 0.0 representing no color channel contribution. For example, black would be represented by setting the red, green, and blue channels to 0.0 and white would be specified by setting all three components to 1.0.

In the next section, you will see that the color of a primitive can be specified in different ways depending on the rendering method you are using. Immediate mode uses the glColor() set of functions:

```
void glColor{34}{bsifd ubusui}(T components);
void glColor{34}{bsifd ubusui}v(T components);
```

The first set of functions takes each color channel value individually. The variations ending in "v" take an array of values. The byte, short, and integer versions of the functions map the values to between 0.0 and 1.0 where the maximum possible integer value is mapped to 1.0.

When using vertex arrays and vertex buffer objects, the primitive colors are specified as arrays of data. You will learn more about this in the next section.

Handling Primitives

So, what are primitives? Merriam-Webster's dictionary defines a primitive as "an unsophisticated person." Well, that doesn't help much, so we'll give it a shot; simply put, primitives are basic geometric entities such as points, lines, and triangles.

You will be using thousands of these primitives to make your games, so it is important to know how they work. Before we get into specific primitive types though, we need to talk about how primitives are drawn in OpenGL.

Over the years, OpenGL has gained several methods of rendering primitives. Each new method has been designed to improve rendering performance. OpenGL 1.0 supported immediate mode (which is the method of drawing you have seen so far). Soon after in OpenGL 1.1, vertex arrays were introduced, and then, a few releases later in OpenGL 1.5, Vertex Buffer Objects (VBO) made it into the core. We're going to give you a quick overview of immediate mode and vertex arrays, before moving onto a more detailed explanation of VBOs, which are now the recommended way to render primitives. Immediate mode and vertex arrays have been marked for removal in a future version of OpenGL; however, they are still available in version 3.0 and are widely used in existing code, so it is still a good idea to learn how to use them.

Immediate Mode

To render using this immediate mode, you must first tell OpenGL that you are about to draw a primitive, then send a series of points that make up the primitive, and finally tell OpenGL that you are finished drawing.

To notify OpenGL that you are about to start rendering primitives, you need to use the following function:

```
void glBegin(GLenum mode);
```

`glBegin()` tells OpenGL two things: 1) that you are ready to start drawing and, 2) the primitive type you want to draw. You specify the primitive type with the mode parameter, which can take on any of the values in Table 3.3.

Figure 3.1 illustrates examples of each of the primitive types that you can draw with OpenGL through the `glBegin()` function.

Each call to `glBegin()` needs to be accompanied by a call to `glEnd()`, which has the following form:

`void glEnd();`

Table 3.3 Valid glBegin() Parameters

Parameter	Definition
GL_POINTS	Individual points.
GL_LINES	Individual line segments composed of pairs of vertices.
GL_LINE_STRIP	Series of connected lines.
GL_LINE_LOOP	Closed loop of connected lines, with the last segment automatically created.
GL_TRIANGLES	Single triangles as vertex triplets.
GL_TRIANGLE_STRIP	Series of connected triangles.
GL_TRIANGLE_FAN	Set of triangles containing a common central vertex (the central vertex is the first one specified in the set).
GL_QUADS	Quadrilaterals (polygons with 4 vertices).
GL_QUAD_STRIP	Series of connected quadrilaterals.
GL_POLYGON	Convex polygon with an arbitrary number of vertices.

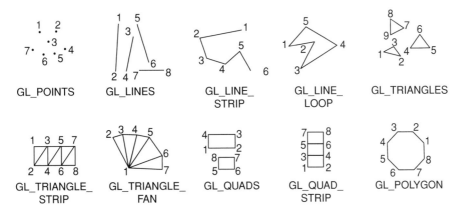

Figure 3.1
OpenGL primitive types.

Table 3.4 Valid glBegin()/glEnd() Functions

Function	Description
`glVertex*()`	Sets vertex coordinates
`glColor*()`	Sets the current color
`glSecondaryColor()`	Sets the secondary color
`glIndex*()`	Sets the current color index
`glNormal*()`	Sets the normal vector coordinates
`glTexCoord*()`	Sets the texture coordinates
`glMultiTexCoord*()`	Sets texture coordinates for multitexturing
`glFogCoord*()`	Sets the fog coordinate
`glArrayElement()`	Specifies attributes for a single vertex based on elements in a vertex array
`glEvalCoord*()`	Generates coordinates when rendering Bezier curves and surfaces
`glEvalPoint*()`	Generates points when rendering Bezier curves and surfaces
`glMaterial*()`	Sets material properties (affect shading when OpenGL lighting is used)
`glEdgeFlag*()`	Controls the drawing of edges
`glCallList*()`	Executes a display list
`glCallLists*()`	Executes display lists

As you can see, `glEnd()` takes no parameters. There really isn't much to say about `glEnd()`, other than it tells OpenGL that you are finished rendering the primitive type you specified in `glBegin()`. Note that `glBegin()`/`glEnd()` blocks may not be nested.

Not all OpenGL functions can be used inside a `glBegin()`/`glEnd()` block. In fact, only variations of the functions listed in Table 3.4 may be used. Using any other OpenGL calls will generate a `GL_INVALID_OPERATION` error.

In between the calls to `glBegin()` and `glEnd()` you must specify the points that make up your primitive. To do this, you use the `glVertex*()` family of functions that take the form:

```
void glVertex{234}{dfis}();
```

or

```
void glVertex{234}{dfis}v();
```

The version of `glVertex()` that is used most often is `glVertex3f()` which takes three floating-point values that represent the x, y, and z coordinates of the vertex. The versions of the function ending in "v" take an array of values as the only parameter.

As an example, the following code will draw a triangle using immediate mode:

```
glBegin(GL_TRIANGLES);
glVertex3f(-1.0f, -0.5f, 0.0f);
glVertex3f(1.0f, -0.5f, 0.0f);
glVertex3f(0.0f, 1.0f, 0.0f);
glEnd();
```

You can draw more than one triangle by adding more vertices in multiples of three between `glBegin()` and `glEnd()`.

Vertex Arrays

Although okay for simple primitives, immediate mode is not very efficient when it comes to describing the vertices that make up a complex model. A complex model will most likely be loaded from a file on disk, or it might be generated procedurally using code. Either way, you are going to be handling a lot of vertex data that will need to be sent to OpenGL. Once loaded/generated, you will be storing the vertices in some kind of container such as an array. Using immediate mode to send these vertices to OpenGL will mean iterating over the array and sending the vertices one at a time. Vertex arrays alleviate this problem by specifying the format and location of an array so that OpenGL can use that data directly. This avoids the need to write a big loop to process the vertices, a method that could involve millions of calls to functions such as `glVertex*()` and `glColor*()`. Not only that, but OpenGL will also be able to better optimize the rendering if it knows about all the data at once.

Vertex arrays have other advantages too. Imagine rendering a cube using triangles. A cube is made up of eight vertices, and 12 triangles. Each of the vertices will be used by several triangles, but using immediate mode, you must specify the same vertex several times, once for each triangle that uses it. Vertex arrays allow you to share the vertices between the triangles, meaning less data for you to store, and less for OpenGL to process.

N o t e

In the examples in the rest of the book, we will be using the `std::vector` container to store vertex data. `vector` is part of the C++ Standard Template Library (STL) and provides a dynamically resizing array that manages its own memory. A vector guarantees that data is stored contiguously in memory, so we can access the data in the same way as a traditional C-style array. You will notice that when passing a pointer into OpenGL functions that require an array, we instead use a pointer to the first element of the vector.

Table 3.5 Array Type Flags

Flag	Meaning
GL_COLOR_ARRAY	Enables an array containing primary color information for each vertex
GL_EDGE_FLAG_ARRAY	Enables an array containing edge flags for each vertex
GL_INDEX_ARRAY	Enables an array containing indices to a color palette for each vertex
GL_NORMAL_ARRAY	Enables an array containing the vertex normal for each vertex
GL_TEXTURE_COORD_ARRAY	Enables an array containing the texture coordinate for each vertex
GL_VERTEX_ARRAY	Enables an array containing the position of each vertex
GL_SECONDARY_COLOR_ARRAY	Enables an array containing secondary colors

Enabling Arrays

Before you can use vertex arrays, you must enable them. In this case, you don't use glEnable() as you might expect; instead, you use the glEnableClientState() function, which has the following definition:

```
void glEnableClientState(GLenum cap);
```

glEnableClientState() takes a parameter that specifies the type of array that we want to enable. This can be any of the values listed in Table 3.5. When you are done with an array, you can disable it using glDisableClientState(), which has the following definition:

```
void glDisableClientState(GLenum cap);
```

Vertex arrays are used to send vertex attributes other than their 3D position. They can also be used to send colors, normals (directional vectors used in lighting), and texture coordinates (used to position a texture on a surface). Each property that you want to specify must be enabled individually using glEnableClientState().

Note

The term vertex array can be a little confusing. Vertex arrays are a series of arrays that we declare to OpenGL, which store different per-vertex attributes (such as colors, normals, etc.). One of these arrays must store vertex positions and this type is called a vertex array, hence the confusion.

Working with Arrays

Once you have enabled the array type that you want to use, you must tell OpenGL where the data for this array is, and in what format it is stored. For this you use the gl*Pointer() set of functions—the function you use depends on the vertex property you are specifying, the most important is of course the positional data:

```
void glVertexPointer(GLint size, GLenum type, GLsizei stride, const GLvoid *array);
```

This array contains the position of each vertex. size must be 2, 3, or 4 and type can be set to GL_SHORT, GL_INT, GL_FLOAT, or GL_DOUBLE.

For example, let's say that you have stored your amazing high-polygon model in an array of floats, and each of the three floats in the array represent a single vertex (x, y, and z). You would declare this array to OpenGL using the following glVertexPointer() call (assuming myArray is the array storing the data):

```
glVertexPointer(3, GL_FLOAT, 0, &myArray[0]);
```

In this example, you state that each vertex has three elements (x, y, z) and each element is a floating-point type. The stride parameter (zero in this case) refers to the amount of padding in bytes between each vertex; this is useful if you store other data besides vertices in the array. We have no other data so no padding is needed. Finally, we pass in the pointer to the start of the array. If you wanted to specify other properties, you would store them in arrays in the same way (see Figure 3.2) and use the appropriate gl*Pointer() functions to describe them to OpenGL. Let's take a look at the other gl*Pointer() functions now:

```
void glColorPointer(GLint size, GLenum type, GLsizei stride, const GLvoid *array);
```

This array contains the primary color data for each vertex. size is the number of color components that can either be 3 (red, green, blue) or 4 (red, green, blue,

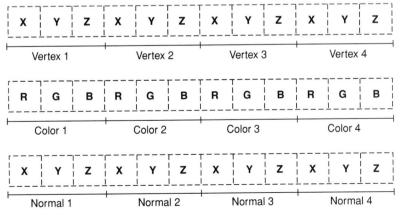

Figure 3.2
A possible array layout for positions, colors, and normals.

alpha). type can be GL_BYTE, GL_UNSIGNED_BYTE, GL_SHORT, GL_UNSIGNED_SHORT, GL_INT, GL_UNSIGNED_INT, GL_FLOAT, or GL_DOUBLE.

```
void glEdgeFlagPointer(GLsizei stride, const GLboolean *array);
```

Edge flags allow you to hide certain edges of the polygons for rendering in wireframe mode (for example, if a square was made up of two triangles, in wireframe you may want to hide the diagonal edge). In this case, there is no type or size parameter, just an array of Boolean values and the stride.

```
void glIndexPointer(GLenum type, GLsizei stride, const GLvoid *array);
```

The naming of this function causes some confusion. glIndexPointer() does not, as you might guess, specify an array of primitive indices, but instead it provides a list of color indices for palletized display modes. It is unlikely that you will be using this kind of display in your applications. type can be set to GL_SHORT, GL_INT, GL_FLOAT, or GL_DOUBLE.

```
void glNormalPointer(GLenum type, GLsizei stride, const GLvoid *array);
```

This specifies an array of directional normal vectors, essentially the direction in which each vertex is "facing." A normal is used for calculating lighting. Normals are always made up of three components (x, y, and z) so there is no need for a size parameter. type can be GL_BYTE, GL_SHORT, GL_INT, GL_FLOAT, or GL_DOUBLE.

```
void glTexCoordPointer(GLint size, GLenum type, GLsizei stride, const GLvoid *array);
```

This array provides a texture coordinate for each vertex. size is the number of coordinates per vertex and it must be 1, 2, 3, or 4. type can be set to GL_SHORT, GL_INT, GL_FLOAT, or GL_DOUBLE.

```
void glSecondaryColorPointer(GLint size, GLenum type, GLsizei stride, const GLvoid * pointer);
```

Finally, this array contains a list of secondary colors. size is the number of components per color, which is always three (red, green, and blue). The types allowed are the same as glColorPointer().

Rendering Using Vertex Arrays

Once you have told OpenGL where to find the vertex data using the gl*Pointer() functions, you are ready to begin rendering. Pay special attention to these functions as they are just as relevant for rendering with vertex buffer objects, which are covered later in this chapter.

glDrawArrays() Once you have enabled the arrays, and told OpenGL where they are, you are ready to draw the primitives. There are several methods that can be used to render vertex arrays, the most commonly used is glDrawArrays(), which has the following definition:

```
void glDrawArrays(GLenum mode, GLint first, GLsizei count);
```

glDrawArrays() renders a series of primitives using the currently bound vertex arrays. mode is the type of primitive to render. The valid arguments for mode are the same as those you can pass to glBegin(). first is the starting index of the elements to render (in the arrays), and count is the number of elements to draw. Let's take a look at a simple example that renders a triangle. First, in the application initialization you store the three vertices that make up the triangle in an array; for a more complex model, you would probably load the vertex positions from a file here.

```
m_vertices.push_back(-2.0f); //X
m_vertices.push_back(-2.0f); //Y
m_vertices.push_back(0.0f);  //Z

m_vertices.push_back(2.0f);  //X
m_vertices.push_back(-2.0f); //Y
m_vertices.push_back(0.0f);  //Z

m_vertices.push_back(0.0f); //X
m_vertices.push_back(2.0f); //etc..
m_vertices.push_back(0.0f);
```

Then in rendering, we enable the array of vertex positions and tell OpenGL where the data can be found. Next, we use glDrawArrays() to render the three vertices, and finally disable the vertex array:

```
glEnableClientState(GL_VERTEX_ARRAY); //Enable the vertex array
//Tell OpenGL where the vertices are
glVertexPointer(3, GL_FLOAT, 0, &m_vertices[0]);
//Draw the triangle, starting from vertex index zero
glDrawArrays(GL_TRIANGLES, 0, 3);
//Finally disable the vertex array
glDisableClientState(GL_VERTEX_ARRAY);
```

glDrawElements()   glDrawArrays() is suitable if every vertex for every primitive is listed sequentially in the array, but sometimes vertices are shared by two or more primitives. In this situation, we can use another method, glDrawElements(). glDrawElements() takes a list of indices into the vertex array which are stored in the order you want to render them. The glDrawElements() function has the following specification:

```
void glDrawElements(GLenum mode, GLsizei count, GLenum type, const GLvoid *indices);
```

Like glDrawArrays(), mode is the type of primitive that you want to draw. This time count is the number of indices that you want to render, type is the data type of the index array, and finally indices is a pointer to the start of the array.

Let's look at an example: the next section of code renders two triangles that make up a square; two of the vertices are shared between the triangles. In the example, m_vertices is a std::vector of floats and m_indices is a std::vector of unsigned integers.

First in the initialization, we store our four vertices, each made up of three floating-point numbers (x, y, z):

```
m_vertices.push_back(-2.0f); //X
m_vertices.push_back(-2.0f); //Y
m_vertices.push_back(0.0f);  //Z

m_vertices.push_back(2.0f);  //X
m_vertices.push_back(-2.0f); //Y
m_vertices.push_back(0.0f);  //Z

m_vertices.push_back(2.0f); //X
m_vertices.push_back(2.0f); //etc..
m_vertices.push_back(0.0f);

m_vertices.push_back(-2.0f);
m_vertices.push_back(2.0f);
m_vertices.push_back(0.0f);
```

Then, still in initialization, we specify the triangle indices into the vertex array:

```
//First triangle, made up of the 1st, 2nd and 4th vertices
//(zero-based array though)
m_indices.push_back(0);
m_indices.push_back(1);
m_indices.push_back(3);
```

```
//Second triangle, made up of the 2nd, 3rd and 4th vertices
m_indices.push_back(1);
m_indices.push_back(2);
m_indices.push_back(3);
```

So now, we have an array of four vertices and six indices. In the rendering, we can do the following to render the triangles:

```
glEnableClientState(GL_VERTEX_ARRAY); //Enable the vertex array
//Tell OpenGL where the vertices are
glVertexPointer(3, GL_FLOAT, 0, &m_vertices[0]);
//Draw the triangles, we pass in the number of indices, the data type of
//the index array (GL_UNSIGNED_INT) and then the pointer to the start of
//the array
glDrawElements(GL_TRIANGLES, m_indices.size(), GL_UNSIGNED_INT,
&m_indices[0]);

//Finally disable the vertex array
glDisableClientState(GL_VERTEX_ARRAY);
```

The full source code for this example can be found on the CD under the "shared vertices" folder. Figure 3.3 shows a screenshot of the running application.

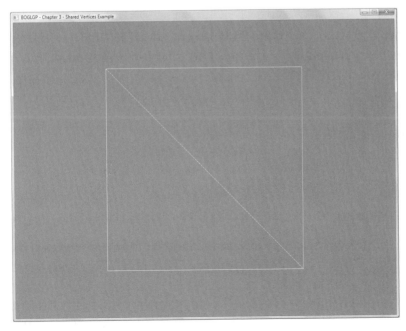

Figure 3.3
Sharing vertices between triangles.

glDrawRangeElements()   This function is almost an extension to `glDrawEle-ments()`. The difference is that `glDrawRangeElements()` allows you to specify a range of vertices to use. For example, if you have a vertex array containing 1,000 vertices, but you know that the object you are about to draw accesses only the first 100 vertices, you can use `glDrawRangeElements()` to tell OpenGL that you're not using the whole array at the moment. This may allow the OpenGL to more efficiently transfer and cache your vertex data. The proto-type is as follows:

```
void glDrawRangeElements(GLenum mode, GLuint start, GLuint end, GLsizei count,
GLenum type, const GLvoid * indices);
```

`mode`, `count`, `type`, and `indices` have the same purpose as the corresponding parameters in `glDrawElements()`. `start` and `end` correspond to the lower and upper bounds of the vertex indices contained in indices.

glMultiDrawArrays()   The last drawing method we are going to cover is `glMultiDrawArrays()`. This is really just a convenience function that allows you to render multiple arrays in a single call. The prototype of the function is as follows:

```
void glMultiDrawArrays(GLenum mode, GLint *first, GLsizei *count, GLsizei
primcount)
```

You will notice that `first` and `count` are now arrays, and the final parameter indicates how many elements are in each array. This function is the equivalent of the following source code:

```
for (int i = 0; i < primcount; ++i)
{
    if (count[i] > 0)
        glDrawArrays(mode, first[i], count[i]);
}
```

Vertex Buffer Objects

Vertex arrays are a lot more efficient at describing large amounts of vertex data than Immediate mode; however, the data you specify is still being read from variables in your program that are stored in your system's memory (RAM) rather than your graphics card's memory (VRAM). This data must continually be sent to the GPU. It would be a lot faster if we could just store the data in buffers on the graphics card. VBOs provide this functionality. VBOs allow you to create buffers of memory where you can store and update vertex data and then use it for fast rendering of primitives.

To use a VBO, you need to perform the following steps:

1. Generate a name for the buffer.

2. Bind (activate) the buffer.

3. Store data in the buffer.

4. Use the buffer to render the data.

5. Destroy the buffer.

Generating a Name

To generate a name for the vertex buffer object, you need to use the `glGenBuffers()` function. It has the following format:

```
void glGenBuffers(GLsizei n, GLuint *buffers);
```

`n` represents the number of buffer names we want to generate. `buffers` is a pointer to a variable or array that can store `n` buffer names. `glGenBuffers()` returns a series of integer names that are guaranteed to have never been generated before by a previous call to `glGenBuffers()`, unless the names have previously been deleted using the `glDeleteBuffers()`, which looks like this:

```
void glDeleteBuffers(GLsizei n, const GLuint *buffers);
```

Passing the same parameters to `glDeleteBuffers()` as `glGenBuffers()` will release all the names that were generated. Here's an example showing how to generate and delete a single buffer name:

```
GLuint bufferID;
glGenBuffers(1, &bufferID); //Generate the name and store it in bufferID

// Do some initialization and rendering with the buffer

glDeleteBuffers(1, &bufferID); //Release the name
```

It is worth noting that the only thing that `glGenBuffers()` does is generate a name and mark it as in use, the actual buffer isn't generated until it is bound.

Binding the Buffer

Once you have generated a name for your buffer, you need to bind it so you can work with it. Binding a buffer makes it current; all buffer-related OpenGL calls and rendering will operate on the currently bound buffer. `glBindBuffer()` is the function that you must use to activate a buffer; it takes two arguments:

```
void glBindBuffer(GLenum target, GLuint buffer);
```

`target` can be `GL_ARRAY_BUFFER`, `GL_ELEMENT_ARRAY_BUFFER`, `GL_PIXEL_PACK_BUFFER`, or `GL_PIXEL_UNPACK_BUFFER`, but the two options relevant to VBOs are `GL_ARRAY_BUFFER` or `GL_ELEMENT_ARRAY_BUFFER` (the other options are related to pixel buffer objects, which allow for storage of pixel data, rather than vertex data). `GL_ARRAY_BUFFER` is used when the buffer is for per-vertex data (positions, colors, normals, etc.); `GL_ELEMENT_ARRAY_BUFFER` is used when indices will be stored in the buffer.

`buffer` is the buffer name previously generated by `glGenBuffers()`. A `buffer` value of zero is special; if `buffer` is zero, the call will unbind any currently bound buffer.

Filling the Buffer

So now you have a buffer generated and bound ready to receive some data. At the time of creation, the buffer is zero-sized; to fill it with data you call `glBufferData()`.

```
void glBufferData(GLenum target, GLsizeiptr size, const GLvoid *data, GLenum usage);
```

`target` can be `GL_ARRAY_BUFFER` or `GL_ELEMENT_ARRAY_BUFFER` (the same as `glBindBuffer()`). `size` is the size in bytes of the vertex array, and `data` is a pointer to the array data to be copied (i.e., your array of vertex positions). Finally, `usage` is a hint to OpenGL telling it how you intend to use this buffer. It can be `GL_STREAM_DRAW`, `GL_STREAM_READ`, `GL_STREAM_COPY`, `GL_STATIC_DRAW`, `GL_STATIC_READ`, `GL_STATIC_COPY`, `GL_DYNAMIC_DRAW`, `GL_DYNAMIC_READ`, or `GL_DYNAMIC_COPY`. Each constant is a combination of two parts: the first is a word describing how often the buffer will be accessed, and the second is the expected type of access. Explanations of the possible keywords can be found in Tables 3.6 and 3.7.

Remember, the `usage` is just a hint for performance; you can still use the buffer as you want, but it may not be optimal if an incorrect usage hint is specified.

Table 3.6 Buffer Frequency Values

Value	Meaning
STREAM	The data will be modified only once, and accessed only a few times.
STATIC	The data will be altered once and accessed multiple times (this hint is good for static geometry).
DYNAMIC	The buffer will be modified a lot and accessed many times (this is suitable for animated models).

Table 3.7 Buffer Access Values

Value	Meaning
DRAW	The contents of the buffer will be altered by the application and will be used for rendering using OpenGL.
READ	The contents will be filled by OpenGL and then subsequently read by the application.
COPY	The contents will be modified by OpenGL and then later used by OpenGL as the source for rendering.

Calling glBufferData() on a buffer object that already contains data will cause the old data to be destroyed and replaced with the new data. If you run out of video memory while attempting to create a store, then the call will fail with a GL_OUT_OF_MEMORY error, which can be checked using glGetError().

Rendering with Buffers and Vertex Arrays

When rendering with VBOs, you follow much the same process as regular vertex arrays. However, when a vertex buffer object is bound the array parameter of the gl*Pointer() functions becomes an offset (in bytes) into the currently bound buffer, instead of a pointer to an array variable. Let's look at the example we used earlier; the following line uses glVertexPointer() to describe an array of vertex positions for rendering with vertex arrays:

```
glVertexPointer(3, GL_FLOAT, 0, &myArray[0]);
```

When using vertex buffer objects, this becomes:

```
//Bind the buffer that stores the vertex data
glBindBuffer(GL_ARRAY_BUFFER, bufferObject);
//Tell OpenGL the vertices start at the beginning of this data
glVertexPointer(3, GL_FLOAT, 0, BUFFER_OFFSET(0));
```

This assumes that myArray was loaded into a valid buffer with the name stored in bufferObject. To revert back to standard vertex arrays, you can call glBind-Buffer() with zero as the buffer parameter, then the final parameter of the gl*Pointer() functions will again be treated as a pointer to an array variable.

The offset is useful if you are storing more than one type of data in the buffer. For example, you could store vertex coordinates in the first half of a buffer, and vertex colors in the second half. In this case, you would use the offset in glColorPointer() to indicate to OpenGL where in the array the color data starts.

Tip

The vertex buffer object specification defines a macro called BUFFER_OFFSET to prevent compiler warnings when passing an integer offset as the array parameter. It is defined as follows:

```
#define BUFFER_OFFSET(i) ((char *)NULL + (i))
```

i is the offset in bytes.

You can use a buffer to store indices too. If a buffer is bound using GL_ELEMENT_ARRAY_BUFFER as the target, rendering functions that take an array of indices such as glDrawElements() or glDrawRangeElements() instead take an offset (in bytes) into the bound buffer.

Now that we have covered the core concepts of rendering with vertex buffer objects, we'll now move onto some solid examples of using them to render primitives.

Drawing Points in 3D

It doesn't get any more primitive than a point, so that's what we'll render first. When rendering using GL_POINTS mode, every vertex position you send to OpenGL is rendered as a dot on the screen. Let's look at an example that renders a single point. First, before rendering, we initialize an array with a single point in the center of the screen two units back, and then create a vertex buffer object:

```
GLfloat vertex [] = {0.0f, 0.0f, -2.0f };
glGenBuffers(1, &m_vertexBuffer); //Generate a buffer for the vertices
glBindBuffer(GL_ARRAY_BUFFER, m_vertexBuffer); //Bind the vertex buffer
glBufferData(GL_ARRAY_BUFFER, sizeof(GLfloat) * 3, &vertex[0], GL_STATIC_DRAW);
//Send the data to OpenGL
```

To render the point, we bind the buffer and set the vertex pointer (note the offset is zero as we want to point at the beginning of the bound buffer). Then once we've enabled the vertex array, we use glDrawArrays() to render a single point.

```
glBindBuffer(GL_ARRAY_BUFFER, m_vertexBuffer);
glVertexPointer(3, GL_FLOAT, 0, BUFFER_OFFSET(0));

glEnableClientState(GL_VERTEX_ARRAY);
glDrawArrays(GL_POINTS, 0, 1);
glDisableClientState(GL_VERTEX_ARRAY);
```

Modifying Point Size

By default, points have a size of 1.0. If you look at the example program for the previous section, you will notice you can barely see the point in the center. You can increase the size of the point by using glPointSize(), which has the following prototype:

```
void glPointSize(GLfloat size)
```

The result is a square point with a width of size, centered at the vertex coordinate that you specified. If point anti-aliasing is disabled (which is the default behavior), then the point size is rounded to the nearest integer, which is the pixel size of the point. The point size will never be rounded to less than 1.

Anti-aliasing Points

Although you can specify primitives with high precision, there are a finite number of pixels on the screen. This can cause the edges of primitives to look jagged. The process of smoothing these jagged edges is known as anti-aliasing. You can enable the anti-aliasing of points by enabling point smoothing, which is done by passing GL_POINT_SMOOTH to glEnable(). You can disable point smoothing again by passing the same parameter to glDisable().

When point smoothing is enabled, the supported range of point sizes may be limited. The OpenGL specification only requires that point smoothing is supported on points with a size of 1.0, but some implementations may allow other sizes. If an unsupported size is used, then the point size will be rounded to the nearest supported value. With anti-aliasing enabled, the current point size is used as the diameter of a circle centered at the x and y window coordinates of the point you specified.

Note

It is worth noting that blending needs to be enabled for anti-aliasing to work. Blending is discussed in Chapter 8, "Blending, Lighting, and Fog."

A Pointy Example

The accompanying CD includes an example application called "Pointy Example," which can be found in the folder for this chapter. The program displays a series of points that gradually increase in size. Let's look at the most important parts of the code. First, during initialization we generate a row of 15 points spaced 0.5 units apart on the x-axis.

```
for (float point = -4.0f; point < 5.0; point+=0.5f)
{
    m_vertices.push_back(point); //X
    m_vertices.push_back(0.0f);  //Y
    m_vertices.push_back(0.0f);  //Z
}

glGenBuffers(1, &m_vertexBuffer); //Generate a buffer for the vertices
glBindBuffer(GL_ARRAY_BUFFER, m_vertexBuffer); //Bind the vertex buffer
glBufferData(GL_ARRAY_BUFFER, sizeof(float) * m_vertices.size(),
            &m_vertices[0], GL_STATIC_DRAW); //Send the data to OpenGL
```

Then during rendering, we draw the points one at a time, increasing the point size before rendering each one.

```
float pointSize = 0.5f;
for (unsigned int i = 0; i < m_vertices.size() / 3; ++i)
{
    glPointSize(pointSize);
    glDrawArrays(GL_POINTS, i, 1); //Draw the point at i
    pointSize += 1.0f;
}
```

Figure 3.4 shows a screenshot of the points example.

Drawing Lines in 3D

Drawing lines in 3D isn't much different from drawing points, except this time we send the two end vertices for each line. Let's look at how to draw a single line, starting with the initialization code:

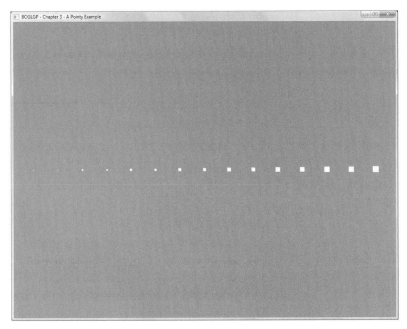

Figure 3.4
Screenshot of the points example.

```
GLfloat vertex [] = {-1.0f, 0.0f, -2.0f,
                      1.0f, 0.0f, -2.0f };
glGenBuffers(1, &m_vertexBuffer); //Generate a buffer for the vertices
glBindBuffer(GL_ARRAY_BUFFER, m_vertexBuffer); //Bind the vertex buffer
glBufferData(GL_ARRAY_BUFFER, sizeof(GLfloat) * 6, &vertex[0],
GL_STATIC_DRAW); //Send the data to OpenGL
```

Notice we've added an extra vertex to the array, and increased the size of the buffer passed to glBufferData(). During rendering, the only changes from the point drawing is the mode passed to glDrawArrays(), and the number of vertices has increased to 2:

```
glBindBuffer(GL_ARRAY_BUFFER, m_vertexBuffer);
glVertexPointer(3, GL_FLOAT, 0, 0);

glEnableClientState(GL_VERTEX_ARRAY);
glDrawArrays(GL_LINES, 0, 2);   //We are now drawing lines
glDisableClientState(GL_VERTEX_ARRAY);
```

Modifying Line Width

The default width of a line is 1.0. You can change this value using the aptly named glLineWidth().

```
void glLineWidth(GLfloat width);
```

It is worth noting that OpenGL 3.0 deprecated line widths greater than 1.0, but larger widths are still available in a backwards-compatible context.

Anti-aliasing Lines

Anti-aliasing lines works in pretty much the same way as points. You can enable it by passing GL_LINE_SMOOTH to glEnable() and disable it using glDisable(). Similar to point smoothing, line smoothing is only guaranteed to be available on lines with a width of 1.0.

Line Width Example

Included on the CD is an application called "Lines." This application simply renders a column of lines, each with a different width. Let's look at the important parts of the code again. During initialization, we must generate the vertices that make up the lines:

```
for (float line = -3.0f; line < 3.0f; line+=0.5f)
{
    m_vertices.push_back(-2.0f); //X
    m_vertices.push_back(line);  //Y
    m_vertices.push_back(-6.0f);  //Z

    m_vertices.push_back(2.0f); //X
    m_vertices.push_back(line);  //Y
    m_vertices.push_back(-6.0f);  //Z
}

glGenBuffers(1, &m_vertexBuffer); //Generate a buffer for the vertices
glBindBuffer(GL_ARRAY_BUFFER, m_vertexBuffer); //Bind the vertex buffer
glBufferData(GL_ARRAY_BUFFER, sizeof(float) * m_vertices.size(),
            &m_vertices[0], GL_STATIC_DRAW); //Send the data to OpenGL
```

The rendering code is again similar to the point rendering, except this time we change the width of the lines using glLineWidth() instead of glPointSize(). Also, notice that i is incremented by two each iteration so that we draw the next line in the array each time.

```
float lineWidth = 0.5f;
for (unsigned int i = 0; i < m_vertices.size() / 3; i+=2)
```

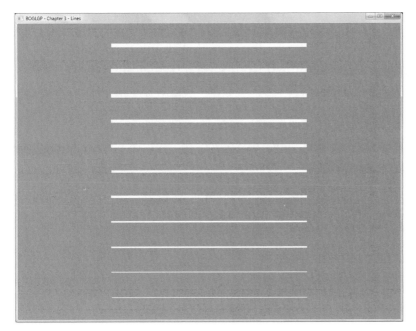

Figure 3.5
Screenshot of the lines example.

```
{
    glLineWidth(lineWidth);
    glDrawArrays(GL_LINES, i, 2); //Draw the line at i
    lineWidth += 1.0f;
}
```

You can see the result of this code in Figure 3.5.

Drawing Triangles in 3D

Although you can do some interesting things armed with points and lines, it is polygons that make up the majority of the scene in a game. Although OpenGL provides modes for rendering quadrilaterals and arbitrary sided polygons, it's generally a good idea to stick with triangles. Rendering with triangles has several advantages; most 3D hardware works with triangles internally as they are easier and faster to rasterize (interpolation of colors etc. is easier across a triangle than a quad) and the points of a triangle are always on the same plane in 3D space. Triangles are always convex and they make non-rendering tasks such as collision detection simpler to calculate. The ARB has even marked quadrilateral and polygon rendering modes for removal in a future version of OpenGL. If you have a list of vertices that you want to turn into an arbitrary sided polygon, have no fear! If you refer back to Figure 3.1, you'll notice that triangle fans allow you to render a complex polygon by building it from several triangles. Neat, huh? Also, rendering four points with a triangle strip will produce a quadrilateral made of two triangles. For this reason, we won't be covering rendering with the GL_QUADS, GL_QUAD_STRIP, or GL_POLYGONS modes. If you do want to use them, rendering occurs in the same way; you just have to switch the mode passed to glDrawArrays() or glDrawElements().

As we have done with points and lines, let's take a look at how you can render a single triangle. We build the vertex list in much the same way:

```
GLfloat vertex [] = {-1.0f, -0.5f, -2.0f,
                      1.0f, -0.5f, -2.0f,
                      0.0f, 0.5f, -2.0f};
glGenBuffers(1, &m_vertexBuffer); //Generate a buffer for the vertices
glBindBuffer(GL_ARRAY_BUFFER, m_vertexBuffer); //Bind the vertex buffer
glBufferData(GL_ARRAY_BUFFER, sizeof(GLfloat) * 9, &vertex[0],
GL_STATIC_DRAW); //Send the data to OpenGL
```

The only changes from rendering lines are the mode we pass to glDrawArrays() and of course the number of vertices we want to render.

```
glBindBuffer(GL_ARRAY_BUFFER, m_vertexBuffer);
glVertexPointer(3, GL_FLOAT, 0, 0);

glEnableClientState(GL_VERTEX_ARRAY);
glDrawArrays(GL_TRIANGLES, 0, 3);
glDisableClientState(GL_VERTEX_ARRAY);
```

As is the case with points and lines, to render more than one triangle you specify more vertices in the array, increase the size of the buffer passed to glBufferData() to match, and change the vertex count passed to glDrawArrays().

Polygon Mode Example

On the CD, you will find an example called "Polygon Mode," which shows three different methods of rendering polygons. You can change the way that polygons are rendered by using glPolygonMode(), which has the following definition:

```
void glPolygonMode(GLenum face, GLenum mode);
```

`face` indicates which side of the polygons will change their rendering type. This can be `GL_FRONT`, `GL_BACK`, or `GL_FRONT_AND_BACK` (we will cover front and back facing in the next section). `mode` can either be `GL_POINT` (the polygon face is rendered using points at each vertex), `GL_LINE` (the face is drawn using lines), or `GL_FILL` (normal rendering).

In the example, we show three rotating squares, each made up of a triangle strip and each rotating in a clockwise direction. Each square is given a different polygon mode. Starting from the left, each square is rendered using the following configuration:

```
glPolygonMode(GL_FRONT_AND_BACK, GL_LINE);
glPolygonMode(GL_FRONT_AND_BACK, GL_POINT);
glPolygonMode(GL_FRONT_AND_BACK, GL_FILL);
```

Note

In the example, we have set the drawing mode for both front and back faces of the polygons at the same time. Currently, it is possible to set the modes of front and back faces individually by passing `GL_FRONT` or `GL_BACK` as the first parameter to `glPolygonMode()`. Feel free to use this functionality; just note that it has been marked for removal in a future version of OpenGL, so it won't work in a forward-compatible context.

Polygon Face Culling

Despite being infinitely thin, polygons have two sides: front and back. Some functions in OpenGL (like `glPolygonMode()`) may change the rendering behavior for one or both sides.

Sometimes you will know that the viewer can only see one side of a polygon; for example, the polygons of a solid, opaque box will only ever have the front side visible. In this situation, it is possible to prevent OpenGL from rendering and processing the backside of the primitive. OpenGL can do this automatically through the process known as *culling*. To use culling, you must enable it by passing `GL_CULL_FACE` to `glEnable()`. Then you can specify which face to cull by using `glCullFace()`, which has the following definition:

```
void glCullFace(GLenum mode);
```

`mode` can be `GL_FRONT`, `GL_BACK`, or `GL_FRONT_AND_BACK`, although obviously culling both faces won't draw anything at all! The default setting is `GL_BACK`.

You may have noticed that culling is only useful if you can determine which side of the polygon is the front, and which is the back. The front and back face are determined by *polygon winding*—the order in which you specify the vertices. Looking at the polygon head-on, you can choose any vertex with which to begin describing it. To finish describing it, you have to proceed either clockwise or counterclockwise around its vertices; OpenGL can use winding to automatically determine whether a polygon face is front or back facing. By default, OpenGL treats polygons with counterclockwise ordering as front facing and polygons with clockwise ordering as back facing. The default behavior can be changed using `glFrontFace()`:

```
void glFrontFace(GLenum mode);
```

`mode` should be `GL_CCW` if you want to use counterclockwise orientation for front-facing polygons and `GL_CW` if you want to use clockwise orientation.

Anti-aliasing Polygons

As with points and lines, you can also choose to anti-alias polygons. You control polygon anti-aliasing by passing `GL_POLYGON_SMOOTH` to `glEnable()` and `glDisable()`. As you might expect, it is disabled by default.

Summary

In this chapter, you learned a little more about the OpenGL state machine. You know how to use `glGet()` and `glIsEnabled()` to query the values of OpenGL parameters. You've also seen how to get information on the OpenGL implementation using `glGetString()` and `glGetStringi()`, and how to find errors using `glGetError()`.

You have learned about the different types of primitives that can be rendered using OpenGL and also have seen three different methods of rendering them: immediate mode, vertex arrays, and vertex buffer objects. Now that you understand basic rendering, it's time to move onto more interesting things.

What You Have Learned

- You can query the OpenGL state machine using `glGet()` and `glIsEnabled()`. Primitives are drawn by passing a series of vertices to OpenGL either one at a time (using immediate mode) or in an array (vertex arrays and vertex buffer objects). You understand how to generate vertex buffer objects, fill them with your primitive data, and use those buffers in rendering with vertex arrays. You know how to render points, lines, and triangles in OpenGL and how to enable anti-aliasing for each type. You know how to vary the size of points and lines by using `glPointSize()` and `glLineWidth()`, respectively.

■ You can change the way OpenGL renders polygons using `glPolygonMode()` and how to cull either the front or back faces by passing `GL_CULL_FACE` to `glEnable()` and using `glCullFace()` to choose the side to cull. You know that front facing polygons are determined by the winding of their vertices, and how to change whether front faces are specified using clockwise or counterclockwise vertex winding using `glFrontFace()`.

Review Questions

1. How is culling enabled?

2. How do you find the current OpenGL version?

3. By default, is the front face of a polygon rendered with vertices in a clockwise winding or a counterclockwise winding?

4. What is passed to `glEnable()` to enable polygon smoothing?

On Your Own

1. Write an application that displays a pyramid with four sides (excluding the bottom). The sides of the pyramid should be formed using a triangle-fan and the bottom should be made of a triangle-strip. All polygons should be rendered using vertex buffer objects and each vertex should be a different color.

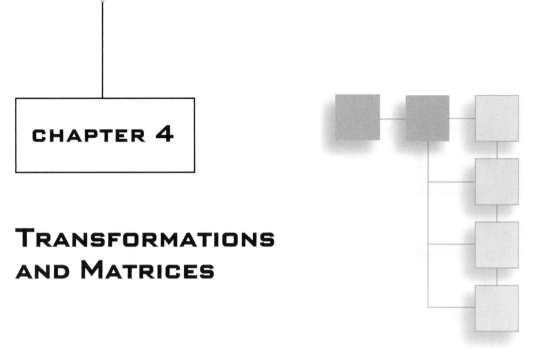

CHAPTER 4

TRANSFORMATIONS AND MATRICES

Now it's time to take a short break from learning how to create objects *in* the world and focus on learning how to move the objects *around* in the world. This is a vital ingredient to generating realistic 3D gaming worlds; without it, the 3D scenes you create would be static, boring, and totally non-interactive. OpenGL makes it easy for the programmer to move objects around using various coordinate transformations, discussed in this chapter. You will also look at how to use your own matrices with OpenGL, which provides you with the power to manipulate objects in many different ways.

In this chapter, you'll learn about:

- The basics of coordinate transformations

- The camera and viewing transformations

- OpenGL matrices and matrix stacks

- Projections

- Using your own matrices with OpenGL

Understanding Coordinate Transformations

Set this book down and stop reading for a moment. Look around you. Now, imagine that you have a camera in your hands, and you are taking photographs of your surroundings. For instance, you might be in an office and have your walls, this book, your desk, and maybe your computer near you. Each of these objects has a shape and geometry described in a *local coordinate system*, which is unique for every object, is centered on the object, and doesn't depend on any other objects. They also have some sort of position and orientation in the world space. You have a position and orientation in world space as well. The relationship between the positions of these objects around you and your position and orientation determines whether the objects are behind you or in front of you. As you are taking photographs of these objects, the lens of the camera also has some effect on the final outcome of the pictures you are taking. A zoom lens makes objects appear closer to or farther from your position. You aim and click, and the picture is "rendered" onto the camera film (or onto your memory card if you have a digital camera). Your camera and its film also have settings, such as size and resolution, which help define how the final picture is rendered. The final image you see in a picture is a product of how each object's position, your position, your camera's lens, and your camera's settings interact to map your surrounding objects' three-dimensional features to the two-dimensional picture.

Transformations work the same way. They allow you to move, rotate, and manipulate objects in a 3D world, while also allowing you to project 3D coordinates onto a 2D screen. Although transformations seem to modify an object directly, in reality, they are merely transforming the object's local coordinate system into another coordinate system. When rendering 3D scenes, vertices pass through four types of transformations before they are finally rendered on the screen:

- **Modeling transformation.** The modeling transformation moves objects around the scene and moves objects from local coordinates into world coordinates.

- **Viewing transformation.** The viewing transformation specifies the location of the camera and moves objects from world coordinates into eye or camera coordinates.

- **Projection transformation.** The projection transformation defines the viewing volume and clipping planes and maps objects from eye coordinates to clip coordinates.

- **Viewport transformation.** The viewport transformation maps the clip coordinates into the two-dimensional viewport, or window, on your screen.

Table 4.1 OpenGL Transformations

Transformation	Description
Viewing	In 3D graphics, specifies the location of the camera (not a true OpenGL transformation)
Modeling	In 3D graphics, handles moving objects around the scene (not a true OpenGL transformation)
Projection	Defines the viewing volume and clipping planes
Viewport	Maps the projection of the scene into the rendering window
Modelview	Combination of the viewing and modeling transformations

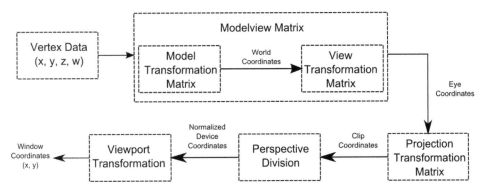

Figure 4.1
The vertex transformation pipeline.

While these four transformations are standard in 3D graphics, OpenGL includes and combines the modeling and viewing transformation into a single modelview transformation. We will discuss the modelview transformation in "The Modelview Matrix" section of this chapter.

Table 4.1 shows a summary of all these transformations.

When you are writing your 3D programs, remember that these transformations execute in a specific order. The modelview transformations execute before the projection transformations. Figure 4.1 shows the general order in which these vertex transformations are executed.

Eye Coordinates

One of the most critical concepts to transformations and viewing in OpenGL is the concept of the camera, or eye coordinates. In 3D graphics, the current

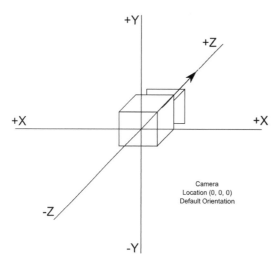

Figure 4.2
The default viewing matrix in OpenGL looks down the negative z-axis.

viewing transformation matrix, which converts world coordinates to eye coordinates, defines the camera's position and orientation. In contrast, OpenGL converts world coordinates to eye coordinates with the modelview matrix. When an object is in eye coordinates, the geometric relationship between the object and the camera is known, which means our objects are positioned relative to the camera position and are ready to be rendered properly. Essentially, you can use the viewing transformation to move a camera about the 3D world, while the modeling transformation moves objects around the world. In OpenGL, the default camera (or viewing matrix transformation) is always oriented to look down the negative z-axis, as shown in Figure 4.2.

To give you an idea of this orientation, imagine that you are at the origin and you rotate to the left 90 degrees (about the y-axis); you would then be facing along the negative x-axis. Similarly, if you were to place yourself in the default camera orientation and rotate 180 degrees, you would be facing in the positive z direction.

Viewing Transformations

The viewing transformation is used to position and aim the camera. As already stated, the camera's default orientation is to point down the negative z-axis while positioned at the origin (0, 0, 0). You can move and change the camera's orientation through translation and rotation commands, which, in effect, manipulate the viewing transformation.

Remember that the viewing transformation must be specified before any other modeling transformations. This is because transformations in OpenGL are applied in reverse order. By specifying the viewing transformation first, you are ensuring that it gets applied after the modeling transformations.

How do you create the viewing transformation? First, you need to clear the current matrix. You accomplish this through the `glLoadIdentity()` function, specified as

`void glLoadIdentity();`

This sets the current matrix equal to the *identity matrix* and is analogous to clearing the screen before beginning rendering.

Tip

The identity matrix is the matrix in which the diagonal element values in the matrix are equal to 1, and all the other (non-diagonal) element values in the matrix are equal to 0, so that given the 4×4 matrix M: $M(0,0) = M(1,1) = M(2,2) = M(3,3) = 1$. Multiplying the identity matrix I by a matrix M results in a matrix equal to M, such that $I \times M = M$.

After initializing the current matrix, you can create the viewing matrix in several different ways. One method is to leave the viewing matrix equal to the identity matrix. This results in the default location and orientation of the camera, which would be at the origin and looking down the negative z-axis. Other methods include the following:

- Using the `gluLookAt()` function to specify a line of sight that extends from the camera. This is a function that encapsulates a set of translation and rotation commands and will be discussed later in this chapter in the "Using `gluLookAt()`" section.

- Using the translation and rotation modeling commands `glTranslate()` and `glRotate()`. These commands are discussed in more detail in the "Using `glRotate()` and `glTranslate()`" section in this chapter; for now, suffice it to say that this method moves the objects in the world relative to a stationary camera.

- Creating your own routines that use the translation and rotation functions for your own coordinate system (for example, polar coordinates for a camera orbiting around an object). This concept will be discussed in this chapter in the "Creating Your Own Custom Routines" section.

Modeling Transformations

The modeling transformations allow you to position and orient a model by moving, rotating, and scaling it. You can perform these operations one at a time or as a combination of events. Figure 4.3 illustrates the three built-in operations

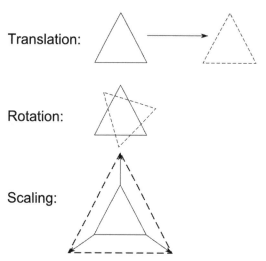

Translation:

Rotation:

Scaling:

Figure 4.3
The three modeling transformations.

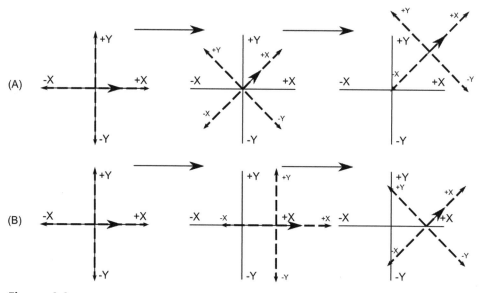

Figure 4.4
a.) A rotation followed by a translation. b.) A translation followed by a rotation.

that you can use on objects:

- **Translation.** This operation is the act of moving an object along a specified vector.

- **Rotation.** This is where an object is rotated about a vector.

- **Scaling.** This is when you increase or decrease the size of an object. With scaling, you can specify different values for different axes. This gives you the ability to stretch and shrink objects non-uniformly.

The order in which you specify modeling transformations is very important to the final rendition of your scene. For example, as shown in Figure 4.4, rotating and then translating an object has a completely different effect than translating and then rotating the object. Let's say you have an arrow located at the origin that lies flat on the x-y plane, and the first transformation you apply is a rotation of 30 degrees around the z-axis. You then apply a translation transformation of +5 units along the x-axis. The final position of the triangle would be (5, 4.33) with the arrow pointing at a 30-degree angle from the positive x-axis. Now, let's swap the order and say you translate the arrow by +5 units along the x-axis first. Then you rotate the arrow 30 degrees about the z-axis. After the translation, the arrow would be located at (5, 0). When you apply the rotation transformation, the arrow would still be located at (5, 0), but it would be pointing at a 30-degree angle from the x-axis.

Projection Transformations

The projection transformation defines the viewing volume and clipping planes. It is performed after the modeling and viewing transformations. You can think of the projection transformation as determining which objects belong in the viewing volume and how they should look. It is very much like choosing a camera lens that is used to look into the world. The field of view you choose when creating the projection transformation determines what type of lens you have. For instance, a wider field of view would be like having a wide-angle lens, where you could see a huge area of the scene without much detail. With a smaller field of view, which would be similar to a telephoto lens, you would be able to look at objects as though they were closer to you than they actually are.

OpenGL offers two types of projections:

- **Perspective projection.** This type of projection shows 3D worlds exactly as you see things in real life. With perspective projection, objects that are farther away appear smaller than objects that are closer to the camera.

▪ **Orthographic projection.** This type of projection shows objects on the screen in their true size, regardless of their distance from the camera. This projection is useful for CAD software, where objects are drawn with specific views to show the dimensions of an object (i.e., front, left, top views), and can also be used for isometric games.

Viewport Transformations

The last transformation is the *viewport transformation*. This transformation maps the clip coordinates created by the perspective transformation onto your window's rendering surface. You can think of the viewport transformation as determining whether the final image should be enlarged or shrunk, depending on the size of the rendering surface.

Fixed-Function OpenGL and Matrices

Now that you've learned about the various transformations involved in OpenGL, let's take a look at how you actually use them. Transformations in OpenGL rely on the *matrix* for all mathematical computations. As you will soon see, OpenGL has what is called the *matrix stack,* which is useful for constructing complicated models composed of many simple objects. You will be taking a look at each of the transformations and look more into the matrix stack in this section.

Before we begin, it is worth noting that the matrix stack was marked as deprecated in OpenGL 3.0, mainly because it is functionality that can be provided by a third-party library and when moving to a programmable pipeline (see Chapter 6, "Moving to a Programmable Pipeline") you must take care of your own matrices. Still, the current matrix functionality will be around for a while yet and it is utilized in most of the code that is available at the time of writing. Also, the concept of the matrix stack and the different matrices we will be discussing are vital for 3D computer graphics. It's only the responsibility of managing them that has become the developer's. Now, let's begin by taking a look at the *modelview matrix.*

The Modelview Matrix

The *modelview matrix* defines the coordinate system that is used to place and orient objects. This 4×4 matrix can either transform vertices or it can be transformed itself by other matrices. Vertices are transformed by multiplying a vertex vector by the modelview matrix, resulting in a new vertex vector that has been transformed. The modelview matrix itself can be transformed by multiplying it by another 4 × 4 matrix.

Before calling any transformation commands, you must specify whether you want to modify the modelview matrix or the projection matrix. Modifying either matrix is accomplished through the OpenGL function `glMatrixMode()`, which is defined as

```
void glMatrixMode(GLenum mode);
```

In order to modify the modelview matrix, you use the argument `GL_MODELVIEW`. This sets the modelview matrix to the current matrix, which means that it will be modified with subsequent transformation commands. Doing this looks like:

```
void glMatrixMode(GL_MODELVIEW);
```

Other arguments for `glMatrixMode()` include `GL_PROJECTION`, `GL_COLOR`, or `GL_TEXTURE`. `GL_PROJECTION` is used to specify the projection matrix; `GL_COLOR` is used to indicate the color matrix, which we won't be covering; and `GL_TEXTURE` is used to indicate the texture matrix, which we will discuss in Chapter 7, "Texture Mapping."

Usually at the beginning of your rendering loop, you will want to reset the modelview matrix to the default position (0, 0, 0) and orientation (looking down the negative z-axis). To do this, you call the `glLoadIdentity()` function, which loads the identity matrix as the current modelview matrix, thereby positioning the camera at the world origin and default orientation. Here's a snippet of how you might reset the modelview matrix:

```
glMatrixMode(GL_MODELVIEW);
glLoadIdentity(); // reset the modelview matrix
// ... do other transformations
```

Translation

Translation allows you to move an object from one position in the world to another position in the world. The OpenGL function `glTranslate()` performs this functionality and is defined as follows:

```
void glTranslate{fd}(TYPE x, TYPE y, TYPE z);
```

The parameters x, y, and z specify the amount to translate along the x, y, and z axes, respectively. For example, if you execute the command

```
glTranslatef(3.0f, 1.0f, 8.0f);
```

any subsequently specified objects will be moved three units along the positive x-axis, one unit along the positive y-axis, and eight units along the positive z-axis, to a final position of (3, 1, 8).

Suppose you want to move a cube from the origin to the position (5, 5, 5). You first load the modelview matrix and reset it to the identity matrix, so you are starting at the origin (0, 0, 0). You then perform the translation transformation on the current matrix to position (5, 5, 5) before calling your renderCube() function. In code, this looks like

```
glMatrixMode(GL_MODELVIEW);          // set current matrix to modelview
glLoadIdentity();                    // reset modelview to identity matrix
glTranslatef(5.0f, 5.0f, 5.0f);      // move to (5, 5, 5)
renderCube();                        // draw the cube
```

Figure 4.5 illustrates how this code executes.

How about a translation example? On the CD under Chapter 4, you will find an example called Translation that illustrates a very simple oscillating translation along the z-axis. The example renders a flat square plane at the origin, but

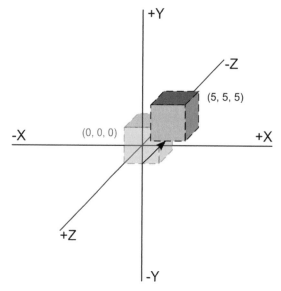

Figure 4.5
Translating a cube from the origin to (5, 5, 5).

because the world coordinate system is being translated, the square plane appears to be moving into and away from the view. Here is the code from the `prepare()` function, which performs the oscillation logic:

```
//If we are moving in the -z direction, decrement the position
if (m_currentDirection == FORWARD) {
    m_zPosition -= speed * dt;
} else { //otherwise we are moving backwards so increment the position
    m_zPosition += speed * dt;
}


//If we hit either the near or far limit, reverse the direction
if (m_zPosition >= nearLimit) {
    m_currentDirection = FORWARD;
    m_zPosition = nearLimit;
} else if (m_zPosition <= farLimit) {
    m_currentDirection = BACKWARD;
    m_zPosition = farLimit;
}
```

The `dt` value in the code above is the time passed since the last frame. Making transformations dependant on time keeps everything running at the same speed regardless of the power of the computer. The code either increases or decreases the value used to translate the world along the z-axis, depending on the "direction" we are currently heading. When the translation value reaches an extreme (defined as the `nearLimit` and `farLimit` variables), then we change the "direction" of the translation. This code in the `prepare()` function is called prior to the `render()` function, which looks like this:

```
void Example::render()
{
    glClear(GL_COLOR_BUFFER_BIT | GL_DEPTH_BUFFER_BIT);
    //Load the identity matrix (reset to the default position and orientation)
    glLoadIdentity();
    //Bind the color array, and set the color pointer to point at it
    glBindBuffer(GL_ARRAY_BUFFER, m_colorBuffer);
    glColorPointer(3, GL_FLOAT, 0, 0);
    //Bind the vertex array and set the vertex pointer to point at it
    glBindBuffer(GL_ARRAY_BUFFER, m_vertexBuffer);
    glVertexPointer(3, GL_FLOAT, 0, 0);
    //Translate using our zPosition variable
    glTranslatef(0.0, 0.0, m_zPosition);
```

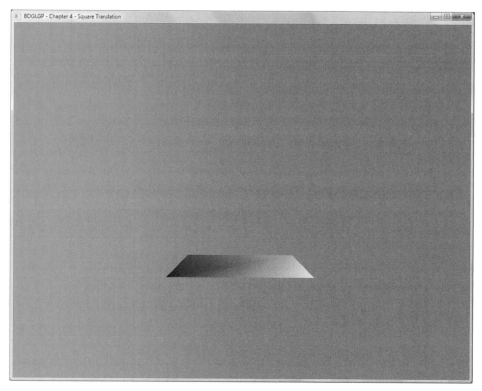

Figure 4.6
A screenshot of the Square Translation example.

```
    //Draw the square as a triangle strip
    glDrawArrays(GL_TRIANGLE_STRIP, 0, 4);
}
```

The render() function is very simple. After clearing the color and depth buffers, we load the identity matrix to initialize to the default world position and orientation; we then bind our vertex buffers and translate along the z-axis using the value determined in the prepare() function, and then draw the square. The resulting execution shows a plane that moves back and forth along the z-axis. A screenshot is shown in Figure 4.6.

Rotation

Rotation in OpenGL is accomplished through the glRotate() function, which is defined as

```
void glRotate{fd}(TYPE angle, TYPE x, TYPE y, TYPE z);
```

glRotatef(45.0f, 0.0f, 0.0f, 1.0f);

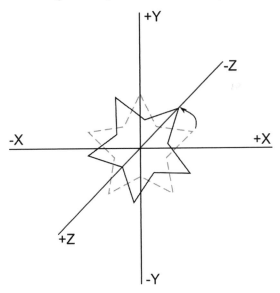

Figure 4.7
The glRotatef() function takes the angle of rotation and a vector for the axis of rotation as parameters.

With this function, you are performing a rotation around the vector specified by the x, y, and z parameters. The angle of rotation is specified by angle and is measured in degrees in the counterclockwise direction.

For example, if you wanted to rotate around the y-axis 135 degrees in the counterclockwise direction, you would use the following:

```
glRotatef(135.0f, 0.0f, 1.0f, 0.0f);
```

The value of 1.0f for the y argument specifies a vector pointing in the direction of the positive y-axis. Figure 4.7 illustrates how the glRotate() function works.

If you wanted to rotate clockwise, you would set the angle of rotation as a negative number. To rotate around the y-axis 135 degrees in the clockwise direction, you use the following code:

```
glRotatef(-135.0f, 0.0f, 1.0f, 0.0f);
```

What if you wanted to rotate around an arbitrary axis? You can accomplish this by specifying the arbitrary axis vector in the x, y, and z parameters. By drawing a line from the relative origin to the point represented by (x, y, z), you can see the arbitrary axis around which you will rotate. For instance, if you rotate 90 degrees glRotatef(90.0f, 1.0f, 1.0f, 0.0f);

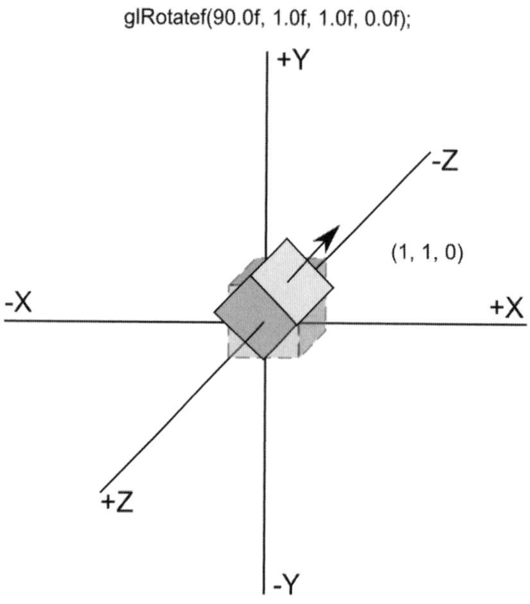

Figure 4.8
Rotation about an arbitrary axis.

about the axis specified by the vector (1, 1, 0), you rotate about the axis that goes from the relative origin to the point (1, 1, 0). In code, this looks like the following:

```
glRotatef(90.0f, 1.0f, 1.0f, 0.0f);
```

Figure 4.8 illustrates how it works.

Rotating about a single axis is fine, but most applications rotate their objects about multiple axes. The order in which you specify rotations is very important when doing this because each rotation you apply changes the local coordinate system of the rotations. For instance, if you rotate an object 60 degrees about the x-axis and then rotate that same object 45 degrees about the y-axis in subsequent calls to glRotate(), then the resultant orientation of that object is a result of the two rotations occurring one after the other within the context of the object's local coordinate system. The first rotation will be applied as expected, and the object will be rotated 60 degrees about the x-axis. However, the second rotation about the y-axis will not be in the context of the world coordinate system. Instead, the y-axis rotation occurs in the context of the object's local coordinate system. Because the object has already been rotated 60 degrees about the x-axis, the object's new y-axis has also been rotated 60 degrees counterclockwise. Your

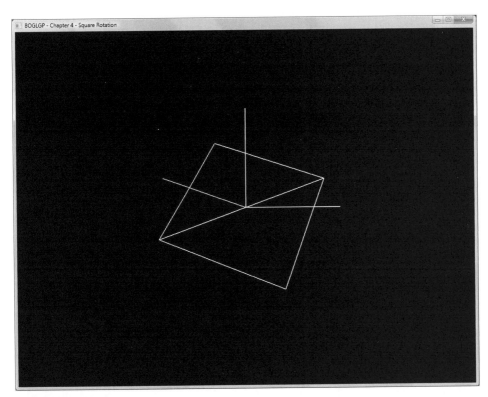

Figure 4.9
A screenshot of the rotation example.

second rotation about the y-axis will actually be in this new configuration. Let's look at an example; maybe it will make more sense.

Included on the CD in Chapter 4 you will find an example entitled Rotation. A screenshot of this example is shown in Figure 4.9. If you build and run the example, you will see the same plane we created in the Translation example, except this time it is rotating about the origin instead of translating along the z-axis. Also being drawn in this example are two sets of lines representing the coordinate system's x- and y-axes.

The white lines represent the world coordinate system's x- and y-axes, while the yellow lines represent the x- and y-axes in the object's local coordinate system. The important part of this example is the following lines in the render() method:

```
glRotatef(m_xRotation, 1.0f, 0.0f, 0.0f);
glRotatef(m_yRotation, 0.0f, 1.0f, 0.0f);
//Draw the square as a triangle strip
glDrawArrays(GL_TRIANGLE_STRIP, 0, 4);
```

You will notice when the example executes that the plane is always rotating about the same world x-axis properly, which also seems to be altering the location of the y-axis. This is because the rotation about the x-axis is specified first, while we are still in the original orientation of the world coordinate system. Once we rotate along the x-axis, though, the orientation of the world coordinate system changes to reflect that rotation, and as you can see from the example, the orientation of the y-axis changes (the yellow line perpendicular to the plane). Then when we rotate about the y-axis, the rotation occurs in the new orientation that has been created as a result of the x-axis rotation. Hopefully, through this example you can see how much the order of rotation about different axes matters. Take some time to modify the Square Rotation example to see how different rotation orders can affect the final rotational outcome of an object.

Scaling

Scaling, in its most simple definition, increases or decreases the size of an object or coordinate system. In other words, when using scaling operations, vertex coordinates for an object are multiplied by a scaling factor for each axis. This means that if you would normally place a vertex at the location (1, 1, 1) without scaling, then applying a scaling factor of 2.0 along each axis would place the vertex at the location (2, 2, 2). Scaling is performed in OpenGL through the glScale() function, which is defined as

```
void glScale{fd}(TYPE x, TYPE y, TYPE z);
```

The values passed to the x, y, and z parameters specify the scale factor along each axis. For example, this line applies a scaling factor of 2.0 along each axis:

```
glScalef(2.0f, 2.0f, 2.0f);
```

If you were to draw a 1 × 1 × 1 unit cube after executing the above line, then the cube would really be drawn as a 2 × 2 × 2 cube. Now, let's say you took that cube, and you wanted to double its width (the x-axis) without changing its height (the y-axis) and depth (the z-axis). You would use the following:

```
glScalef(2.0f, 1.0f, 1.0f);
```

What if you wanted to shrink an object? Well, because the scaling factors are each multiplied by the vertices, you simply choose a value less than one, like this:

```
glScalef(0.5f, 0.5f, 0.5f);
```

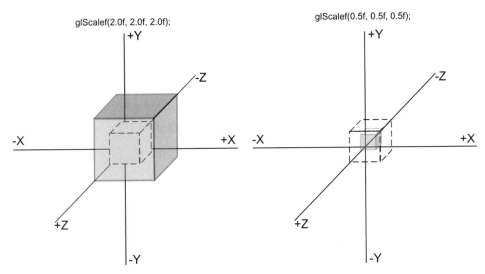

glScalef(2.0f, 2.0f, 2.0f);

glScalef(0.5f, 0.5f, 0.5f);

Figure 4.10
The effect of calling `glScale()`.

This line will shrink an object by half its original size. A value of 0.2 would shrink it by one-fifth, 0.1 by one-tenth, and so on. If you pass a negative value to `glScale()` then the object will be flipped, which is useful for simulating reflections (see Chapter 12 for an example). If you set a scaling factor to 1.0, then the axis the scaling factor belongs to will not be scaled. As you might have guessed from this, scaling is equivalent to multiplying by the scaling factor. Values between 0.0 and 1.0 will shrink the object, and values greater than 1.0 will enlarge the object. Figure 4.10 illustrates the `glScale()` function.

In the examples so far in this chapter, you've seen an object move around for translation, and you've seen an object rotate for rotation. So naturally, now you are going to see an example for scaling of an object shrinking and expanding. On the CD, you will find an example entitled "Scaling" in the Chapter 4 folder. Taking a look at the `prepare()` function in the `Example` class, you will see:

```
//If we are increasing the scale then increment the scale variable
if (m_increasing) {
    m_scale += speed * dt;
} else { //otherwise decrement
    m_scale -= speed * dt;
}
//If we hit either the min or max limit, reverse the scaling direction
if (m_scale >= maxLimit) {
```

```
    m_increasing = false;
} else if (m_scale <= minLimit) {
    m_increasing = true;
}
```

Before we render each frame, the prepare() function increases or decreases our scaling factor within a range of 0.1 units to 2.0 units. We pass the scaling factor to the glScale() function in the render() function below:

```
void Example::render()
{
    glClear(GL_COLOR_BUFFER_BIT | GL_DEPTH_BUFFER_BIT);
    glLoadIdentity();

    //Bind the color array, and set the color pointer to point at it
    glBindBuffer(GL_ARRAY_BUFFER, m_colorBuffer);
    glColorPointer(3, GL_FLOAT, 0, 0);

    //Bind the vertex array and set the vertex pointer to point at it
    glBindBuffer(GL_ARRAY_BUFFER, m_vertexBuffer);
    glVertexPointer(3, GL_FLOAT, 0, 0);

    glTranslatef(0.0f, 0.0f, -10.0f); //Move 10 units back
    glScalef(m_scale, m_scale, m_scale); //Scale using our scaling variable
    //Draw the square as a triangle strip
    glDrawArrays(GL_TRIANGLE_STRIP, 0, 4);
}
```

The render() function sets up the camera 10 units back and rotated onto the z-axis so that we can view the plane from above. It then calls the glScale() function, passing the scale factor to all three axis parameters. The result is a plane that increases and decreases in size with the value of the scale factor. Although you can't see the plane changing shape, Figure 4.11 is a screenshot of the Square Scaling example.

Matrix Stacks

The modelview matrix we've been playing with so far is actually only one matrix at the top of a stack of matrices, which is naturally called the OpenGL matrix stack. There are four types of matrix stacks in OpenGL:

- The modelview matrix stack

- The projection matrix stack

Figure 4.11
A screenshot of the Square Scaling example. Exciting!

- The color matrix stack

- The texture matrix stack

The modelview matrix is the top matrix of the modelview matrix stack, and the projection matrix is the top matrix of the projection matrix stack. Figure 4.12 gives some more information about these matrix stacks.

The texture matrix stack is used for the transformation of texture coordinates, and the color matrix can be used to modify colors.

The modelview matrix stack allows you to save the current state of the transformation matrix, perform other transformations, and then return to the saved transformation matrix without having to store or calculate the transformation matrix on your own. The projection, texture, and color matrix stacks allow you to do the same thing.

Using the modelview matrix stack essentially allows you to transform from one coordinate system to another while being able to revert to the original coordinate

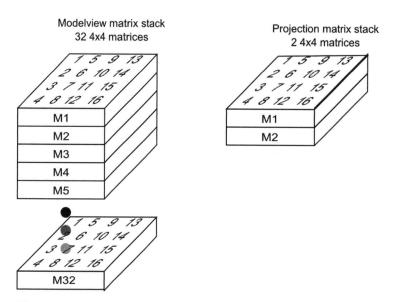

Figure 4.12
The modelview and projection matrix stacks are made up of 32 4 × 4 matrices and two 4 × 4 matrices, respectively, for the Microsoft OpenGL implementation.

system. For instance, if we position ourselves at the point (10, 5, 7), and we then push the current modelview matrix onto the current stack, then our current transformation matrix is reset to the local coordinate system centered around the point (10, 5, 7). This means that any transformations we do are now based on the coordinate system at (10, 5, 7). So if we then translate 10 units down the positive x axis with glTranslate(10.0f, 0.0f, 0.0f), we are at the position (10, 0, 0) in the current transformation matrix, but in the world we are positioned at (20, 5, 7). When the matrix stack is popped, we revert to the original transformation matrix and therefore the original coordinate system, which means we are again positioned at (10, 5, 7).

Two functions allow you to push and pop the matrix stacks: glPushMatrix() and glPopMatrix(). The glPushMatrix() function copies the current matrix and pushes it onto the stack and is defined as:

```
void glPushMatrix();
```

If you push too many matrices onto the stack, then OpenGL gives a GL_STACK_OVERFLOW error. The modelview matrix stack is guaranteed to have a stack depth of at least 32, and all of the other matrix stacks have a depth of at least 2. You can find out if your implementation supports larger stacks by calling

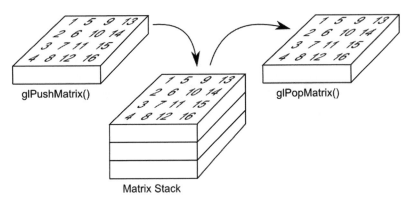

Figure 4.13
Pushing and popping on the matrix stack.

glGet() with GL_MAX_MODELVIEW_STACK_DEPTH, GL_MAX_PROJECTION_STACK_DEPTH, GL_MAX_COLOR_STACK_DEPTH, or GL_MAX_TEXTURE_STACK_DEPTH.

The glPopMatrix() function pops off the top matrix on the stack and discards its contents. All other matrices in the stack are moved up one position. glPopMatrix() is defined as

```
void glPopMatrix();
```

If you try to use this function when there is only one matrix in the stack, OpenGL will give a GL_STACK_UNDERFLOW error.

Figure 4.13 shows how the glPushMatrix() and glPopMatrix() functions operate on the matrix stack.

The Robot Example

On the CD, you will find the source code for an OpenGL demo called Robot Example that shows an animated walking robot around which the camera rotates. The robot is constructed of cubes that you scale to different shapes and sizes to give the robot arms, legs, feet, a torso, and a head. The glPushMatrix() and glPopMatrix() functions are used to position the robot's body parts in coordinates relative to the center of the robot. Take special note of these functions as you trace through the source code.

Figure 4.14 shows a screenshot of the Robot example.

There are two functions that you should focus on as you browse through the source code. The first is the animate() method in the Robot class:

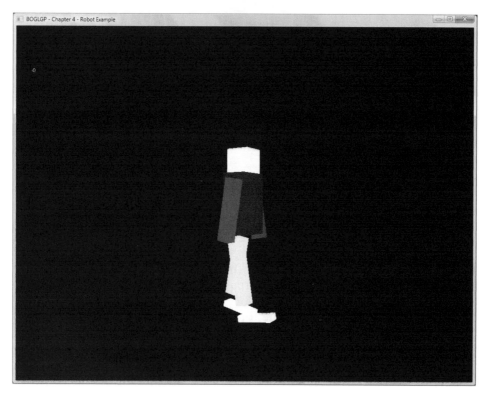

Figure 4.14
A screenshot of the Robot example

```
void Robot::animate(float dt)
{
    const float armRotationSpeed = 20.0f;
    const float maxArmAngle = 15.0f;
    const float legRotationSpeed = 30.0f;
    const float maxLegAngle = 15.0f;

    for (unsigned int side = 0; side < MAX_SIDES; ++side) {
     // arms
        if (m_armStates[side] == FORWARD_STATE) {
            m_armAngles[side] += armRotationSpeed * dt;
        } else {
            m_armAngles[side] -= armRotationSpeed * dt;
        }
        // change state if exceeding angles
        if (m_armAngles[side] >= maxArmAngle) {
            m_armStates[side] = BACKWARD_STATE;
        } else if (m_armAngles[side] <= -maxArmAngle) {
        m_armStates[side] = FORWARD_STATE;
```

```
        }
        // legs
        if (m_legStates[side] == FORWARD_STATE) {
            m_legAngles[side] += legRotationSpeed * dt;
        } else {
            m_legAngles[side] -= legRotationSpeed * dt;
        }
    // change state if exceeding angles
        if (m_legAngles[side] >= maxLegAngle) {
            m_legStates[side] = BACKWARD_STATE;
        } else if (m_legAngles[side] <= -maxLegAngle) {
            m_legStates[side] = FORWARD_STATE;
        }
    }
  }
}
```

The animate() method modifies the angle of rotation of the legs and arms of the robot, as well as determining the direction each arm and leg is moving. As you've seen in previous examples, we use the delta time (dt) parameter to keep the movement frame rate independent. The m_armAngles and m_legAngles arrays store each arm's and leg's angles (array index 0 is for the left limb, array index 1 for the right), respectively; the m_armStates and m_legStates arrays store the current direction each arm and leg is moving, respectively.

The method that does the main rendering work is probably the most interesting. This is the render() method of the Robot class:

```
void Robot::render(float xPos, float yPos, float zPos)
{
    glPushMatrix();
        glTranslatef(xPos, yPos, zPos); // move to (0, 0, -30)
        // draw head and torso parts
        renderHead(0.0f, 3.5f, 0.0f);
        renderTorso(0.0f, 0.0f, 0.0f);
    // move the left arm away from the torso and rotate it to give "walking"
effect
    glPushMatrix();
        glTranslatef(0.0f, -0.5f, 0.0f);
        glRotatef(m_armAngles[LEFT], 1.0f, 0.0f, 0.0f);
        renderArm(2.0f, 0.0f, 0.0f);
    glPopMatrix();
```

```
        // move the right arm away from the torso and rotate it to give "walking"
    effect
        glPushMatrix();
            glTranslatef(0.0f, -0.5f, 0.0f);
            glRotatef(m_armAngles[RIGHT], 1.0f, 0.0f, 0.0f);
            renderArm(-2.0f, 0.0f, -0.0f);
        glPopMatrix();
        // move the left leg away from the torso and rotate it to give "walking"
    effect
        glPushMatrix();
            glTranslatef(0.0f, -0.5f, 0.0f);
            glRotatef(m_legAngles[LEFT], 1.0f, 0.0f, 0.0f);
            renderLeg(-1.0f, -5.0f, -0.5f);
        glPopMatrix();
        // move the right leg away from the torso and rotate it to give "walking"
    effect
        glPushMatrix();
            glTranslatef(0.0f, -0.5f, 0.0f);
            glRotatef(m_legAngles[RIGHT], 1.0f, 0.0f, 0.0f);
            renderLeg(1.0f, -5.0f, -0.5f);
        glPopMatrix();
    glPopMatrix(); //pop back to original cooordinate system
}
```

The renderRobot() method draws the entire robot at the specified position. To simplify the code, the method calls several other methods that each render a certain part of the robot's body. These methods are renderHead(), renderTorso(), renderArm(), and renderLeg(). renderLeg() also calls another method, render-Foot(). In turn, each of these methods draws its respective part at the specified position, relative to the position of the robot itself because we use the glPush-Matrix() and glPopMatrix() functions to position and rotate each robot part.

Projections

We've mentioned projection transformations several times now and even used them in code, so it's high time we discussed how they work. As we've pointed out, there are two general classes of projection transformations available in OpenGL: orthographic (or parallel) and perspective. We'll look at both of these in detail.

By setting a projection transformation, you are, in effect, creating a viewing volume, which serves two purposes. The first is that the viewing volume defines a number of clipping planes, which determine the portion of your 3D world that is visible at any given time. Objects that are outside this volume are not rendered.

The second purpose of the viewing volume is to determine how objects are drawn. This depends on the shape of the viewing volume, which is the primary difference between orthographic and perspective projections.

Before specifying any kind of projection transformation, though, you need to make sure that the projection matrix is the currently selected matrix stack. As you saw earlier with the modelview matrix, this is done with a call to `glMatrixMode()`:

```
glMatrixMode(GL_PROJECTION);
```

In most cases, you will want to follow this up with a call to `glLoadIdentity()` to clear out anything that may be stored in the projection matrix, so that previous transformations aren't accumulated. Unlike with the modelview matrix, it is rare to make many changes to the projection matrix.

Once the projection matrix stack is selected, you're ready to specify your projection. We'll look at orthographic projections first and then at the more commonly used perspective transformations.

Orthographic

As we mentioned before, orthographic, or parallel, projections are those that involve no perspective correction. In other words, no adjustment for distance from the camera is made; objects appear the same size onscreen whether they are close or far away. Although this may not look as realistic as perspective projections, it has a number of uses. Traditionally, orthographic projections are included in OpenGL for applications such as CAD, but they can also be used for 2D games or isometric games.

OpenGL provides the `glOrtho()` function to set up orthographic projections:

```
glOrtho(GLdouble left, GLdouble right, GLdouble bottom, GLdouble top,
GLdouble near, GLdouble far);
```

`left` and `right` specify the x-coordinate clipping planes, `bottom` and `top` specify the y-coordinate clipping planes, and `near` and `far` specify the distance to the z-coordinate clipping planes. Together, these coordinates specify a box-shaped viewing volume. More precisely, opposite planes are parallel to each other, and adjacent planes are perpendicular.

Because orthographic projections are commonly used to create 2D scenes, the OpenGL Utility Library provides an additional routine to set up orthographic projections for scenes in which you won't really be using the z-coordinate:

```
gluOrtho2D(GLdouble left, GLdouble right, GLdouble bottom, GLdouble top);
```

`left`, `right`, `bottom`, and `top` are as with `glOrtho()` above. Using `gluOrtho2D()` is equivalent to calling `glOrtho()` with near set to −1.0 and far set to 1.0. When using `gluOrtho2D()`, you'll normally want to send vertices that contain two components (the x- and y-coordinates) because the z-coordinate isn't needed.

It's common in this case to use integer coordinates and to set the view volume to match the x- and y-coordinates of the viewport.

Perspective

Although orthographic projections can be interesting, perspective projections create more realistic-looking scenes, so that's what you'll likely be using more often. In perspective projections, as an object gets farther from the viewer, it appears smaller on the screen—an effect commonly referred to as foreshortening. The viewing volume for a perspective projection is a frustum, which looks like a pyramid with the top cut off, with the narrow end toward the viewer. That the far end of the frustum is larger than the near end is what creates the foreshortening effect. The way this works is that OpenGL transforms the frustum so that it becomes a cube. This transformation affects the objects inside the frustum as well, so objects at the wide end of the frustum are compressed more than objects at the narrow end. The greater the ratio between the wide and narrow ends, the more an object is shrunk. If the ends of the frustum are close in size, there won't be much perspective correction (if they are the same, there will be no correction at all, which is what happens with orthographic projections).

There are a couple of ways you can set up the view frustum, and thus the perspective projection. The first we'll look at is the following:

```
void glFrustum(GLdouble left, GLdouble right, GLdouble bottom, GLdouble top,
GLdouble near, GLdouble far);
```

`left`, `right`, `top`, and `bottom` together specify the x- and y-coordinates on the near clipping plane, and near and far specify the distance to the near and far clipping planes. Thus, the top-left corner of the near clipping plane is at (left, top, −near), and the bottom-right corner is at (right, bottom, −near). The corners of the far clipping plane are determined by casting a ray from the viewer through the corners of the near clipping plane and intersecting them with the far clipping plane. So, the closer the viewer is to the near clipping plane, the larger the far clipping plane is, and the more foreshortening is apparent.

Using glFrustum() enables you to specify an asymmetrical frustum, which may be useful in some instances, but it's not typically what you'll want to do. In addition, thinking about what the viewer can see in terms of a frustum is not particularly intuitive. Instead, it's easier to think about the field of view—that is, how wide of an angle the viewer can see. The OpenGL Utility Library provides a function that allows you to directly specify the field of view, and then calculates the frustum for you. This function is as follows:

```
void gluPerspective(GLdouble fov, GLdouble aspect, GLdouble near, GLdouble far);
```

fov specifies, in degrees, the angle around the y-axis that is visible to the user. aspect is the aspect ratio of the screen, which is the width divided by the height. This determines the field of view around the x-axis. near and far have the same meanings they've had in the other projection functions in this section.

One thing we haven't mentioned in our discussion of setting up a frustum is how to determine an appropriate ratio between the width of the far and near end (that is, how wide the field of view is). The appropriate field of view is highly application dependent. If you want to create a fish-eye effect, a very wide field of view may be appropriate. For a realistic perspective, something around 45–90 degrees usually works well. In general, you'll want to experiment to see what looks right for your particular application.

Setting the Viewport

Some of the projection functions we've just discussed are closely related to the size of the viewport (for example, the aspect ratio in gluPerspective()). You know that the viewport transformation happens after the projection transformation, so now is as good a time as any to discuss it.

In essence, the viewport specifies the dimensions and orientation of the 2D window into which you'll be rendering. It is set using glViewport():

```
void glViewport(GLint x, GLint y, GLsizei width, GLsizei height);
```

x and y specify the coordinates of the lower-left corner of the viewport, and width and height specify the size of the window in pixels.

When a rendering context is first created and attached to your window, the viewport is automatically set to match the dimensions of the window. That may be good enough for some applications, but in most cases, you'll want to update your viewport any time the window is resized. Although the viewport generally matches your window size, there is nothing requiring it to be the same size. There may be times when you want to limit rendering to a sub-region of your window, and setting a smaller viewport is one way to do this.

Projection Example

To get a better idea of the differences between the two major projection types, we've included a simple demo that allows you to view the same scene in each mode. The demo starts off with a perspective projection; pressing the spacebar enables you to toggle between orthographic (shown in Figure 4.15) and perspective (shown in Figure 4.16) projections.

The relevant portion of this demo is in the updateProjection() and onResize() methods of the Example class, which are listed here for convenience:

```
void Example::updateProjection()
{
```

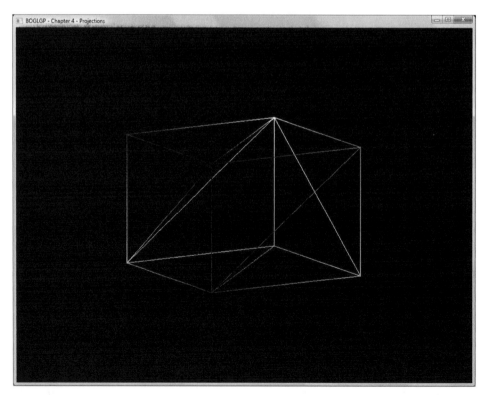

Figure 4.15
Orthographic projection.

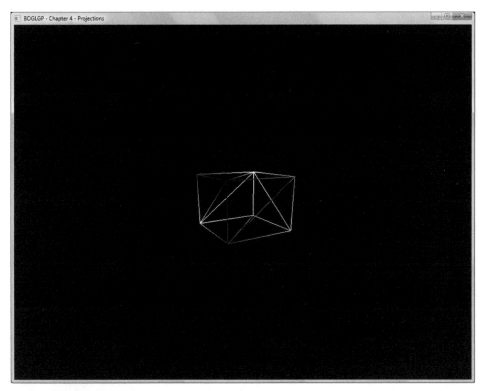

Figure 4.16
Perspective projection.

```
    glMatrixMode(GL_PROJECTION);
    glLoadIdentity();

    if (m_perspective) {
        // set the perspective with the appropriate aspect ratio
        glFrustum(-1.0, 1.0, -1.0, 1.0, 1.0, 1000.0);
    } else {
        // set up an orthographic projection with the same near clip plane
        glOrtho(-1.0, 1.0, -1.0, 1.0, 1.0, 1000.0);
    }

    glMatrixMode(GL_MODELVIEW);
    glLoadIdentity();
}
void Example::onResize(int width, int height)
{
    if (height == 0) //Prevent a divide by zero
```

```
    {
        height = 1;
    }

    // set the viewport to the new window size
    glViewport(0, 0, width, height);

    //set the projection based on the m_perspective flag
    updateProjection();
}
```

Manipulating the Viewpoint

In this section, we are going to introduce you to several options for manipulating the viewpoint, or the "camera." Your first option is to use the gluLookAt() function, which allows you to specify the position of the viewpoint, a directional vector from the viewpoint, and an up vector from the viewpoint to orient and position the viewpoint. The second option is to use a combination of the glTranslate() and glRotate() functions to orient and position the viewpoint. Finally, you can use your own custom routines to define the viewpoint behavior. For instance, you might want the viewpoint to be oriented through the polar coordinate system.

Let's look at these options.

Using gluLookAt()

Now let's take a look at the gluLookAt() function, which is defined as

```
void gluLookAt(GLdouble eyex, GLdouble eyey, GLdouble eyez, GLdouble centerx,
GLdouble centery, GLdouble centerz, GLdouble upx, GLdouble upy, GLdouble upz);
```

You can use this function to define the camera's location and orientation instead of the modeling transformations glTranslate() and glRotate(). The first set of three parameters (eyex, eyey, eyez) specifies the location of the camera. The value (0, 0, 0) would naturally specify the origin. The next set of parameters (centerx, centery, centerz) specifies where the camera is pointing. From this, OpenGL can determine the forward direction of the camera.

The last set of parameters (upx, upy, upz) is a vector that tells which direction is the up direction. Figure 4.17 shows how all of these parameters work on the camera with the gluLookAt() function.

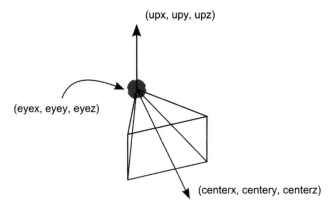

gluLookAt(GLdouble eyex, GLdouble eyey, GLdouble eyez, GLdouble centerx, GLdouble centery,
         GLdouble centerz, GLdouble upx, GLdouble upy, GLdouble upz);

Figure 4.17
The gluLookAt() parameters specify the location and orientation of the camera.

Here is a short code snippet that uses the gluLookAt() function.

```
glClear(GL_COLOR_BUFFER_BIT | GL_DEPTH_BUFFER_BIT);
glLoadIdentity();

/* We set the camera at position (0, 0, 10) looking down the negative z-axis (0, 0,
-100). The orientation of the camera is determined using the up vector (0, 1, 0)
*/
gluLookAt(0.0, 0.0, 10.0,   //Position
          0.0, 0.0, -100.0,   //Point camera is looking at
          0.0, 1.0, 0.0); //Up vector

glEnableClientState(GL_VERTEX_ARRAY);
glBindBuffer(GL_ARRAY_BUFFER, m_vertexBuffer);
glVertexPointer(3, GL_FLOAT, 0, 0);
glDrawArrays(GL_TRIANGLES, 0, 3);
```

As you can see, the gluLookAt() function is rather easy to use. By manipulating the parameters, you can move the camera to any position and orientation that you want.

Using glRotate() and glTranslate()

A drawback to gluLookAt() is that you must link the GLU library with your application. What if you don't want to use the GLU library, but you want to get the same functionality? One solution is to simply use the glRotate() and glTranslate() modeling-transformation functions as discussed earlier in this chapter. The code below uses the modeling functions to produce the same effect on the camera as the previous gluLookAt() code.

```
glClear(GL_COLOR_BUFFER_BIT | GL_DEPTH_BUFFER_BIT);
glLoadIdentity();
/* We move the modeling transformation to (0.0, 0.0, -10.0). Moving the world
10 units along the negative z-axis effectively moves the camera to the position
(0.0, 0.0, 10.0)
*/
glTranslatef(0.0f, 0.0f, -10.0f);

//Render a triangle
glEnableClientState(GL_VERTEX_ARRAY);
glBindBuffer(GL_ARRAY_BUFFER, m_vertexBuffer);
glVertexPointer(3, GL_FLOAT, 0, 0);
glDrawArrays(GL_TRIANGLES, 0, 3);
```

In this case, there isn't a serious difference in code from the gluLookAt() function because all you are doing is moving the camera along the z-axis. But if you were orienting the camera at an odd angle, you would need to use the glRotate() function as well, which leads to the next way of manipulating the camera: your own custom routines.

Creating Your Own Custom Routines

Suppose you want to create your own flight simulator. In a typical flight simulator, the camera is positioned in the pilot's seat, so it moves and is oriented in the same manner as the plane. Plane orientation is defined by pitch, yaw, and roll, which are rotation angles relative to the center of gravity of the plane (in your case, the pilot/camera position). Using the modeling-transformation functions, you could create the following function to create the viewing transformation:

```
void planeView(GLfloat planeX, GLfloat planeY, GLfloat planeZ,
            GLfloat roll, GLfloat pitch, GLfloat yaw)
{
    // roll is rotation around the z axis
    glRotatef(roll, 0.0f, 0.0f, 1.0f);
    // yaw, or heading, is the rotation around the y axis
    glRotatef(yaw, 0.0f, 1.0f, 0.0f);
    // pitch is rotation about the x axis
    glRotatef(pitch, 1.0f, 0.0f, 0.0f);
    // move to the plane's world coordinates
```

```
    glTranslatef(-planeX, -planeY, -planeZ);
}
```

Using this function places the camera in the pilot's seat of your airplane regardless of the orientation or location of the plane. This is just one of the uses of your own customized routines. Other uses include applications of polar coordinates, such as rotation about a fixed point, and use of the modeling-transformation functions to create what is called "*Quake*-like movement," where the mouse and keyboard can be used to control the camera.

The greatest degree of camera control can be obtained by manually constructing and loading your own matrices, which will be covered in the next section.

Using Your Own Matrices

Up until now, we've talked about functions that allow you to modify the matrix stacks without really having to worry about the matrices themselves. This is great because it allows you to do a lot without having to understand matrix math, and the functions OpenGL provides for you are actually quite powerful and flexible. Eventually, though, you may want to create some advanced effects that are possible only by directly affecting the matrices. This will require that you know your way around matrix math, which we're assuming as a prerequisite to reading this book. However, we'll at least show you how to load your own matrix, how to multiply the top of the matrix stack by a custom matrix, and one example of using a custom matrix.

Loading Your Matrix

Before you can load a matrix, you need to specify it. OpenGL matrices are column-major 4×4 matrices of floating-point numbers, laid out as in Figure 4.18.

$$\begin{bmatrix} m_0 & m_4 & m_8 & m_{12} \\ m_1 & m_5 & m_9 & m_{13} \\ m_2 & m_6 & m_{10} & m_{14} \\ m_4 & m_7 & m_{11} & m_{15} \end{bmatrix}$$

Figure 4.18
The column-major matrix format used by OpenGL.

As the matrices are 4 × 4, you may be tempted to declare them as two-dimensional arrays, but there is one major problem with this. In C and C++, two-dimensional arrays are row major. For example, to access the bottom-left element of the matrix in Figure 4.18, you might think you'd use matrix[3][0], which is how you'd access the bottom-left corner of a 4 × 4 C/C++ two-dimensional array, but because OpenGL matrices are column major, you'd really be accessing the top-right element of the matrix. To get the bottom-left element, you'd need to use matrix[0][3]. This is the opposite of what you're used to in C/C++, making it counterintuitive and error prone. Rather than using two-dimensional arrays, it's recommended that you use a one-dimensional array of 16 elements. The nth element in the array corresponds to element mn in Figure 4.18.

As an example, if you want to specify the identity matrix you could use:

```
GLfloat identity[16] = { 1.0, 0.0, 0.0, 0.0, 0.0, 1.0, 0.0, 0.0, 0.0, 0.0, 1.0,
0.0, 0.0, 0.0, 0.0, 1.0 };
```

That's easy enough. So, now that you've specified a matrix, the next step is to load it. This is done by calling glLoadMatrix():

```
void glLoadMatrix{fd}(const TYPE matrix[16]);
```

When glLoadMatrix() is called, whatever is at the top of the currently selected matrix stack is replaced with the values in the matrix array, which is a 16-element array as specified previously.

Multiplying Matrices

In addition to loading new matrices onto the matrix stack (and thus losing whatever information was previously in it), you can multiply the contents of the active matrix by a new matrix. Again, you'd specify your custom matrix as above and then call the following:

```
void glMultMatrix{fd}(const TYPE matrix[16]);
```

Again, matrix is an array of 16 elements. glMultMatrix() uses post-multiplication; in other words, if the active matrix before the call to glMultMatrix() is Mold, and the new matrix is Mnew, then the new matrix will be Mold × Mnew. Note that the ordering is important; because matrix multiplication is not commutative, Mold × Mnew in most cases will not have the same result as Mnew × Mold.

Summary

In this chapter, you learned how to manipulate objects in your scene by using transformations. You've also examined how to change the way in which the scene itself is viewed, through setting up projections. In the process, you've learned about the projection and modelview matrices and how to manipulate them using both built-in functions and matrices you define yourself. You now have the means to place objects in a 3D world, to move and animate them, and to move around the world.

What You Have Learned

- Transformations allow you to move, rotate, and manipulate objects in a 3D world, while also allowing you to project 3D coordinates onto a 2D screen.

- The viewing transformation specifies the location of the camera.

- The modeling transformation moves objects around the 3D world.

- The projection transformation defines the viewing, volume, and clipping planes.

- The viewport transformation maps the projection of the scene into the viewport, or window, on your screen.

- The OpenGL modelview transformation is a combination of the modeling and viewing transformations.

- The viewpoint is also called the "camera" or "eye coordinates."

- Translation is the act of moving an object along a vector.

- Rotation is the act of rotating an object about a vector-defined axis.

- Scaling is the act of increasing or decreasing the size of an object.

- Perspective projection shows 3D worlds exactly as you see things in real life. Objects that are farther away appear smaller than objects that are closer to the camera.

- Orthographic projection shows objects on the screen in their true size, regardless of their distance from the camera.

- The modelview matrix defines the coordinate system that is used to place and orient objects. You set the modelview matrix to the current matrix by using the `glMatrixMode()` function with `GL_MODELVIEW` as the parameter. Using `GL_PROJECTION` as the parameter sets the current matrix to the projection matrix.

- `glLoadIdentity()` restores the current matrix to the identity matrix.

- Translation is performed in OpenGL with the `glTranslate()` function.

- Rotation is performed in OpenGL with the `glRotate()` function.

- Scaling is performed in OpenGL with the `glScale()` function.

- Saving and restoring the current matrix is accomplished via the `glPushMatrix()` and `glPopMatrix()` functions.

- The `glOrtho()` and `gluOrtho2D()` functions are used to set up orthographic projections.

- The `glFrustum()` and `gluPerspective()` functions are used to set up perspective projections.

- `gluLookAt()` can be used to position and orient the OpenGL viewpoint.

- Use the `glLoadMatrix()` function to load a user-defined matrix as the current OpenGL matrix.

- Use the `glMultMatrix()` function to multiply the current OpenGL matrix by a user-defined matrix.

Review Questions

1. How do you store the current matrix so that it can be restored later?

2. Write the line of code that will position an object at (10, 5, 0).

3. Name three different matrix stacks in OpenGL.

4. Write the line of code that will halve the size of the objects that are rendered after.

5. Which command allows you to rotate an object?

6. Which command allows you to load your own matrix in to the current matrix stack?

7. How do you restore a matrix that was previously pushed onto the stack?

On Your Own

1. Write a program that renders a pyramid that rotates constantly around the y-axis and moves backwards and forwards along the z-axis.

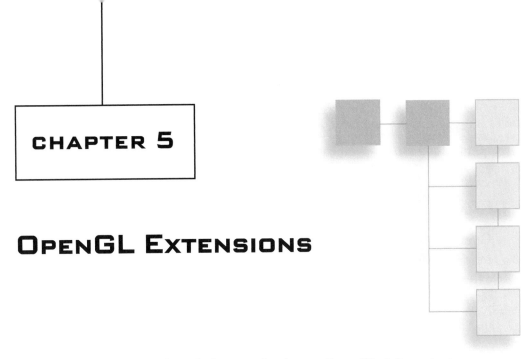

CHAPTER 5

OpenGL Extensions

In Chapter 2, we mentioned that to obtain an OpenGL 3.0 context, you were required to use OpenGL extensions. Now it's time to look at the extension mechanism in more detail. In this chapter, you will learn:

- What an OpenGL extension is

- How to discover which extensions are supported

- Why extensions are necessary on the Windows platform

- How to access extensions

- How to use the GLee library to transparently use the most cutting-edge features

What Is an Extension?

An OpenGL extension is really just that; an extension to the OpenGL standard. In fact, just like OpenGL, each extension is recorded in a specification document. This document describes, in detail, some extra functionality that allows you to render faster, in better quality or more easily. Extensions allow graphics card vendors to quickly provide access to the most cutting-edge features of their chipsets, without waiting for updates to the OpenGL specification.

Extension specifications are hosted at the OpenGL extension registry, which can be found at http://www.opengl.org/registry/.

An OpenGL extension specification usually contains the following information:

- **Name**—The name of the extension

- **Name Strings**—Unique identifiers for the extension

- **Overview**—This section is a short description of the purpose of the extension, why there is the need for the extended functionality and what the extension provides

- **New procedures and functions**—Prototypes of any new API functions that have been added as part of this specification

- **New tokens**—Any new constants that are defined by the extension

- **Dependencies**—Any other extensions that this extension relies on

Extension Naming

Every OpenGL extension must have a unique name to identify it. There is a standard naming convention for extensions; all extensions must start with a prefix, words are separated with underscores instead of spaces, and everything after the prefix is usually lowercase. For example:

```
PREFIX_extension_name
```

When a vendor creates an extension, they name it with their own unique prefix. For example, NVIDIA uses the prefix NV, whereas Apple unsurprisingly uses APPLE. If an extension is adopted by more than one vendor, the prefix is changed to EXT to reflect this. Eventually the ARB might officially approve the extension; in that case, the prefix becomes ARB. Table 5.1 shows some of the prefixes in use.

Name Strings

As mentioned earlier, in every specification document there is a section called "Name Strings." These strings are values unique to the extension that are listed as part of the `GL_EXTENSIONS` string(s) that can be obtained using `glGetString()` or `glGetStringi()` if the extension is supported by the OpenGL implementation.

Table 5.1 OpenGL Extension Prefixes

Prefix	Meaning/Vendor/Category
ARB	Extension approved by the Architecture Review Board
EXT	Extension agreed upon by two or more vendors
APPLE	Apple Inc.
ATI	AMD/ATI
MESA	Open Source implementation of the OpenGL specification
NV	NVIDIA
SGI	Silicon Graphics Inc.
SGIS	Silicon Graphics Inc. (specialized)
SGIX	Silicon Graphics Inc. (experimental)
SUN	Sun Microsystems
WIN	Microsoft

Normally, the name string for an extension is the extension name prefixed by GL_, WGL_ (for Windows extensions), GLX_ (for X extensions), or GLU_ (for extensions to the GLU library).

Although each extension normally only has one name string, occasionally one may have several, especially if the extension added functionality specific to the windowing system.

Functions and Tokens

Extensions can add new functions, new tokens, or both to OpenGL. If the extension provides new functions, you will need to get a pointer to them before you can use them. This is explained in the "Obtaining a Function Entry Point" section a little later.

Any new functions are required to follow the naming conventions defined by OpenGL; each function is prefixed by a lower case "gl" and then the rest of the function name uses a capital letter at the beginning of each word. Finally, each function name is suffixed with the prefix used in the extension name (e.g., ARB). For example:

```
glFunctionNameARB()
```

If the extension is later moved into the core, the suffix would be dropped from the function names that it provides.

Some extensions may not specify any new functions for OpenGL, but instead will just provide a new token to pass to an existing function. A token is a constant or enumerant such as `GL_TEXTURE_2D` or `GL_FLOAT`.

Any new tokens must follow the consistent naming from the rest of OpenGL. This means that they should be all capital letters, with spaces replaced by underscores and prefixed with `GL_`. Again the token will have the extension name prefix appended. For example:

```
GL_SOME_NEW_TOKEN_ARB
```

If an extension just provides new tokens (and no new functions), it is much easier to use as you do not need to obtain any function pointers. Instead, you can just download the latest `glext.h` header file from the OpenGL extension registry, which provides the latest extension tokens and function definitions. There are also `wglext.h` and a `glxext.h` for platform-specific extension tokens, for Windows and X, respectively.

Obtaining a Function's Entry Point

The `glext.h`, `wglext.h`, and `glxext.h` header files provide you with the definitions of the latest extension functions, but definitions aren't much use without the actual function implementations! As the implementations are unavailable when you compile your code, you need to link to them dynamically at runtime. This involves querying the graphics drivers for a function pointer to the function you want to use. This is platform specific, but the general idea is the same on all platforms.

First, you must declare a pointer to a function. Each function has its own parameters and return type, which make defining function pointers pretty ugly. Fortunately, the previously mentioned headers provide us with some typedefs to make the function pointers a little more readable. Next, you call a platform-specific function to find the address of the function you want, and assign it to the function pointer. If the function pointer is NULL after this call, then the extension that provides the function is not available. Now you can use the function pointer in the same way as a regular function.

Let's break this down with an example. We'll obtain a pointer to the `glGetStringi()` function. You will need to use this later to find out which other extensions are supported. After including `glext.h` we must declare a function pointer like so:

```
PFNGLGETSTRINGIPROC glGetStringi = NULL;
```

That's easy enough. PFNGLGETSTRINGIPROC is the typedef for the function pointer type, which is defined in glext.h. The next step is to get the address of the glGetStringi() function and assign it to our pointer. On Windows, we use the wglGetProcAddress() function for this (on X you would use glXGetProcAddress()) which has the following definition:

```
PROC wglGetProcAddress(LPCSTR lpszProcName);
```

Let's take a look at how to use it to get our glGetStringi() function pointer:

```
glGetStringi = (PFNGLGETSTRINGIPROC) wglGetProcAddress("glGetStringi");
```

We cast the returned value to our pointer type before assigning it to our function pointer. If the function was unavailable, wglGetProcAddress() would return NULL. You should check this before attempting to use the function pointer; otherwise, your program may crash. For example:

```
if (glGetStringi != NULL) {
      //We can use glGetStringi
}
```

Extensions on Windows

The original intention of the extension mechanism was to provide cutting-edge functionality that was not part of the core of OpenGL. On platforms besides Windows, this is still the case. However, on the Windows platform, you must use extensions to access any functionality after OpenGL 1.1. To understand why, we need to look at what is required to use OpenGL in your applications.

When you develop an OpenGL application, you must include the OpenGL header files, which give you access to the function and token definitions available. You also need to link your application (on Windows) to OPENGL32.lib and possibly GLU32.lib. These library files are required to access the functionality in the dynamic link libraries OPENGL32.dll and GLU32.dll, respectively.

This is where the problem lies—Microsoft hasn't kept up to date with OpenGL releases and the headers, libraries, and DLLs are heavily out of date. To use any new functionality you must use the extension mechanism.

Finding Supported Extensions

Before using an OpenGL extension, it's a good idea to first check that it is present on the running system. As previously mentioned, you can get available extensions by using glGetStringi() and passing GL_EXTENSIONS as the first parameter. glGetStringi() takes an integer index as a second parameter. To get a list of all extensions supported by the OpenGL implementation, you must iterate from 0 to NUM_EXTENSIONS - 1 calling glGetStringi() each time with the new index. But how big is NUM_EXTENSIONS? To find out, you need to pass GL_NUM_EXTENSIONS to glGetIntegerv() like so:

```
GLint numExtensions = 0;
glGetIntegerv(GL_NUM_EXTENSIONS, &numExtensions);
```

After this call, numExtensions will hold the number of extensions supported by the current OpenGL implementation. The only thing left to do is to grab the extension strings one by one and store them in an array:

```
for (int i = 0; i < numExtensions; i++)
{
    //Get the extension at i
    string extension = (const char*) glGetStringi(GL_EXTENSIONS, i);
    //Add the extension to the string list
    extensions.push_back(extension);
}
```

As described in the "Obtaining a Function's Entry Point" section, before you can use the glGetStringi() function, you will need to get a pointer to it. Then you can use the function to query the available extensions. We can bring all these steps together to create a function that returns an array of all supported extensions:

```
vector<string> getSupportedExtensions()
{
    PFNGLGETSTRINGIPROC glGetStringi = NULL;
    glGetStringi = (PFNGLGETSTRINGIPROC)wglGetProcAddress("glGetStringi");

    vector<string> extensions;
    if (glGetStringi == NULL)
    {
        //Return empty array
        return extensions;
    }

    GLint numExtensions = 0;
    //Get the number of supported extensions
```

```
glGetIntegerv(GL_NUM_EXTENSIONS, &numExtensions);
for (int i = 0; i < numExtensions; i++)
{
    //Get the extension at i
    string extension = (const char*) glGetStringi(GL_EXTENSIONS, i);
    //Add the extension to the string list
    extensions.push_back(extension);
}
return extensions;
}
```

Note

You may notice that we cast the return of `glGetStringi()` to `const char*`. This is because `glGetStringi()` returns a string made up of unsigned characters (`const Glubyte*`), but we require them as signed characters to assign to the string instance.

Determining whether or not an extension is supported just consists of iterating over the array looking for the extension string you require. The `isExtension-Supported()` function below does just that.

```
bool isExtensionSupported(const string& ext)
{
    //Get a list of extensions
    vector<string> extensions = getSupportedExtensions();

    /*Go through all the extensions and if the current one matches the one we are
    looking for then return true */
    for (vector<string>::iterator it = extensions.begin(); it != extensions.end
(); ++it)
    {
        if (*it == ext)
        {
            return true;
        }
    }

    /* If we go through all the extensions and none match then return false */
    return false;
}
```

WGL Extensions

In addition to the standard OpenGL extensions, there are some extensions that are specific to the Windows system. These extensions provide additions that are very specific to the windowing system and the way it interacts with OpenGL. To get these Windows-specific extensions, you should use the `wglGetExtensions-StringARB()` function which (like `glGetStringi()`) is itself an extension (ARB_extension_string). To get access to this function, you will need to use `wglGetProcAddress()` and check that the returned function pointer is not NULL before using it. The format of this function is as follows:

```
const char* wglGetExtensionsStringARB(HDC hdc);
```

The only parameter is the handle to the rendering context. This function differs from `glGetStringi()` in that it returns the extension strings as a space-delimited list; it is the same as the older `glGetString(GL_EXTENSIONS)` in this respect.

Defining Tokens

If you are using an up-to-date version of `glext.h` and `wglext.h` or `glxext.h` all your extension tokens will be defined already, but you can also define extension tokens yourself. If an extension specifies any new tokens, they will be listed in the associated specification document on the OpenGL registry. For example, in the NV_half_float specification under the "New Tokens" heading, you will find a token called HALF_FLOAT_NV with the value 0x140B. To define this you simply use:

```
#define GL_HALF_FLOAT_NV        0x140B
```

Notice that we prefix the GL_ to the constant defined in the specification to match the naming convention of the other tokens.

Introduction to GLee

If you are using only a few extension functions, then obtaining the function pointers and managing them is not too difficult. However, when you begin using many extension functions they very quickly become hard to manage, and obtaining the function pointers clutters up your initialization code. Fortunately, there are existing libraries that transparently initialize function pointers, specify tokens, and give you an easy way of checking if an extension is supported. The two most common libraries that provide this functionality are GLee (OpenGL Easy Extension library) and GLEW (OpenGL Extension Wrangler library). We'll be covering GLee here but GLEW's usage is very similar. GLee is developed and maintained by Ben Woodhouse; it is available for Linux and Windows and is also compatible with OSX and FreeBSD. It is released under a non-restrictive modified BSD license. The latest version of GLee with OpenGL 3.0 support is on the CD; however, you can check for updates at http://elf-stone.com/glee.php.

Setting Up GLee

The GLee source package provides a header file (for inclusion in your code), a source file (glee.c), and a library (glee.lib). There are two options for using GLee in your applications: you can add the source file to your project, which is then compiled with the rest of your code, or you can tell the compiler to link to the glee library instead. Either way, you just need to extract the zip file containing GLee and copy the files to a location where you can include them in your project. This can either be in a folder local to the project or it can be in your compiler's include and library directories.

Using GLee

Before you can use GLee, you must include the header file glee.h. glee.h replaces the need to include gl.h; in fact, your code will produce a descriptive compiler error if you include gl.h before glee.h. The latest releases of GLee don't require any special initialization, so once the header file has been included, you can begin checking for extensions.

GLee internally holds a boolean variable for each extension that stores whether or not the extension is available. The name of each of these variables is the same as the name string, but with GLEE_ prefixed instead of GL_. For example, if you wanted to see if the vertex buffer object extension is available (which will always be the case in a GL 3.0 context), you would use the following:

```
if (GLEE_ARB_vertex_buffer_object)
{
    glBindBufferARB(...);
    ...
}
```

Platform-specific extensions (WGL/GLX) are treated slightly differently; in this case, the whole name string is prefixed with GLEE_ and includes the WGL_ or GLX_ part of the name. For example GLEE_WGL_ARB_pbuffer.

You can check which version of OpenGL is supported by checking the value of the variable `GL_VERSION_x_y` where x and y are the major and minor version numbers, respectively.

Using GLee with Core Extensions

Over the lifetime of OpenGL, many features that started off as extensions became part of the core specification. GLee allows you to use these features without using the extension suffix. For example, vertex buffer objects were moved into the core specification, so you can use:

```
glBindBuffer(...);
```

instead of:

```
glBindBufferARB(...);
```

If you are using the former version, make sure that you check the `GLEE_VERSION_x_y` flag to see if the driver supports the OpenGL version that the extension was promoted to the core.

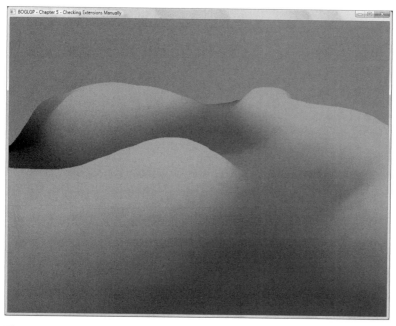

Figure 5.1
A screenshot from the terrain example.

Extensions in Action

As the examples in this book are written for OpenGL 3.0, every single example uses an extension of some sort. However, so far we've done the extension checking manually. Included on the CD under the Chapter 5 folder you will find two versions of the same application. The program renders a simple heightmap-based terrain, which we will build on in later chapters to make more realistic. One version of the application checks for and loads extensions manually; the other uses GLee to manage the extensions.

Summary

OpenGL extensions are essential on the Windows platform and are required to create and use an OpenGL 3.0 context as well as access all the advanced features. On all platforms they provide access to the cutting-edge functionality on the latest graphics cards. You should now understand how to check for an extension's availability and how to get access to the functions provided by that extension. You've seen how libraries such as GLee can make accessing extensions easy, and accessing post-OpenGL 1.1 functionality on Windows transparent.

What You Have Learned

- Extensions exist to enable hardware vendors to innovate and add new features quickly

- The OpenGL registry keeps a database of all OpenGL extension specifications

- When programming, the key elements to an extension are the extension string, function, pointers, and tokens

- Libraries such as GLee make using and managing extensions easy

Review Questions

1. What function is used to return a list of supported extensions, and what should its first argument be?

2. What does the ARB prefix indicate?

3. `glGetStringi()` is available in which OpenGL version?

4. What are extensions for?

On Your Own

1. Write a program that reads the extensions available on your OpenGL implementation and writes the list to a text file.

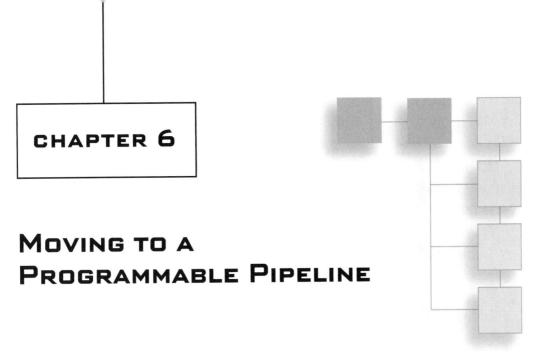

CHAPTER 6

MOVING TO A PROGRAMMABLE PIPELINE

In the previous chapters, we have used several methods of rendering—starting from immediate mode and then moving to vertex arrays and finally using vertex arrays with VBOs. All of these methods use the fixed-function pipeline. The fixed-function pipeline is still available in OpenGL and will be available for some time, but gradually fixed-function techniques will be removed from the OpenGL specification in favor of shader-based rendering. GLSL and shader techniques are a massive topic so this chapter will provide a brief introduction rather than a complete reference.

In this chapter, you will learn:

- The OpenGL Shading Language

- How to use GLSL shaders to render primitives

- How to manage your own transformation matrices

The Future of OpenGL

Over the lifetime of OpenGL, many features have been added to improve the performance of rendering complex scenes. Unfortunately, the API has become very large, with a whole array of options to choose from for each particular rendering task. Such a large number of options makes it very difficult to determine which technique will perform the most efficiently; in other words, it has became difficult to find what's known as the "fast path." The introduction of the deprecation model in OpenGL 3.0 promises to rectify this situation. The majority of the API (specifically the fixed-function part) has been marked as deprecated; the remaining functions provide the fastest methods of rendering.

Here is a list of the main functionality deprecated in Version 3.0. If you have some previous knowledge of OpenGL (or you read the first edition of this book), this list may be of interest to you.

- Color Index mode

- OpenGL shading language versions 1.10 and 1.20 (now replaced with 1.30)

- Immediate mode

- Fixed-function vertex processing

- Matrix stacks

- Client vertex arrays

- Rectangles

- Raster position

- Non-sprite points

- Wide lines and line stipple

- Quadrilateral and polygon primitives

- Separate polygon drawing mode

- Polygon stipple

- Pixel drawing

- Bitmaps

- Texture wrap mode—GL_CLAMP

- Display lists

- The selection buffer

- The accumulation buffer

- Alpha test

- Attribute stacks

- Evaluators

- Unified extension string

It's quite a lot isn't it! Most of the above functionality is now implemented using shaders, and some parts (such as the matrix stack) can be implemented in separate libraries. There are a few items listed above that are no longer relevant because they have been replaced by more efficient methods (e.g., display lists), and some have been removed because they don't really belong in a rendering API (e.g., the selection buffer). By the end of this chapter, you will understand how to render using future-proof, non-deprecated functionality by replacing the fixed-function features we have relied on so far (vertex arrays and the matrix stack) with new techniques using shaders.

What Is GLSL?

GLSL or the OpenGL Shading Language is used to write programs that run on the GPU. The language is defined in a specification document developed by the ARB that can be found on the opengl.org registry alongside the OpenGL specification. GLSL is a high-level language that borrows many elements from C and C++, so the syntax should be quite familiar.

There are two main types of shaders: vertex shaders, which operate on every vertex sent to the graphics card, and fragment (also known as pixel) shaders, which operate on every pixel to be rasterized.

When you use shaders, you effectively replace whole sections of the pipeline; this provides a huge amount of flexibility and control, but it does mean that some of the functionality that was automatically taken care of using fixed-function rendering will become your responsibility to handle when using shaders. Figure 6.1 shows the stages of the pipeline that can be replaced using GLSL shaders.

Vertex Shaders

As we have already covered, OpenGL takes a series of vertices to build geometric primitives. These are then transformed, clipped, and rasterized to produce the pixels in the framebuffer as output. Vertex shaders are programs that operate on

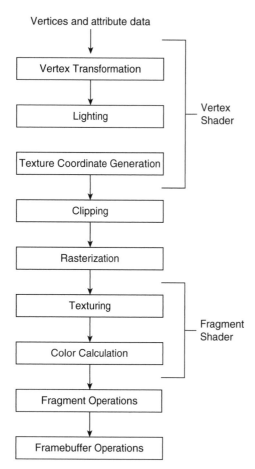

Figure 6.1
Pipeline stages that can be replaced by GLSL shaders.

each vertex that is sent to the graphics card by a rendering command such as glDrawArrays(). It is the responsibility of this shader to calculate the final position of the vertex (usually using the projection and modelview matrices) and also to calculate per-vertex attributes such as colors. One important thing to note is that a vertex shader only knows about a single vertex at a time; it is not possible to extract information on neighboring vertices. The only output that is required by a vertex shader is the position. This must be stored in a built-in variable, which is a four-element floating-point vector (vec4) called gl_Position. The shader can output other variables, which can then be used as inputs to the fragment shader. These outputs are normally interpolated across the surface of the primitive and each fragment receives the interpolated value that corresponds with its position on the surface. So, for example, imagine a vertex shader that outputs a single floating-point value. If the shader operates on two neighboring vertices and outputs 0.0 for the first, and 1.0 for the second, then (assuming linear inter-polation), the fragment exactly halfway between the two vertices would receive the value 0.5 as an input. This is how colors, texture coordinates, etc. are smoothly interpolated across a surface. Once the vertex processing stage is complete, the graphics card takes back control until the fragment processing stage. When using a vertex shader, you will need to manually handle the following:

- Vertex transformation (using modelview and projection matrices)

- Texture coordinate generation

- Lighting calculations

- Color application

- Normal transformation

Vertex transformation and color application are explained later in this chapter. Texture coordinates are covered in Chapter 7, "Texture Mapping" and Lighting and Normals are covered in Chapter 8, "Blending, Lighting, and Fog."

Note

> As we discussed in Chapter 1 there is a third kind of shader called a geometry shader. Geometry shaders are still relatively new and currently only available as an extension. They are generally used for advanced effects and are beyond the scope of this book.

Fragment Shaders

It is the job of the fragment shader to calculate the final output color of a pixel that will be stored in the frame buffer. Fragment shaders take the outputs from the vertex shader (which may have been interpolated) as input variables; you can use these inputs to color or texture the fragment, or achieve more advanced effects such as bump mapping and per-pixel lighting. Fragment shaders need to output a single, user-defined, four-element vector that makes up the color of the pixel. When using a fragment shader you must handle the following parts of the pipeline:

- Computing per-pixel colors

- Applying textures

- Calculating per-pixel fog

- Applying per-pixel lighting

The GLSL Language

Now that you have a general idea of what GLSL is for, it's time to look at how to use it. We'll cover the language itself first before moving on to the details of how the shaders are loaded, compiled, and used in OpenGL. There have been three versions of GLSL since its introduction; the first version was labeled 1.10, the second 1.20, and finally, coinciding with the release of OpenGL 3.0, 1.30. We will be covering version 1.30 in this chapter; versions 1.10 and 1.20 have been marked as deprecated.

Shader Structure

A GLSL shader must contain at least a single function called `main()`. This function has the same purpose as the `WinMain()` or `main()` function in a C or C++ program; it is executed when the shader program begins, and the shader ends when the function completes. The definition of the main method is as follows:

```
void main(void)
```

As you can see, the `main()` function doesn't return anything; any output that the shader generates is passed via variables which have a qualifier of `out` (we'll discuss variable qualifiers later). Variables that are passed into or out of a shader must be declared in global scope. It is normal for a list of these variables to be declared at the top of the shader before the `main()` function. Following is an example of a simple vertex shader; you'll notice the variables listed above `main()`. The first line is a preprocessor directive.

```
#version 130

uniform mat4 projection_matrix;
uniform mat4 modelview_matrix;

in vec3 a_Vertex;
in vec3 a_Color;
out vec4 color;
```

```
void main(void)
{
    vec4 pos = modelview_matrix * vec4(a_Vertex, 1.0);
    gl_Position = projection_matrix * pos;
    color = vec4(a_Color, 1.0);
}
```

Preprocessor

GLSL borrows the idea of a preprocessor from C. Preprocessor directives are evaluated before compilation of the shader source code and can alter the final code that is compiled. The full list of preprocessor directives and their functions are shown in Table 6.1.

Variables

Variables are fundamental to any programming language and GLSL is no different. Like C++, GLSL variables obey rules of scope. A scope block is defined inside a pair of curly braces ({...}), and variables are declared inside the curly braces and have no presence outside of that scope. A variable can exist in local scope (between two curly braces), global scope (at the top of the shader), or a variable can exist across more than one shader (program scope). For a variable to exist between shaders, it must be declared with the correct qualifiers in both shaders (e.g., in and out).

Table 6.1 Preprocessor Directives

Directive	Function
#	Ignore
#define	Define a constant or macro
#undef	Undefine a previously defined constant
#if / #ifdef / #ifndef / #else / #elif / #endif	Conditional compilation
#error	Insert an error into the shader log output
#pragma	Declare implementation-specific options
#line	Use to override the line numbering recognized by the compiler
#version	Choose which version of GLSL to use (the current version is 1.30)
#extension	Use to enable extended functionality available to the GLSL implementation

Data Types

Like C and C++, GLSL is a statically typed language. Each variable that is declared must specify a data type that it will hold throughout the lifetime of the variable. GLSL provides a few familiar data types such as "float" for floating-point numbers and "int" for integers, but as you saw in the vertex shader example, GLSL also has some other base types specific to shader programming. These data types include vectors and matrices with various dimensions. Table 6.2 contains a list of all the data types in GLSL.

Table 6.2 GLSL Data Types

Data Type	Description
void	Used as the return type for functions that don't return a value
bool	Stores a true or false value
int	A signed integer
uint	An unsigned integer
float	A floating-point number
vec2, vec3, vec4	two-, three-, or four-element floating-point vector
bvec2, bvec3, bvec4	two-, three-, or four-element Boolean vector
ivec2, ivec3, ivec4	two-, three-, or four-element integer vector
uvec2, uvec3, uvec4	two-, three-, or four-element unsigned integer vector
mat2, mat3, mat4	2x2, 3x3, or 4x4 floating-point matrix
mat2x2, mat3x3, mat4x4	Equivalent to mat2, mat3, and mat4
mat2x3, mat2x4	Non-square floating-point matrices with two columns
mat3x2, mat3x4	Non-square floating-point matrices with three columns
mat4x2, mat4x3	Non-square floating-point matrices with four columns
sampler1D, sampler2D, sampler3D, usampler1D, usampler2D, usampler3D, isampler1D, isampler2D, isampler3D	Handles for accessing one-, two-, or three-dimensional textures (floating-point, unsigned integer, and integer access)
samplerCube, usamplerCube, isamplerCube	Handle for accessing a cube-mapped texture
sampler1DShadow, sampler2DShadow, samplerCubeShadow	Handle for accessing one- or two-dimensional depth textures or a cube map of depth textures
sampler1DArray, sampler2DArray, usampler1DArray, usampler2DArray, isampler1DArray, isampler2DArray	Handle for accessing one- or two-dimensional array textures
sampler1DArrayShadow, sampler2DArrayShadow	Handle for accessing one- or two-dimensional array depth textures

Note

Samplers are a handle to a texture map. Samplers allow access to the pixel data of the texture and are required for many different effects. We will discuss textures and samplers in detail in the next chapter.

Variables must be declared before they are first used and are declared in the same way as in C—by specifying the type before the variable name. You can initialize a variable when it is declared like so:

```
int i = 0;
```

More complex variable types (vectors and matrices) are made up of multiple components; a vec2, for example, is made up of two floating-point elements. For vectors, these elements can be addressed individually by adding a period (.) to the variable name and then using the component name to select a component. For vectors, the component names that are available are as follows:

- {x, y, z, w}—When accessing vectors that represent points

- {r, g, b, a}—For accessing vectors that represent colors

- {s, t, p, q}—For accessing vectors that represent texture coordinates

The different component naming is just for aesthetic purposes. x, r, and s all refer to the same component. Matrix components are accessed using the array-style notation:

```
mat4[column][row]
```

column and row have to be within the bounds of the matrix. Attempting to access outside the bounds of the matrix results in undefined behavior.

Like other languages, you can define arrays of variables in GLSL. Arrays must be indexed with a zero-based integer constant. Negative indexes are illegal. An array declaration in GLSL is similar to its C counterpart:

```
vec3 array[3]; //An array of 3 vectors
```

GLSL arrays may be initially declared without specifying a size, although they must be redeclared with a size before first use, for example:

```
vec3 array[];     //Declaration of an array without the size specified
vec3 array[3];    //Redeclared with the size of the array before first use
```

Once a size has been specified, you cannot redeclare the array again. GLSL arrays can be initialized with data on the same line that they are defined; the syntax in GLSL differs slightly from C as GLSL types use constructors rather than an initialization list of values:

```
float array[3] = float[3](0.0, 1.0, 2.0); //Initializes the 3 floats
float array[3] = float[](0.0, 1.0, 2.0); //Does the same thing, the second 3 is
optional
```

Once declared, the length of an array can be determined later in the shader by using the built-in length() method:

```
float array[3];
int arrayLength = array.length();   //arrayLength will be 3 after this is
executed
```

Structures

Custom data types can be defined by grouping variables together in C++-style structures. A structure must contain at least one data member. Structures are defined by using the struct keyword and an identifier, followed by the variables inside curly braces:

```
struct Light {
    vec3 color;
    vec3 position
};
Light firstLight;
firstLight.color = vec3(0.0, 1.0, 2.0);
```

It is illegal to nest a structure declaration inside another structure. It is, however, perfectly fine for a structure to contain an instance of another structure:

```
struct B {
    struct A { //Invalid!
        int a;
    };
};

struct A { int a; }
struct B {
    A a; // OK.
};
```

Table 6.3 GLSL Operators

Precedence	Operator Class	Operators	Associativity
1 (highest)	parenthetical grouping	()	N/A
2	array subscript, function call and constructor structure, field or method selector, swizzler, post fix increment and decrement	[] () . ++ --	Left to Right
3	prefix increment and decrement unary	++ -- + - ~ !	Right to Left
4	multiplicative	* / %	Left to Right
5	additive	+ -	Left to Right
6	bit-wise shift	<< >>	Left to Right
7	relational	< > <= >=	Left to Right
8	equality	== !=	Left to Right
9	bit-wise and	&	Left to Right
10	bit-wise exclusive or	^	Left to Right
11	bit-wise inclusive or	|	Left to Right
12	logical and	&&	Left to Right
13	logical exclusive or	^^	Left to Right
14	logical inclusive or	||	Left to Right
15	selection	?:	Right to Left
16	assignment, arithmetic assignment	= += -= *= /= %= <<= >>= &= ^= |=	Right to Left
17 (lowest)	sequence	,	Left to Right

Operators

GLSL data types support basic operators such as addition, subtraction, multiplication, division, assignment, equality, and comparison (less than, greater than). Table 6.3 shows the full list of all available GLSL operators:

The operators work on integer, unsigned integer, and floating-point types, as you would expect. On types such as vectors that are made up of several components (e.g., x, y, z), the operators work on a component-by-component basis. The one exception is multiplications involving matrices, which work using standard linear algebra rules.

When using operators you should make sure that the types in the expression match; for example, you can multiply an integer with another integer type, but not a floating type. If you want to mix types, you need to use constructors to mimic the behavior of casting. We'll discuss this in the "Constructors" section later.

Table 6.4 Storage Type Qualifiers

Qualifier	Effect
None	A local variable that can be read and written
const	A variable that is not writable
in	A variable that has been copied in from a previous stage (e.g., an attribute passed from the program to the vertex shader)
out	A variable that is copied out to a later stage of processing (e.g., a variable passed from the vertex shader to the fragment shader)
uniform	A variable passed in from the application that doesn't change during the rendering of the current primitive
centroid in	Same as in, but using centroid interpolation
centroid out	Same as out, but using centroid interpolation

Variable Qualifiers

Variable qualifiers modify a variable's behavior in some way. A variable without a qualifier will behave as you would expect; the variable would be readable and writable and will respect the scope in which it is declared. Table 6.4 shows the full list of nondeprecated-type qualifiers and the effect they have on a variable. Centroid interpolation, which appears in the table, is sometimes used to avoid artifacts when using multisampling. As this is an advanced subject, we won't go into centroid interpolation in detail.

Extra qualifiers can be specified for output variables from a vertex shader and input variables into a fragment shader. These extra qualifiers are listed in Table 6.5 and affect the interpolation of the variable.

The final type of qualifier is used on variables that are passed into functions. These qualifiers can be found in Table 6.6.

Table 6.5 Interpolation Qualifiers

Qualifier	Meaning
smooth	Perspective correct interpolation
flat	No interpolation
noperspective	Linear interpolation

Table 6.6 Parameter Qualifiers

Qualifier	Meaning
None	Same as in
in	The variable is an input to the function
out	The variable passed will be the destination of a function output
inout	The variable can be both the input and output of the function

The different variable qualifiers may be used in the following situations:

- Global variables can use `const`, `in`, `out`, and `uniform`

- Local variables can only use `const`

- Function arguments can use `const`, `in`, `out`, and `inout`

Shader Inputs

There are two methods for passing in variable values from an OpenGL application: uniforms and attributes.

Uniforms

A variable with a uniform qualifier has its value passed into the shader from the application and remains constant between the shader stages; uniforms do not change on a per-vertex or per-fragment basis. Uniforms cannot be the target of an assignment inside the shader. Their value can only be set by the application. They can be accessed by all stages of the shader program if the variable is declared identically in each shader. Uniform values are passed into the shader program using the `glUniform*()` OpenGL API functions, which are described later.

Vertex Attributes

A vertex attribute is a regular global variable marked with the `in` qualifier in a vertex shader. The value of a vertex attribute is specified by the application on a per-vertex basis using the `glVertexAttribPointer()` function. `glVertexAttrib Pointer()` will be discussed in detail in the "Sending Data to the Shaders" section.

Statements

GLSL contains the same flow control statements that you find in C and C++. Branching logic can be achieved by using the `if` and `if-else` statements, which behave in the same way as C, aside from one minor difference; it is not legal to define a variable inside an `if` statement:

```
if (condition)   //This is legal
{
    // do something
}

if (bool someVariable = condition)   //This is not legal
{
    // do something
}
```

Looping logic can be achieved using the `for`, `while`, and `do-while` constructs, which behave identically to their C++ counterparts. Like in C++, variables can be declared inside the `for` or `while` statements, which are then local to the loop.

Constructors

GLSL data types have built-in constructors that can be used to create new variables initialized with data. We have already seen an instance of constructor usage in the "Arrays" section to initialize an array with data. You will no doubt use constructors a lot in GLSL code, not only to initialize new variables, but also to copy data from a variable of one type to another. For example, let's assume that we have a color value stored as a three-element floating-point vector (`vec3`). However, the output of our fragment shader expects a four-element vector. We can copy the data to our output variable by using a `vec4` constructor, which takes two arguments, a `vec3` variable, and a floating-point value for the fourth component:

```
out vec4 ourColorOutput;
void main(void)
{
    vec3 color = vec3(1.0, 0.0, 0.0); //A 3-element vector initialized with a
constructor

    //A constructor is used to copy the data to a 4-element vector
    ourColorOutput = vec4(color, 1.0);
}
```

Table 6.7 GLSL Constructors

Constructor	Purpose
int(bool)	Converts a Boolean value to an integer (result is 1 if the value is true, or 0 if it's false)
int(float)	Converts a float value to an integer (decimal part is dropped)
int(uint)	Converts an unsigned integer to a signed integer
float(bool)	Converts a Boolean value to a float (result is 1.0 if the value is true, or 0.0 if it's false)
float(int)	Converts an integer value to a float
float(uint)	Converts an unsigned integer value to a float
bool(float)	Converts a float value to a Boolean (non-zero is true)
bool(int)	Converts an integer value to a Boolean (non-zero is true)
bool(uint)	Converts an unsigned integer to a Boolean (non-zero is true)
uint(bool)	Converts a Boolean value to an unsigned integer (result is 1 if the value is true or 0 if it's false)
uint(float)	Converts a float value to an unsigned integer (decimal part is dropped; if the float is negative then behavior is undefined)
uint(int)	Converts a signed integer value to an unsigned integer
vec2(float)	Initializes both components of the vector to the passed value
vec2(float, float)	Initializes the vector with the two floats
vec2(vec3)	Drops the last component of the vec3 and constructs a vec2 from the remaining components
vec3(float)	Initializes all components with the passed float
vec3(float, float, float)	Initializes the vec3 with the three floats
vec3(vec4)	Drops the last component of the vec4 and constructs a vec3 from the remaining components
vec3(vec2, float)	Constructs a vec3 from using the vec2 as the first two components and the float as the final one
bvec3(int, float, uint)	Uses Boolean conversions on each parameter
mat2(float)	Initializes the diagonal of the matrix to float; all other elements are set to zero
mat2(vec2, vec2)	Initializes the two columns using the two vectors
mat2(float, float, float, float)	Initializes the matrix with the two elements of the first column, and then the two elements of the second column

There are many different constructors for each type so that new objects can be initialized with different types of data. Table 6.7 lists the main constructors that you will use regularly.

Table 6.7 is not an exhaustive list for brevity; the vector constructors following the same rules are extended to vec4 and the matrix constructors are extended to the different matrix sizes (mat3, mat4, mat3x2, etc.) and follow the same patterns of available parameters.

Swizzling

Some constructors allow you to pass in more than one type of argument to construct an object of the sum of their components; for example, a vec3 and a float (totaling four components) can be used to construct a vec4. Sometimes, however, you may want to construct a three-component vector from a four-component vector, but not necessarily using the first three components. You might want to construct a vec3 using the y, z, and w components for instance. You could construct such a vector like so:

```
vec4 fourVec(1.0, 2.0, 3.0, 4.0);
vec3 threeVec = vec3(fourVec.y, fourVec.z, fourVec.w);
```

GLSL provides a shorthand method of doing this called "swizzling." Using swizzling, you can do the same conversion like this:

```
vec4 fourVec(1.0, 2.0, 3.0, 4.0);
vec3 threeVec = fourVec.yzw;
```

Swizzling works on all vector types, and you can use any combination of component names from the same name set (xyzw, rgba, or stpq). Here are some examples:

```
vec4 vector;
vector.x; //Returns a float
vector.xyz; //Returns a vec3
vector.rg; //Returns a vec2
vector.xyza; //Illegal, a is not part of the same naming set
```

You can also assign values to certain elements by using the same component syntax on the left-hand side of an assignment:

```
vec4 vector = vec4(1.0, 2.0, 3.0, 4.0);
vector.xw = vec2(1.0, 2.0); //vector is now 1.0, 2.0, 3.0, 2.0
vector.xy = vec3(0.0, 1.0); // vector is now 0.0, 1.0, 3.0, 2.0
vector.xx = vec2(1.0, 0.0); // Illegal, you cannot use the same component twice
```

Defining Functions

Functions in GLSL will seem very familiar as they are declared in the same way as C with the following syntax:

```
returnType functionName(typeA arg1, typeB arg2, ... typeZ argn)
{
    return returnValue;
}
```

Function declarations differ from C in that each parameter may include one of the following qualifiers: in, out, inout, or const (whereas C only has const). Functions in GLSL can be overloaded (like C++ methods); two functions can have the same name but different parameters and the correct version will be called depending on the parameters passed in.

Built-in Functions

GLSL provides a large number of built-in functions that are automatically available for use in a shader. Some of these functions are simple convenience functions you could write yourself (max() is one example). Others provide access to hardware functionality which is impossible to recreate manually (e.g., the texture() function, which allows access to a texture) and a few are designed to be hardware accelerated (i.e., trigonometry functions). There are far too many built-in functions to cover in this chapter, but Table 6.8 describes some of the most commonly used functions. A full list of all built-in functions can be found in section 8 of the GLSL specification.

GLSL Deprecated Functions

Before we cover how to use GLSL shaders in your OpenGL applications, we'll just briefly talk about deprecated functionality. Despite only quite recently being promoted to core, GLSL didn't escape the wrath of the new deprecation model completely. The following features have been deprecated or redesigned:

- The attribute and varying keywords have been replaced by in and out.

- gl_ClipVertex has been replaced by gl_ClipDistance.

- gl_FragData and gl_FragColor have been deprecated.

- Built-in attributes have been deprecated in favor of user-defined attributes.

- Mixing of fixed-function vertex or fragment stages with shader programs. Vertex and fragment shaders should always be used together.

- All built-in texture function names have changed.

- gl_FogFragCoord and gl_TexCoord have been replaced in favor of user-defined variables.

- The built-in function ftansform() has been deprecated.

- gl_MaxVaryingFloats has been replaced by gl_MaxVaryingComponents.

Table 6.8 Built-in GLSL Functions

Syntax	Description
`TYPE radians(TYPE degrees)`	Converts degrees to radians
`TYPE degrees(TYPE radians)`	Converts radians to degrees
`TYPE sin(TYPE angle)`	The standard sine function
`TYPE cos(TYPE angle)`	The standard cosine function
`TYPE tan(TYPE angle)`	The standard tangent function
`TYPE acos(TYPE x)`	Arc cosine function
`TYPE asin(TYPE x)`	Arc sine function
`TYPE atan(TYPE y, TYPE x)`	Arc tangent function
`TYPE pow(TYPE x, TYPE y)`	Returns x raised to the y power
`TYPE exp(TYPE x)`	Returns the natural exponentiation of x
`TYPE log(TYPE x)`	Returns the natural logarithm of x
`TYPE sqrt(TYPE x)`	Returns the square root of x
`TYPE abs(TYPE x)`	Returns x if x >= 0, otherwise it returns −x
`TYPE floor(TYPE x)`	Returns a value equal to the nearest integer less than x
`TYPE ceil(TYPE x)`	Returns a value equal to the nearest integer greater than x
`TYPE mod(TYPE x, float y)`	Returns x − y * float(x / y)
`TYPE min(TYPE x, TYPE y)`	Returns whichever is the lowest value, x or y
`TYPE max(TYPE x, TYPE y)`	Returns whichever is the highest value, x or y
`float length(TYPE x)`	Returns the length of vector x
`float distance(TYPE p0, TYPE p1)`	Returns the distance between p0 and p1
`float dot(TYPE x, TYPE y)`	Returns the dot product of x and y
`vec3 cross(vec3 x, vec3 y)`	Returns the cross product of two vectors
`TYPE normalize(TYPE x)`	Returns a vector with a length of 1 that is in the same direction of x
`TYPE texture(SAMPLER sampler, TYPE p)`	Performs a texture lookup on the texture bound to sampler using texture coordinate p

Using Shaders

To use GLSL programs in your code, you need to use the C API functions that were promoted to core in OpenGL 2.0. There are several steps to using GLSL shaders in your application; these are as follows:

1. Create the shader objects—This will normally consist of creating a program object and two shader objects (fragment and vertex).

2. Send the source to OpenGL—The source for each shader is associated with the corresponding shader objects.

3. Compile the shaders.

4. Attach the shaders to the program object.

5. Link the program.

6. Bind the program ready for use.

7. Send any uniform variables and vertex attributes.

8. Render the objects that use the program.

There are many different ways to load the source code into your application, but in the examples for this chapter, we will assume that the source is stored in a `std::string` instance ready to go.

Note

When you load GLSL source from disk, be careful to preserve the newline characters. GLSL relies on these characters during compilation. If the newline characters are stripped during file loading, your shader will fail to compile.

Creating GLSL Objects

The first thing to do to prepare our GLSL program for use is to generate the objects that hold the state of the program in OpenGL. There are two types of object that we will need to use: shader objects hold the source code and data belonging to the vertex or fragment shaders, and program objects hold information relating to the GLSL program as a whole.

To create the shader objects, you must use the `glCreateShader()` function, which has the following prototype:

```
GLuint glCreateShader(GLenum type);
```

The `glCreateShader()` function will create a new shader object and return a handle to it. Currently, the type parameter can be either `GL_VERTEX_SHADER` or `GL_FRAGMENT_SHADER` (although it is probable that more parameter types will be available in the future). You will most likely make two calls to this function, one for each shader type. The shader objects will eventually need to be attached to a program object, which is created in a similar way using the `glCreateProgram()` function:

```
GLuint glCreateProgram(void);
```

`glCreateProgram()` takes no arguments and returns a handle to a program object. We are now ready to send the shader source code to OpenGL. This is done using the `glShaderSource()` function:

```
void glShaderSource(GLuint shader, GLsizei count, const GLchar **string, const GLint *length);
```

The first parameter is the shader object we want to load the source code into. `string` is an array of C-style strings, and `count` is the number of strings in this array. `length` is an array that stores the character length of the strings in the `string` array. If `length` is `NULL`, all strings in the array are assumed to be null-terminated (and so a length isn't needed). If your shaders are stored in a single C++ string (rather than array of strings), you can send the source to OpenGL using the following code:

```
// Create a temporary pointer to the string
const GLchar* tmp = static_cast<const GLchar*>(m_vertexShader.sour-
ce.c_str());

//Send the source to OpenGL, NULL indicates that the string is null-terminated
glShaderSource(m_vertexShader.id, 1, &tmp, NULL);
```

Once the source code has been sent to the shader objects, we are ready to compile the shaders. Shaders are compiled using the `glCompileShader()` command, which has the following definition:

```
void glCompileShader(GLuint shader);
```

You pass the shader object as the only argument. `glCompileShader()` doesn't return a value to indicate success or failure so to find out whether compilation of the shader was successful, you need to query the compile status using the following function:

```
void glGetShaderiv(GLuint shader, GLenum pname, GLint *params);
```

`glGetShaderiv()` takes the shader object as the first parameter. `pname` is an enum, which specifies the data you want to retrieve about the shader; it can be any of the values in Table 6.9. The result is stored in the variable that `params` points to.

For example, to check if a shader was compiled successfully you could do the following:

```
GLint result;
glGetShaderiv(shaderObject, GL_COMPILE_STATUS, &result);
```

Table 6.9 glGetShaderiv() pname Values

GLenum	Result
GL_COMPILE_STATUS	GL_TRUE if the shader compiled successfully, GL_FALSE otherwise
GL_SHADER_TYPE	GL_VERTEX_SHADER if the shader is a vertex shader object or GL_FRAGMENT_SHADER if it is a fragment shader object
GL_DELETE_STATUS	GL_TRUE if the shader was marked for deletion, GL_FALSE otherwise
GL_INFO_LOG_LENGTH	The length in chars of the information log including the null termination character
GL_SHADER_SOURCE_LENGTH	The length in chars of the source code for this shader

```
if (result == GL_TRUE)
{
    // The shader compiled successfully
}
```

If the compilation fails for any reason, you can obtain more detailed information on the failure by retrieving the information log attached to the shader. We will cover this later on in the chapter.

Once you have compiled the shaders, you are ready to attach them to the program object. The function that does this is called glAttachShader():

```
void glAttachShader(GLuint program, GLuint shader);
```

If you attempt to attach the same shader to the program twice, OpenGL generates a GL_INVALID_OPERATION error. You can attach the shader objects to a program object before they have been compiled, or even before the source code has been loaded. glAttachShader() has a counterpart function called glDetachShader() which takes the same parameters:

```
void glDetachShader(GLuint program GLuint shader);
```

Once the shaders have been attached to the program object, you are ready to link the GLSL program. The link stage performs sanity checks on your program and prepares it for use. Linking may fail for a number of reasons:

- One of the shader objects hasn't compiled successfully.

- The number of active attribute variables has exceeded the number supported by the OpenGL implementation.

- The number of supported or active uniform variables has been exceeded.

- The main function is missing from one of the attached shaders.

- An output variable from the vertex shader is not declared correctly in the fragment shader.

- A function or variable reference cannot be resolved.

- A global variable shared between stages is declared with different types or initial values.

You link a program by using the following function:

```
void glLinkProgram(GLuint program);
```

Again, the function doesn't return whether it is successful or not (because the work is done asynchronously), but you can retrieve the status of the link in a similar way to checking the status of a shader's compilation. To retrieve information on a program object, you use glGetProgramiv():

```
void glGetProgramiv(GLuint program, GLenum pname, GLint *params);
```

The first parameter is the program object you want to query. pname can be any of the parameters in Table 6.10. When the function call completes, the result is stored in params.

Table 6.10 glGetProgramiv() pname Values

GLenum	Result
GL_DELETE_STATUS	Returns GL_TRUE if the program is flagged for deletion, GL_FALSE otherwise
GL_LINK_STATUS	Returns GL_TRUE if the program linked successfully, GL_FALSE otherwise
GL_VALIDATE_STATUS	Returns GL_TRUE if the last validation operation was successful, GL_FALSE otherwise
GL_INFO_LOG_LENGTH	Returns the length in characters of the program's info log, including the null-termination character
GL_ATTACHED_SHADERS	Returns the number of shaders attached to the program
GL_ACTIVE_ATTRIBUTES	Returns the number of active attributes
GL_ACTIVE_ATTRIBUTE_MAX_LENGTH	Returns the length of the longest active attribute name, including the null-termination character
GL_ACTIVE_UNIFORMS	Returns the number of active uniforms
GL_ACTIVE_UNIFORM_MAX_LENGTH	Returns the length of the longest active uniform name, including the null-termination character

Once the program has passed linking, it is ready to use. You can enable a GLSL program by using the `glUseProgram()` function:

```
void glUseProgram(GLuint program);
```

This will bind and enable the program. Any primitives sent to OpenGL while the program is enabled will use the attached shaders for rendering. If you pass 0 as the `program` parameter, then shader will be disabled.

Querying the Information Logs

As has been mentioned, sometimes compilation of a shader or linking of a program may fail for some reason. To help you diagnose the problem, OpenGL stores a log that records the error. There is an info log attached to shader objects and program objects, and it can be retrieved using one of the following functions depending on the type of object:

```
void glGetProgramInfoLog(GLuint program, GLsizei maxLength, GLsizei *length,
GLchar *infoLog);
void glGetShaderInfoLog(GLuint shader, GLsizei maxLength, GLsizei *length,
GLchar *infoLog);
```

The first parameter of each function is the handle to the object you are retrieving the log for. `maxLength` is the size of the buffer you want the info log copied to; OpenGL will copy as much of the log as it can up to `maxLength`. The total length of the string returned (excluding the null-terminator) is stored in `length`. The log is copied into the buffer pointed to by `infoLog`.

Sending Data to Shaders

We've now covered all the information we need to load, compile, link, and use shaders (and retrieve information if something goes wrong!), but the shaders wouldn't be very useful if we couldn't send them any data. We mentioned earlier that there are two ways to pass data from an application into a GLSL program: uniform variables and vertex attributes.

Passing Data to Uniforms

Sending data to uniforms takes a couple of steps. Each GLSL implementation has a limited number of locations to store uniform variables. When you link a GLSL program, each uniform is attached to one of these locations (the GLSL implementation determines which uniform goes in which location). Before you can send data to a uniform, you must first find out its location. glGetUniformLocation() does this by taking the name of a uniform variable as a parameter and returning the location as an unsigned integer. The prototype is as follows:

```
GLuint glGetUniformLocation(GLuint program, const GLchar* name);
```

The first parameter is the program object; the second is the variable name as defined in the shaders.

Tip

Obtaining a uniform location can be quite a slow process so it's a good idea to cache the result of the location lookup the first time you retrieve a uniform's location. This is quite easy to do by using std::map. The GLSLProgram class used in the examples demonstrates how to do this.

Once you have retrieved the location of a uniform variable, then you are ready to send the data to it. There is a family of functions available to send data that all begin with glUniform. They have the following prototypes:

```
void glUniform{1|2|3|4}{f|i}(GLint location, TYPE v);
void glUniform{1|2|3|4}ui(GLint location, TYPE v);

void glUniform{1|2|3|4}{f|i}v(GLint location, GLuint count, const TYPE *v);
void glUniform{1|2|3|4}uiv(GLint location, GLuint count, const TYPE *v);

void glUniformMatrix{2|3|4}fv(GLint location, GLuint count, GLboolean trans-
pose, const GLfloat *v);
void glUniformMatrix{2x3|3x2|2x4|4x2|3x4|4x3}fv(GLint location, GLuint count,
GLboolean transpose, const GLfloat *v);
```

location is the location obtained by using glGetUniformLocation(). In the case of floats, integers, unsigned integers, and vectors, you just need to pass the location and chosen values into one of the first pair of functions. Here are some examples:

```
glUniform1f(floatLocation, 1.0f);
glUniform3f(vectorLocation, 1.0f, 2.0f, 3.0f);
glUniform1i(integerLocation, 1);
glUniformui(unsignedIntLocation, 2);
```

When passing data into uniform arrays, you should use one of the second pair of functions above. In this case count is the number of values in the array, and v is a pointer to an array containing the data. So for example, if your shader had the following uniform defined:

```
vec3 vecArray[4];
```

You could pass data to it like so:

```
float data [] = { 1.0, 1.0, 1.0,
                  2.0, 2.0, 2.0,
                  3.0, 3.0, 3.0,
                  4.0, 4.0, 4.0 };
glUniform3fv(vecArrayLocation, 4, data);
```

The final pair of functions for sending uniform data (the ones that begin glUni formMatrix) behave in a similar way to the last set, but they contain an extra parameter called transpose. If you have stored your data in column-major order then you need to pass GL_FALSE to transpose; otherwise, pass GL_TRUE.

Passing Data to Vertex Attributes

Attributes in GLSL are variables that are defined in the vertex shader with the in qualifier. Passing data to vertex attributes is similar in some ways to passing uniform data. Like uniforms, GLSL provides a number of slots for vertex attributes. However, with vertex attributes, you can either let OpenGL determine which location to store the attribute or you can specify it manually. If you prefer to let OpenGL determine the locations automatically, you can retrieve the location for a variable by using the following function:

```
GLint glGetAttribLocation(GLuint program, const GLchar* name);
```

The arguments are the same as the ones to glGetUniformLocation(). Like glUni formLocation(), the program needs to have been linked for this function to work.

If you would rather specify the location of the attributes yourself, you can do so with glBindAttribLocation(). This function takes three arguments; the first is the program object, then index is the location you want to give this attribute, and finally name is the name of the variable in the shader. The prototype is as follows:

```
void glBindAttribLocation(GLuint program, GLuint index, const GLchar* name);
```

Calls to glBindAttribLocation() should be made before linking the GLSL program—the attribute locations won't take effect until then. Attribute zero is special and should always be used for the vertex position.

Once you have the attribute location (whether it was generated automatically and you queried for it, or you specified it manually), you can send the data to the attribute using glVertexAttribPointer():

```
void glVertexAttribPointer(GLuint index, GLint size, GLenum type, GLboolean
normalized, GLsizei stride, const GLvoid *pointer);
```

glVertexAttribPointer() is very similar to the vertex array functions glVertexPointer(), glColorPointer(), etc. This is because they do a very similar job; glVertexPointer() sets the (now deprecated) built-in attribute gl_Vertex, whereas glVertexAttribPointer() can set any attribute. index is the location of the attribute you want to set, size indicates the number of components per element (this can be between one and four). Type can be any of the following: GL_BYTE, GL_UNSIGNED_BYTE, GL_SHORT, GL_UNSIGNED_SHORT, GL_INT, GL_UNSIGNED_INT, GL_FLOAT, or GL_DOUBLE. If the normalized flag is true then data will be converted to a floating-point value between -1.0 and 1.0 (for signed values) or 0.0 and 1.0 for unsigned values. stride specifies the offset in bytes between attributes in the array, and a value of zero indicates that the attributes are stored consecutively in the array. Finally, pointer is a pointer to the array of data to send to the attribute. If you are using VBOs (which you should be!), this should be an integer offset in bytes into the currently bound buffer.

Vertex attributes must be enabled before rendering for them to take effect; to do this, you must use glEnableVertexAttribArray():

```
void glEnableVertexAttribArray(GLuint index);
```

The sole argument is the attribute location. The attributes can be disabled with a corresponding call to glDisableVertexAttribArray():

```
void glDisableVertexAttribArray(GLuint index);
```

We have covered the basics that you need to know to use shaders. In the following chapters, we will use GLSL almost exclusively to achieve a number of effects including texturing, fog, transparency, and lighting.

The GLSLProgram Class

Included on the CD is a class called GLSLProgram, which makes loading and using shaders easy. This class will be used in the examples from now on. Here's a quick look at how it is used:

```
GLSLProgram* shaderProgram = new GLSLProgram("path/to/vertex/shader", "path/
to/fragment/shader");
```

```
//Load the shader files
if (!shaderProgram->initialize())
{
    //Something went wrong
}

//Bind the attribute locations
shaderProgram->bindAttrib(0, "a_Vertex");
shaderProgram->bindAttrib(1, "a_Color");

//Re link the program
shaderProgram ->linkProgram();
shaderProgram ->bindShader();   //Enable our program

//Send some uniform data
shaderProgram->sendUniform("modelview_matrix", modelviewMatrix);
shaderProgram->sendUniform("projection_matrix", projectionMatrix);

//When done:
delete shaderProgram;
```

Replacing the Fixed-Function Pipeline

Now that we have covered the basics of the GLSL shading language, it's time to find out how to use it to replace the fixed-function vertex and fragment stages of the pipeline. In the next section, we will cover how to transform the vertex positions in the vertex shader, and how to pass colors through the vertex shader and into the fragment shader.

Calculating Vertex Transformations

As the vertex shader replaces the whole transformation logic of the fixed-function pipeline, it is your responsibility to do this manually in GLSL. This isn't as complicated as you might think. As you have seen from the previous example, we pass in the modelview and projection matrices to our shader program as uniform variables. To find the final position of the vertex, you just need to multiply the vertex's local position by the modelview matrix and then multiply the result of that transformation by the projection matrix:

```
// First multiply the current vertex by the modelview matrix
vec4 pos = modelview_matrix * vec4(a_Vertex, 1.0);
```

```
// Then multiply the result by the projection matrix
gl_Position = projection_matrix * pos;
```

The order of multiplication is important when multiplying matrices; if you do the multiplications in the wrong order, you will get an incorrect result.

Tip

In the GLSL examples, we pass the modelview and projection matrices individually for clarity. However, it is more efficient to multiply the modelview and projection matrices once to create a single modelview-projection matrix and then pass that into the shader to multiply it by the vertex position in the shader. This saves a matrix multiplication on each vertex processed.

Applying Colors

Applying colors to your primitives in GLSL is a two-step process. In the vertex shader, you must read the input attribute that contains the color for the vertex. You must pass this to your fragment shader using an out variable. Unless you have specified the flat qualifier, the color will be interpolated before the input to the fragment shader. In the fragment shader, you can pass this color directly out as the final color, or you can perform some logic to change the color (for example, for fog effects, or modulating with a texture) before sending the new color as the output. Let's take a quick look at an example. In your OpenGL application, you should send your colors using a glVertexAttribPointer(); if you have bound the color attribute to slot 1, and the data is stored in a VBO, the code will look like this:

```
//Bind the color array
glBindBuffer(GL_ARRAY_BUFFER, m_colorBuffer);
glVertexAttribPointer((GLint)1, 3, GL_FLOAT, GL_FALSE, 0, 0);
```

When the primitives are rendered, the color for each vertex will be stored in the color attribute variable, which is read in the vertex shader:

```
#version 130

uniform mat4 projection_matrix;
uniform mat4 modelview_matrix;

in vec3 a_Vertex;
in vec3 a_Color; //The color attribute which was passed in from the program
out vec4 color; //The output color which will be passed to the fragment shader
```

```
void main(void)
{
    vec4 pos = modelview_matrix * vec4(a_Vertex, 1.0);
    gl_Position = projection_matrix * pos;
    color = vec4(a_Color, 1.0);
}
```

The color is assigned to the output variable (color) where it is used as the fragment color in the fragment shader. A fragment shader is required to output a four-component color which will be used as the color of the pixel at the end of the fragment processing stage.

```
#version 130

in vec4 color; //The color passed in from the vertex shader (interpolated)
out vec4 outColor; //Define the output of our fragment shader

void main(void)
{
    outColor = color;      //Copy the color to the output
}
```

In the source folder for this chapter, there is an application called "GLSL Terrain." This is an adaptation of the terrain application from Chapter 5, which instead of using fixed-function processing, does all its rendering through simple shaders. The shaders are stored in text files in the data directory; the vertex shader has the file extension .vert, and the fragment shader has the file extension .frag. You can edit these files in any text editor and see the result immediately by re-running the application. In the next chapter, we'll improve the program even further by adding texture to our terrain!

Handling Your Own Matrices

Now that we have covered rendering using a programmable pipeline, we have almost left the fixed-function (deprecated) OpenGL functionality behind. However, there is one last topic we need to cover before your OpenGL applications become fully forwards compatible. Thus far we have been relying on the built-in matrix functions to manage our modelview and projection matrices. If you look at the source code of the GLSL Terrain example you will notice that we pass the modelview and projection matrices into the shaders manually, like so:

```
//Get the current matrices from OpenGL
glGetFloatv(GL_MODELVIEW_MATRIX, modelviewMatrix);
glGetFloatv(GL_PROJECTION_MATRIX, projectionMatrix);

//Send the modelview and projection matrices to the shaders
m_GLSLProgram->sendUniform("modelview_matrix", modelviewMatrix);
m_GLSLProgram->sendUniform("projection_matrix", projectionMatrix);
```

As you can see, the matrices are retrieved from OpenGL. If you want to use a forward-compatible context, you will need to manage the matrices yourself, or use a third-party library to do it for you.

The Kazmath Library

Kazmath is an open-source 3D math library, which was developed by the maintainers of NeHe (http://nehe.gamedev.net/): Carsten Haubold and Luke Benstead (one of the co-authors of this very book!). It provides over 100 math-related functions that manipulate basic structures such as vectors and matrices. One feature that the library provides is its own matrix stack, which you can use almost as a drop-in replacement for the OpenGL matrix functions. A version of Kazmath is included on the CD, but the latest versions can always be found at http://www.kazade.co.uk/kazmath/.

The Robot Example Revisited

On the CD, you will find a version of the robot example from Chapter 4, which only uses nondeprecated functionality. GLSL replaces fixed-function rendering and the matrix stack is replaced by the Kazmath library. The other examples in the book will continue to use the built-in OpenGL matrix stacks for simplicity, but if you intend to use a forward-compatible context, then using the Kazmath library is one possible way of managing your matrices.

Summary

We have covered a lot in this chapter, and some of it may seem quite over-whelming at the moment. But fear not, things will become clearer over the next few chapters as we put GLSL into practice. In this chapter, you have learned that GLSL is a programming language used to write small programs that run on your graphics card's GPU. You should now understand that there are (currently) two main types of shaders that can be used to replace stages in the fixed-function pipeline: vertex and fragment. You have learned about all the major components of the GLSL shading language, including variables and their types and qualifiers and also functions, statements, and constructors. You should now be able to load, compile, and use your own shader programs using the OpenGL C-API functions relating to GLSL. We also briefly covered how you can fully replace the remaining deprecated functionality that we have used so far using a third-party library.

What You Have Learned

- Shaders are programs that run on the GPU

- Vertex and fragment shaders are the two types of shaders available to use in OpenGL without extensions

- GLSL shaders provide a huge amount of flexibility over the fixed-function pipeline

- A vertex shader is required to output the vertex position to the `gl_Position` variable and a fragment shader must output a single four-component color

- GLSL variables can be passed between stages using in and out qualifiers

- Uniform variables can be passed to the shader program from the application

- Vertex attributes are variables passed into the shader program on a per-vertex basis using the `glVertexAttribPointer()` function

- The OpenGL matrix stack can be replaced using a third-party library or by managing your own modelview and projection matrices

Review Questions

1. What does GLSL stand for?

2. What is a shader?

3. How do you specify the required GLSL version for a shader?

4. What is a uniform?

5. What is the difference between a uniform and an attribute?

6. What command attaches a shader to a program?

7. How do you link a GLSL program?

On Your Own

1. Alter the vertex shader in the terrain program so that the whole terrain is rendered in red, overriding the passed in color.

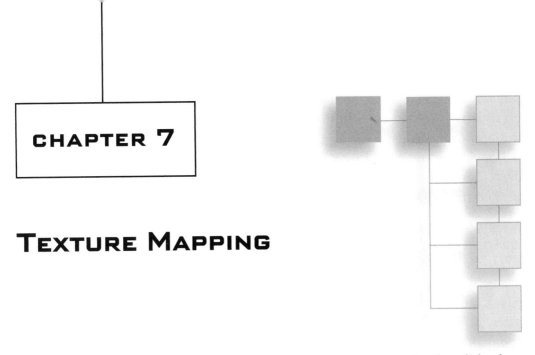

CHAPTER 7

TEXTURE MAPPING

The scenes we have rendered in the previous chapters have used only solid colors to decorate our primitives. Colors are fun, but they are hardly realistic! Using texture mapping can instantly give a massive jump in realism to our rendered scenes.

In this chapter, you will learn:

- The basics of texture mapping
- How to create, use, and delete texture objects
- GLSL texture application
- How to use mipmaps
- Texture filtering
- Texture wrap modes
- How to load Targa images (TGA)

An Overview of Texture Mapping

Texture mapping is the process of applying an image onto the surface of a primitive rather than drawing it using basic colors. For example, if you want to render the walls of a house, rendering them in plain color would be very dull and not very lifelike. The act of applying a brick pattern texture to the wall would greatly improve the scene. In the terrain example used in the previous chapters, the landscape was rendered using different shades of green depending on the hill height. The scene would look far more real if the terrain were patterned with grass. Texture mapping is so essential to providing realism that you'll be hard-pressed to find a game created in the last 10 years that doesn't use it!

A texture map is a rectangular array of color data, and each color element is known as a *texel*. Although a texture map is rectangular, it can still be mapped to any surface by using texture coordinates. The most common form of texture map is a two-dimensional image like a photo, which has a width and a height. Some effects require the use of a one-dimensional texture (with an arbitrary width, but a height of one texel) or even a three-dimensional texture (with a width, height, and depth).

You can compare the application of a texture to a surface to printing an image onto a sheet of paper; no matter which way you rotate or move the paper, the image will still stay in the same place and at the same orientation as the paper.

Using the Texture Map

There are several steps to follow to use texture mapping:

1. Load the texture into memory.

2. Generate an OpenGL texture object.

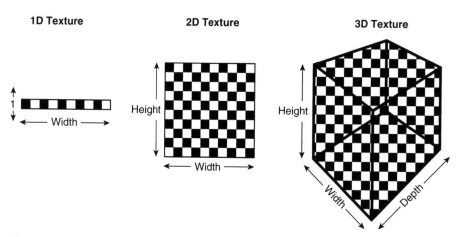

Figure 7.1
One-, two- and three-dimensional textures.

3. Bind the texture object (make it the currently active texture).

4. Upload the image data to the texture object.

5. Specify any filtering/wrapping modes.

6. Send texture coordinate data to OpenGL.

7. Apply the texture in the fragment shader.

The first step is to store the image data (the texel colors, width, height, and color depth) in memory. This information can be loaded from an image file or it can be procedurally generated using code. Before we cover loading the image data from a file, we'll first look at how OpenGL manages textures.

Note

There are many different image formats out there that you can use to store your texture on disk. You will learn how to load the Targa image format in the "Loading Targa Image Files" section later in this chapter. Targa images are well suited for texture storage as they can be compressed, support a large number of colors, and have alpha channel support (something that is very useful for blending techniques like transparency); they are also a simple format to read.

Texture Objects

Textures have a lot of associated information that OpenGL needs to look after. This data includes the texture size, the color data, filtering options, etc. OpenGL binds this data together internally into texture objects. OpenGL hides direct access to these objects, but you can control them with associated integer handles (also known as "texture names") in much the same way as the shader and program objects we covered in the last chapter.

Creating Texture Objects

Once you have loaded your image data (either from file, or procedurally generated) into your application, you need to tell OpenGL to create a texture object for you to upload the data to. A texture object is created automatically the first time you bind a unique texture name. You can generate unique texture names using glGenTextures():

```
void glGenTextures(GLsizei n, GLuint *textures);
```

n specifies the number of unique texture names you want to generate. The new names are stored in the variable pointed to by textures. Each name generated by glGenTextures() is marked as in use by OpenGL internally. This is so that each time you call the function, you can be guaranteed that the names generated are unique. Below are a couple of examples showing how to generate texture names:

```
GLuint firstTexture = 0;            //Output variable
glGenTextures(1, &firstTexture);    //Generate a single unique texture name

GLuint textureNameArray[3];         //An array to hold 3 texture names
glGenTextures(3, textureNameArray); //Generate the names and store them
                                       in the array
```

Once you have generated a unique texture name for your texture, you must bind it before OpenGL creates the associated texture object. You do this by using the glBindTexture() function:

```
void glBindTexture(GLenum target, GLuint texture);
```

target can be one of the following constants: GL_TEXTURE_1D, GL_TEXTURE_2D, GL_TEXTURE_3D, GL_TEXTURE_CUBE_MAP, TEXTURE_1D_ARRAY, or TEXTURE_2D_ARRAY. Each target corresponds with a different texture type. OpenGL uses this information to calculate the dimensionality of the texture. glBindTexture() allows you to switch between texture objects, each time making their associated state current; this is how you would render one object with one texture and then switch to another texture for a different object.

Deleting Texture Objects

When you are completely finished using a texture object, you should delete it. OpenGL allocates memory for every texture object, and if you fail to delete them, it can lead to resource leaks. You can delete texture objects using the glDeleteTextures() function:

```
void glDeleteTextures(GLsizei n, GLuint *textures);
```

Once a texture object has been deleted, its associated name is free for reuse and may be returned by a later call to glGenTextures().

Specifying Textures

Once you have created a texture object, you can copy the image data to it. OpenGL provides a family of three functions to do this, the function you use depends on the dimensionality of the texture. The functions are named `glTexImage1D()`, `glTexImage2D()`, and `glTexImage3D()` for one-dimensional, two-dimensional, and three-dimensional textures, respectively.

Note

There is one occasion where the `glTexImage*()` function doesn't match the dimensionality of the texture you are supplying with data. This special case is when you use a feature known as *texture arrays*. Texture arrays provide a means to fill an array of textures with data in a single call and access them as an array in the fragment shader. Texture arrays are beyond the scope of this book and so won't be covered in detail.

2D Textures

To specify the image data for a two-dimensional texture (which is by far the most common texture target), you use `glTexImage2D()`:

```
void glTexImage2D(GLenum target, GLint level, GLint internalformat, GLsizei
width, GLsizei height, GLint border, GLenum format, GLenum type, const GLvoid
*pixels)
```

`target` must be `GL_TEXTURE_2D`, `GL_PROXY_TEXTURE_2D`, or one of the cube mapping related constants: `GL_TEXTURE_CUBE_MAP_POSITIVE_X`, `GL_TEXTURE_CUBE_MAP_POSITIVE_Y`, `GL_TEXTURE_CUBE_MAP_POSITIVE_Z`, `GL_TEXTURE_CUBE_MAP_NEGATIVE_X`, `GL_TEXTURE_CUBE_MAP_NEGATIVE_Y`, `GL_TEXTURE_CUBE_MAP_NEGATIVE_Z`, or `GL_PROXY_TEXTURE_CUBE_MAP`. Targets beginning with `GL_PROXY` are used to test to see if a given texture format is supported. We won't be discussing them in detail. The cube map related constants will be covered in detail a little later. `GL_TEXTURE_2D` indicates a two-dimensional texture; this is the target parameter you will use most often.

The `level` parameter is used to generate mipmaps at various levels of details. We will cover this parameter in the section called "Mipmaps." The base level is 0, which is what you should pass if you are not using mipmapping.

The `internalformat` parameter specifies the number and type of the components that make up the texture. There are many possible formats for this parameter but the most commonly used are: `GL_RGB`, `GL_RGBA`, and `GL_DEPTH_COMPONENT`. There are also "sized color formats," which extend these base formats by having an additional desired bit depth (e.g., `GL_RGBA8`) and some formats which suffix a letter representing a data type for the channels (e.g., `GL_RGBA32F`). Some common values for `internalformat` can be seen in Table 7.1.

Table 7.1 Common Texture Internal Formats

Format	Description
GL_DEPTH_COMPONENT	Depth values
GL_RGB	Red, green, and blue values
GL_RGBA	Red, green, blue, and alpha values
GL_RGB8	Red, green, and blue values with a requested 8 bits per channel
GL_RGBA8	Red, green, blue, and alpha values with a requested 8 bits per channel
GL_RGBA32F	Red, green, blue, and alpha values with requested 32-bit floating-point storage per channel

Table 7.2 Texture Pixel Formats

Format	Description
GL_DEPTH_COMPONENT	Depth values
GL_RED	Red pixel values (R)
GL_GREEN	Green pixel values (G)
GL_BLUE	Blue pixel values (B)
GL_ALPHA	Alpha values (A)
GL_RGB	Red, green, and blue values (RGB)
GL_RGBA	Red, green, blue, and alpha values (RGBA)
GL_BGR	Blue, green, and red values (BGR)
GL_BGRA	Blue, green, red, and alpha values (BGRA)

Note

It is a good idea to use internal formats that specify a bit depth because by default some OpenGL implementations may use less than 8 bits per channel. Note that formats that specify a bit depth are requests; OpenGL may ignore the bit depth value.

width and height are the dimensions of the texture map that you are specifying.

The border parameter has been deprecated. If set to 1, OpenGL would draw a border around the texture. For forward-compatibility, you should set this to zero. Future versions of OpenGL will generate an INVALID_VALUE error if this parameter is not zero.

The format parameter is the format of the image data that will be passed as the last parameter to this function. The most common values are listed in Table 7.2.

Table 7.3 Common Texture Data Types

Format	Description
GL_UNSIGNED_BYTE	Unsigned 8-bit integer
GL_BITMAP	A single bit (0 or 1)
GL_BYTE	Signed 8-bit integer
GL_UNSIGNED_SHORT	Unsigned 16-bit integer (2 bytes)
GL_SHORT	Signed 16-bit integer (2 bytes)
GL_UNSIGNED_INT	Unsigned 32-bit integer (4 bytes)
GL_INT	Signed 32-bit integer (4 bytes)
GL_HALF_FLOAT	2-byte floating-point type
GL_FLOAT	Single precision floating point (4 bytes)
GL_UNSIGNED_BYTE_3_3_2	Packed into unsigned 8-bit integer. R3, G3, B2
GL_UNSIGNED_BYTE_2_3_3_REV	Packed into unsigned 8-bit integer. B2, G3, R3
GL_UNSIGNED_SHORT_5_6_5	Packed into unsigned 16-bit integer. R5, G6, B5
GL_UNSIGNED_SHORT_5_6_5_REV	Packed into unsigned 16-bit integer. B5, G6, R5
GL_UNSIGNED_SHORT_4_4_4_4	Packed into unsigned 16-bit integer. R4, G4, B4, A4
GL_UNSIGNED_SHORT_4_4_4_4_REV	Packed into unsigned 16-bit integer. A4, B4, G4, R4
GL_UNSIGNED_SHORT_5_5_5_1	Packed into unsigned 16-bit integer. R5, G5, B5, A1
GL_UNSIGNED_SHORT_1_5_5_5_REV	Packed into unsigned 16-bit integer. A1, B5, G5, R5
GL_UNSIGNED_INT_8_8_8_8	Packed into unsigned 32-bit integer. R8, G8, B8, A8
GL_UNSIGNED_INT_8_8_8_8_REV	Packed into unsigned 32-bit integer. A8, B8, G8, R8
GL_UNSIGNED_INT_10_10_10_2	Packed into unsigned 32-bit integer. R10, G10, B10, A2
GL_UNSIGNED_INT_2_10_10_10_REV	Packed into unsigned 32-bit integer. A2, B10, G10, R10
GL_UNSIGNED_INT_24_8	Packed into unsigned 32-bit integer D24, S8*

The type parameter defines the data type of the image data. This can be any of the values in Table 7.3.

The packed values in Table 7.3 are formats where the individual color channels have been packed into a single data type. For example, when using the format GL_UNSIGNED_BYTE_3_3_2, three color channels are stored in a single byte. The red channel takes up the three most significant bits, followed by the green channel, which also takes up three bits, and finally the blue channel, which fills the remaining two bits (the least significant bits of the byte). If the format ends in _REV then the ordering of the color channels is reversed. GL_UNSIGNED_BYTE _2_3_3_REV stores the channels with the blue taking up the most significant two bits, followed by green and then red taking up the three least significant bits. Figure 7.2 shows how data packing works.

GL_UNSIGNED_BYTE_3_3_2

GL_UNSIGNED_BYTE_2_3_3_REV

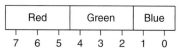

Figure 7.2
Packed data type bit layouts.

Note

There are actually three packing formats missing from Table 7.3. These are GL_UNSIGNED_INT_ 10F_11F_11F_REV, GL_UNSIGNED_INT_5_9_9_9_REV, and GL_FLOAT_32_UNSIGNED_ INT_24_8_REV. These packed types go through a more complicated conversion process than the ones in Table 7.3. We will not be covering this process as it is beyond the scope of this book.

The final parameter to glTexImage2D() is pixels, which is a pointer to the image data stored in memory. The image data will be read using the format indicated by type.

As an example, if you have an image with a width and height of 128 and your image data is stored in an array of unsigned bytes (imageData), where each color channel (r, g, b, a) is allocated 8 bits, you could specify the image to OpenGL with the following call:

```
glTexImage2D(GL_TEXTURE_2D, GL_RGBA8, 128, 128, 0, GL_RGBA, GL_UNSIGNED_BYTE,
imageData);
```

After this call, the texture would be loaded into the currently bound texture object and would be ready for use.

1D Textures

Specifying 1D textures is very similar to specifying 2D textures. The only difference between the two types is that 1D textures always have a height of 1. 1D textures can be used to produce shading effects such as Cel-Shading (a style of cartoon rendering). You specify a 1D texture with glTexImage1D():

```
void glTexImage1D(GLenum target, GLint level, GLint internalformat, GLsizei
width, GLint border, GLenum format, GLenum type, const GLvoid *pixels)
```

The only differences between this function and glTexImage2D() are as follows:

- There is no height parameter

- You should specify GL_TEXTURE_1D as the target parameter

3D Textures

You can imagine 3D textures as lots of 2D textures layered one above another. 3D textures are normally generated procedurally and are accessed using 3D coordinates. You can specify 3D texture data using the glTexImage3D() function:

```
void glTexImage3DEXT(GLenum target, Glint level, GLenum internalformat, GLsizei
width, GLsizei height, GLsizei depth, Glint border, GLenum format, GLenum type,
const GLvoid *pixels)
```

Again, the parameters are the same as glTexImage2D(), with the exception of the additional parameter depth, which specifies the third dimension of the texture.

Cube Map Textures

A cube map texture is a special type of texture target. Cube maps are made up of six individual 2D textures. The cube map is normally used with a three-dimensional texture coordinate, which forms a direction vector that points from the center of a cube to the required texel. The texel lookup is done in two stages. First, given the 3D texture coordinate (s, t, r), the highest magnitude of the three texture coordinate components is used to determine which of the six cube textures is used. Then once the 2D texture has been determined, the components of the 3D texture coordinate are used to calculate a 2D texture coordinate (s, t). Each of the size textures in the cube map is specified using glTexImage2D() along with one of the GL_TEXTURE_CUBE_MAP* target values. The textures that make up the cube map must be square (i.e., their width and height must be the same). To access a cube map in a shader you must use one of the cube map texture samplers (see Table 6.2).

Texture Filtering

When mapping a texture to a polygon, it is very unlikely that a single pixel will map one-to-one with a texel on the image. If the image is being viewed close to the viewport, a pixel may only take up a small part of the texel it is mapped to (the situation is known as *magnification*). Conversely, if the texture is far from the viewport then a single pixel may contain several texels (called *minification*). In these situations, OpenGL must calculate the color of the pixel; the behavior of this calculation is controlled using *Texture filtering*.

You can tell OpenGL how to handle texture filtering by using the `glTexParameter()` functions:

```
void glTexParameter{if}(GLenum target, GLenum pname, TYPE param)
void glTexParameter{if}v(GLenum target, GLenum pname, TYPE param)
```

`target` should be one of `GL_TEXTURE_1D`, `GL_TEXTURE_2D`, `GL_TEXTURE_1D_ARRAY`, `GL_TEXTURE_2D_ARRAY`, `GL_TEXTURE_3D`, or `GL_TEXTURE_CUBE_MAP`. For texture filtering `pname` should be `GL_TEXTURE_MAG_FILTER` or `GL_TEXTURE_MIN_FILTER` depending on the filtering situation you want to set the filtering mode for. When setting the magnification filter, the possible values of `param` are `GL_LINEAR` or `GL_NEAREST`. Using `GL_NEAREST` as the magnification filter tells OpenGL to use the texel nearest to the center of the pixel for the final color. This is sometimes referred to as *point sampling*. It is the cheapest filtering method and can result in blocky textures. Setting `GL_LINEAR` tells OpenGL to use the weighted average of the four texels closest to the center of the pixel. This type of filtering results in smoother textures and is also known as *bilinear filtering*.

When setting the minification filter value, there are a few more possible values available; these are listed in Table 7.4 in order of rendering quality.

Table 7.4 Texture Minification Filter Values

Filter	Description
GL_NEAREST	Uses the texel nearest to the center of the pixel being rendered.
GL_LINEAR	Uses bilinear interpolation.
GL_NEAREST_MIPMAP_NEAREST	Uses the mipmap level closest to the polygon resolution, and uses the GL_NEAREST filtering on that level.
GL_NEAREST_MIPMAP_LINEAR	Uses the mipmap level closest to the polygon resolution, and uses the GL_LINEAR filtering on that level.
GL_LINEAR_MIPMAP_NEAREST	Uses GL_NEAREST sampling on the two levels closest to the polygon resolution, and then linearly interpolats between the two values.
GL_LINEAR_MIPMAP_LINEAR	Uses bilinear filtering to obtain samples from the two levels closest to the polygon resolution, and then linearly interpolates between the two values. This is also known as *trilinear filtering*.

The four mipmap-related filters will make more sense once we have covered mipmaps in the "Mipmaps" section later.

The default filtering settings for a texture are set to GL_LINEAR for the magnification filter and GL_NEAREST_MIPMAP_LINEAR for the minification filter. If you are not using mipmapping with the texture, you should change the minification filter to GL_LINEAR or GL_NEAREST; otherwise, texturing will not work correctly because the default filtering mode requires all mipmap levels have been generated.

Texture Coordinates

Texture coordinates have been referenced a few times in previous chapters and now it's time to cover them in detail. Textures (unlike most of the surfaces you will be rendering) are rectangular in shape so there needs to be some method of mapping them to an arbitrary polygon. Texture coordinates are used to determine where each part of the texture should apply to a polygon face. Each corner of a texture is given a 2D coordinate with (0.0, 0.0) at the lower-left and (1.0, 1.0) at the top-right. Texture coordinates are specified per-vertex when rendering a primitive and then are interpolated for fragment processing. During the fragment processing, the interpolated coordinates are used to look up the color for the pixel in the currently bound texture map. Whereas vertex and vector components are generally labeled as x, y, z, and w, texture coordinates are generally referred to as s, t, r, and q (the exception to this rule is the vector component naming in GLSL shaders, where r is replaced by p to prevent a conflict with the rgba component naming set). Figure 7.3 shows the mapping of coordinates to a texture on a simple polygon.

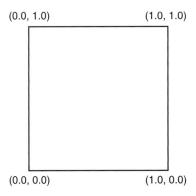

Figure 7.3
Texture coordinate values on a polygon.

Note

While most of the time texture coordinates will range between 0.0 and 1.0, there are occasions when the values may be higher than that. These higher values will be discussed in detail in the "Texture Wrap Modes" section later in the chapter.

Textures can be spread across several polygons by specifying the texture coordinates so that only part of the texture is displayed on each polygon. As an example, a quadrilateral is normally made up of two triangles. If you want to texture a quad seamlessly, you will need to specify the correct texture coordinates for both of the triangles. Look at Figure 7.3 and imagine the diagonal that would be formed if the quad was made up of two triangles. The texture would still be mapped correctly as long as each triangle specified the same texture coordinates for the same vertices.

Applying Texture Coordinates

Texture coordinates are an attribute of a vertex, so if you are using GLSL, you specify texture coordinates using `glVertexAttribPointer()`. You should send the texture coordinate data to GLSL as an array in the same way as color data. To apply the texture coordinates in GLSL you need to do the following:

1. In the vertex shader, you must declare an `out` variable for the current vertex's coordinate, which will be interpolated and used as an input into the fragment shader.

2. The vertex shader should read the input coordinate and assign it to the output variable.

3. The fragment shader should then use this coordinate to perform a texture lookup for the fragment.

Let's look at a concrete GLSL example. First, here is the code for a vertex shader that performs texturing:

```
#version 130

uniform mat4 projection_matrix;
uniform mat4 modelview_matrix;

in vec3 a_Vertex;
in vec3 a_Color;
in vec2 a_TexCoord0;
```

```
out vec4 color;
out vec2 texCoord0;

void main(void)
{
    texCoord0 = a_TexCoord0;
    color = vec4(a_Color, 1.0);
    vec4 pos = modelview_matrix * vec4(a_Vertex, 1.0);
    gl_Position = projection_matrix * pos;
}
```

The input attribute (a_TexCoord) is read by the vertex shader and assigned to the output variable (texCoord0). The fragment shader is where the actual job of applying the texture happens:

```
#version 130

uniform sampler2D texture0;

in vec4 color;
in vec2 texCoord0;

out vec4 outColor;

void main(void) {
    outColor = color * texture(texture0, texCoord0.st);
}
```

You will notice the sampler2D type that has been used. Samplers provide access to a texture unit. In your application, you are required to set the sampler uniform (in this case texture0) to the texture unit that the texture is bound to. We will discuss texture units in greater detail when we cover multitexturing in Chapter 9, "More on Texture Mapping." For now, all you need to know is the default texture unit is 0; so in your application you can set the sampler using the GLSLProgram class like so:

```
m_GLSLProgram->sendUniform("texture0", 0);
```

The texture coordinate passed into the fragment shader will have been interpolated for the current fragment. To get the texel color from the texture using the texture coordinate for this fragment, you can use the `texture()` function:

```
vec4 texture(sampler1D sampler, float P)
vec4 texture(sampler2D sampler, vec2 P)
vec4 texture(sampler3D sampler, vec3 P)
vec4 texture(samplerCube sampler, vec3 P)
float texture(sampler1DShadow sampler, vec3 P)
float texture(sampler2DShadow sampler, vec3 P)
float texture(samplerCubeShadow sampler, vec4 P)
vec4 texture(sampler1DArray sampler, vec2 P)
vec4 texture(sampler2DArray sampler, vec3 P)
float texture(sampler1DArrayShadow sampler, vec3 P)
float texture(sampler2DArrayShadow sampler, vec4 P)
```

`sampler` is the texture sampler used to look up the texel, and `P` is the texture coordinate used to locate the texel. The texel color returned takes into account the texture filtering modes. The texture color can be returned from the fragment shader directly or you can combine the color with other variables. In the preceding example, we multiply the texel color by the interpolated fragment color; the result is a combination of the two.

Texture Parameters

When we covered texture filtering modes, we used the `glTexParameter()` function to set the magnification and minification filters. But that isn't the only use for the `glTexParameter()` function. Let's look again at the definition:

```
void glTexParameter{if}(GLenum target, GLenum pname, TYPE param)
void glTexParameter{if}v(GLenum target, GLenum pname, TYPE param)
```

There are several other possible values for `pname` and `param` that are unrelated to texture filtering but alter the way the currently bound texture is applied. Table 7.5 shows a list of possible values for `pname` and the possible (non-deprecated) values that can be set for `param`.

Texture Wrap Modes

Texture wrap modes allow you to modify how OpenGL interprets texture coordinates outside of the range [0, 1]. Using the `glTexParameter()` function with `GL_TEXTURE_WRAP_S`, `GL_TEXTURE_WRAP_T`, or `GL_TEXTURE_WRAP_R`, you can specify how OpenGL interprets the s, t, and r coordinates, respectively.

Table 7.5 Texture Parameters

Name	Type	Values
GL_TEXTURE_WRAP_S	integer	GL_CLAMP_TO_EDGE, GL_REPEAT, GL_MIRRORED_REPEAT
GL_TEXTURE_WRAP_T	integer	GL_CLAMP_TO_EDGE, GL_REPEAT, GL_MIRRORED_REPEAT
GL_TEXTURE_WRAP_R	integer	GL_CLAMP_TO_EDGE, GL_REPEAT, GL_MIRRORED_REPEAT
GL_TEXTURE_MIN_FILTER	integer	GL_NEAREST, GL_LINEAR, GL_NEAREST_MIPMAP_NEAREST, GL_NEAREST_MIPMAP_LINEAR, GL_LINEAR_MIPMAP_NEAREST, GL_LINEAR_MIPMAP_LINEAR
GL_TEXTURE_MAG_FILTER	integer	GL_NEAREST, GL_LINEAR
GL_TEXTURE_MIN_LOD	float	any value
GL_TEXTURE_MAX_LOD	float	any value
GL_TEXTURE_BASE_LEVEL	integer	any non-negative integer
GL_TEXTURE_MAX_LEVEL	integer	any non-negative integer
GL_TEXTURE_LOD_BIAS	float	any value
GL_TEXTURE_COMPARE_MODE	enum	GL_NONE, GL_COMPARE_R_TO_TEXTURE
GL_TEXTURE_COMPARE_FUNC	enum	GL_LEQUAL, GL_GEQUAL, GL_LESS, GL_GREATER, GL_EQUAL, GL_NOTEQUAL, GL_ALWAYS, GL_NEVER

Note

There are two texture modes that are still available in OpenGL but have been marked as deprecated since OpenGL 3.0 and so won't be covered in detail. These modes are GL_CLAMP and GL_CLAMP_TO_BORDER. Both modes are very similar to GL_CLAMP_TO_EDGE and only differ in the way that texels at the edge of the texture are sampled.

Wrap Mode GL_REPEAT

The default wrap mode is GL_REPEAT. In this mode, textures are tiled if the coordinate goes outside the [0, 1] range. For example, if you specify the texture coordinates (2.0, 2.0), then the texture will be repeated twice in both the s and t directions. Figure 7.4 shows the effect of GL_REPEAT.

Although the default wrap mode is GL_REPEAT, you can revert back to it from another mode by using the following commands:

```
glTexParameteri(GL_TEXTURE_2D, GL_TEXTURE_WRAP_S, GL_REPEAT);
glTexParameteri(GL_TEXTURE_2D, GL_TEXTURE_WRAP_T, GL_REPEAT);
```

This will reset the wrap mode in both the s and t directions.

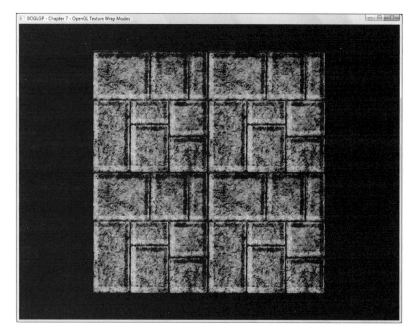

Figure 7.4
Wrap mode GL_REPEAT.

Wrap Mode GL_CLAMP_TO_EDGE

The GL_CLAMP_TO_EDGE wrap mode works by clamping the texture coordinates in the range 0.0 to 1.0. If you specify texture coordinates outside this range, OpenGL will take the edge of the texture and extend it to the remainder of the surface. Figure 7.5 shows GL_CLAMP_TO_EDGE in action.

To set the wrap mode in both the s and t directions to GL_CLAMP_TO_EDGE, you would use the following code:

```
glTexParameteri(GL_TEXTURE_2D, GL_TEXTURE_WRAP_S, GL_CLAMP_TO_EDGE);
glTexParameteri(GL_TEXTURE_2D, GL_TEXTURE_WRAP_T, GL_CLAMP_TO_EDGE);
```

Wrap Mode GL_MIRRORED_REPEAT

The final wrap mode we will cover is GL_MIRRORED_REPEAT. This mode is similar to GL_REPEAT, but instead of repeating the same texture over and over, the image is reflected repeatedly along the s and t directions. Figure 7.6 demonstrates this.

The following lines of code set the wrap mode to GL_MIRRORED_REPEAT:

```
glTexParameteri(GL_TEXTURE_2D, GL_TEXTURE_WRAP_S, GL_MIRRORED_REPEAT);
glTexParameteri(GL_TEXTURE_2D, GL_TEXTURE_WRAP_T, GL_MIRRORED_REPEAT);
```

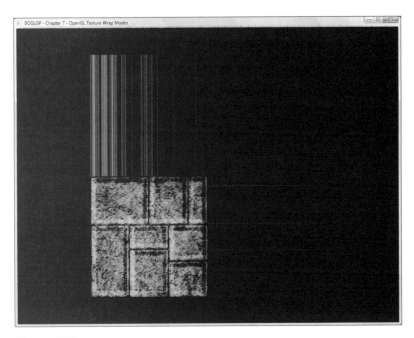

Figure 7.5
Wrap mode `GL_CLAMP_TO_EDGE`.

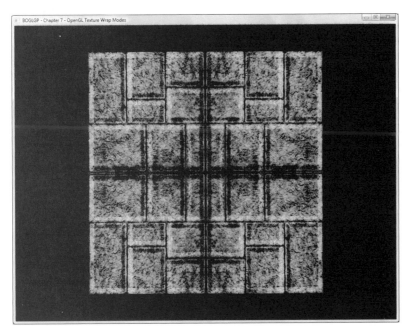

Figure 7.6
Wrap mode `GL_MIRRORED_REPEAT`.

Mipmaps

Mipmaps are a series of precalculated versions of a texture, each half the size of the previous one. For example, if the original texture image has the dimensions 64×64, then a series of images at different mipmap levels will be generated at 32×32, 16×16, 8×8, 4×4, 2×2, and finally 1×1, resulting in seven mipmap levels.

Mipmaps help to combat a visual artifact called *swimming*. Swimming occurs when two adjacent pixels sample the same texture but from texels quite far apart. This tends to happen when the textured surface is far away from the viewport. When the viewport moves, the portions of the texture being sampled change, resulting in the appearance of different colors. Mipmaps reduce this problem because levels with lower resolutions are used for distant polygons, leading to more consistent sampling. Mipmaps have the additional benefit of reducing texture cache misses, since the smaller levels are more likely to remain in the high-speed video memory for as long as they are needed. Figure 7.7 shows a series of mipmaps generated from a base image.

OpenGL performs mipmapping by determining which texture image to use based on the size of the fragment relative to the size of the texels being applied to it. OpenGL chooses the mipmap level that allows as close to a one-to-one mapping as possible. Each level is defined using the glTexImage*() functions. The level parameter of these functions specifies the level of detail, or resolution level, of the image being specified.

By default, you have to specify all levels starting from level 0 to the level at which the texture shrinks to 1×1 (which is the equivalent of $\log_2$ of the largest dimension of the base texture). You can change these limits by using the

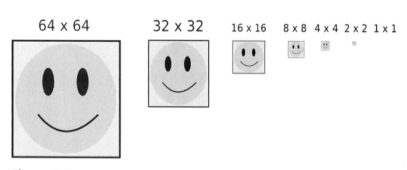

Figure 7.7
A series of mipmaps.

`glTexParameter()` function and specifying pname as GL_TEXTURE_BASE_LEVEL or GL_TEXTURE_MAX_LEVEL, respectively.

Mipmapping is first enabled by specifying one of the mipmapping values for the minification texture filter. You then need to specify the texture mipmap levels using the `glTexImage*()` functions. The following code sets up a seven-level mipmap with a minification filter of GL_NEAREST_MIPMAP_LINEAR and starting at a 64 × 64 base image:

```
glTexParameteri(GL_TEXTURE_2D, GL_TEXTURE_MAG_FILTER, GL_LINEAR);
glTexParameteri(GL_TEXTURE_2D, GL_TEXTURE_MIN_FILTER, GL_NEAREST_MIPMAP_LINEAR);
glTexImage2D(GL_TEXTURE_2D, 0, GL_RGB, 64,64,0, GL_RGB, GL_UNSIGNED_BYTE,
texImage0);
glTexImage2D(GL_TEXTURE_2D, 1, GL_RGB, 32,32,0, GL_RGB, GL_UNSIGNED_BYTE,
texImage1);
glTexImage2D(GL_TEXTURE_2D, 2, GL_RGB, 16,16,0, GL_RGB, GL_UNSIGNED_BYTE,
texImage2);
glTexImage2D(GL_TEXTURE_2D, 3, GL_RGB, 8, 8, 0, GL_RGB, GL_UNSIGNED_BYTE,
texImage3);
glTexImage2D(GL_TEXTURE_2D, 4, GL_RGB, 4, 4, 0, GL_RGB, GL_UNSIGNED_BYTE,
texImage4);
glTexImage2D(GL_TEXTURE_2D, 5, GL_RGB, 2, 2, 0, GL_RGB, GL_UNSIGNED_BYTE,
texImage5);
glTexImage2D(GL_TEXTURE_2D, 6, GL_RGB, 1, 1, 0, GL_RGB, GL_UNSIGNED_BYTE,
texImage6);
```

Mipmaps and the OpenGL Utility Library

The GLU library allows the `gluBuild2DMipmaps()` and `gluBuild1DMipmaps()` functions to build mipmaps automatically for two- and one-dimensional textures, respectively. These functions replace the set of function calls you would normally make to the `glTexImage2D()` and `glTexImage1D()` functions to specify mipmaps.

```
int gluBuild2DMipmaps(GLenum target, GLint components, GLint width,
GLint height, GLenum format, GLenum type, const void *data);
int gluBuild1DMipmaps(GLenum target, GLint components GLint width,
GLenum format, GLenum type, const void *data);
```

The following code uses the `gluBuild2DMipmaps()` function to specify mipmaps in the same way as the previous mipmap example using `glTexImage2D()`:

```
glTexParameteri(GL_TEXTURE_2D, GL_TEXTURE_MAG_FILTER, GL_LINEAR);
```

```
glTexParameteri(GL_TEXTURE_2D, GL_TEXTURE_MIN_FILTER, GL_NEAREST_MIPMAP_
LINEAR);
gluBuild2DMipmaps(GL_TEXTURE_2D, GL_RGB, 64, 64, GL_RGB, GL_UNSIGNED_BYTE,
texImage0);
```

Loading Targa Image Files

Now that we have covered the basics of using textures with OpenGL, it's time to find out how to load them into your application! We'll be covering the Targa image format here, which is a very flexible format that is suited for game textures.

The Targa File Format

The Targa format is divided into two parts: the header, which stores information on the rest of the file, and the data. The header consists of a series of fields, which are arranged in the following structure:

```
struct TargaHeader
{
    unsigned char idLength;
    unsigned char colorMapType;
    unsigned char imageTypeCode;
    unsigned char colorMapSpec[5];
    unsigned short xOrigin;
    unsigned short yOrigin;
    unsigned short width;
    unsigned short height;
    unsigned char bpp;
    unsigned char imageDesc;
};
```

The header provides important information required for loading the rest of the file; of specific importance are the idLength, imageTypeCode, width, height, bpp, and imageDesc fields. idLength holds the length in bytes of an identification string found later in the file. It is likely that you will want to skip the identification string rather than load it; the idLength field indicates how much data to skip. imageTypeCode stores a value indicating the type of image; it can be any of the values in Table 7.6.

width and height are the dimensions of the image in texels. bpp is the color depth of the image, more specifically it is the bits required to store each texel. imageDesc is a single byte of data whose bits store information on the pixel data. The four

Table 7.6 Targa Image Type Codes

Code	Description
0	No image data included
1	Uncompressed color mapped image
2	Uncompressed RGB image
3	Uncompressed black-and-white image
9	Compressed (RLE) color mapped image
10	Compressed (RLE) RGB image
11	Compressed black-and-white image

Table 7.7 Targa Image Origin

First Pixel Position	Bit 5	Bit 4	Hex Value
Bottom left	0	0	0x00
Bottom right	0	1	0x10
Top left	1	0	0x20
Top right	1	1	0x30

least significant bits in the byte store the number of bits per pixel that are for the Alpha channel. The two that we are interested in are bits 4 and 5, which store the corner of the image where the pixel data starts. Some Targa files store the image data upside-down (the data starts from the bottom of the image); these bits let us know whether we need to flip the image after loading. The possible values for these bits are shown in Table 7.7.

After the header follows the identifier string we mentioned earlier. You can skip past this by using the idLength value. Then following that is the image pixel data. This data is stored either in a raw format for an uncompressed Targa or in an RLE compressed format for the compressed version. We won't cover the decompressing algorithm here; if you want to learn more about it then you can study the source code on the CD, or look up the Targa image specification on the Internet, which describes the compression in detail.

The TargaImage Class

On the CD in the source folders for both of this chapter's sample applications, you will find a header and source file called targa.h and targa.cpp, respectively.

This class will load a Targa image and store the data ready for use in OpenGL.
Let's look at the class definition:

```
class TargaImage
{
public:
    TargaImage();
    virtual ~TargaImage();
    //loading and unloading functions
    bool load(const string& filename);
    void unload();

    unsigned int getWidth() const;
    unsigned int getHeight() const;
    unsigned int getBitsPerPixel() const;
    const unsigned char* getImageData() const;

private:
    TargaHeader m_header;
    unsigned int m_width;
    unsigned int m_height;
    unsigned int m_bitsPerPixel;
    unsigned int m_bytesPerPixel;

    vector<unsigned char> m_imageData;

    //Load() calls one of these functions depending on the type
    bool loadUncompressedTarga(istream& fileIn);
    bool loadCompressedTarga(istream& fileIn);

    bool isImageTypeSupported(const TargaHeader& header);
    bool isCompressedTarga(const TargaHeader& header);
    bool isUncompressedTarga(const TargaHeader& header);

    void flipImageVertically();
};
```

The TargaImage class is designed to be simple and easily reusable. It does not call
any OpenGL functions automatically, but instead provides access to the internal
data so you can call these functions whenever you want. Let's look at an example
of the usage of this class:

```
//Declare our TargaImage instance
TargaImage texture;
```

```
//And allocate space for the generated texture name
GLuint texID;

if (!texture.load("data/rock.tga"))
{
    std::cerr << "Could not load the texture" << std::endl;
    return false;
}

glGenTextures(1, &texID);
glBindTexture(GL_TEXTURE_2D, texID);
glTexParameteri(GL_TEXTURE_2D, GL_TEXTURE_MAG_FILTER, GL_LINEAR);
glTexParameteri(GL_TEXTURE_2D, GL_TEXTURE_MIN_FILTER, GL_LINEAR);
glTexImage2D(GL_TEXTURE_2D,0, GL_RGB8, texture.getWidth(),
             texture.getHeight(), 0, GL_RGB, GL_UNSIGNED_BYTE,
             texture.getImageData());
```

Figure 7.8 shows the sample application for this chapter—a textured version of the terrain from the previous chapters.

Figure 7.8
The textured terrain example.

Summary

In this chapter, you learned about texture objects and how OpenGL uses them to store a texture's state. You found out how to bind textures and use them in GLSL by binding sampler uniforms. You learned how to send texture coordinates as a vertex attribute and how to use them in the fragment shader to look up the texel for the fragment. You should understand the reasons for mipmapping and how to control the way that OpenGL performs mipmapping to vary the quality of the output. Finally, you learned about the Targa image format and how to use the TargaImage class to load Targa image files into your applications.

What You Have Learned

- Texture mapping allows you to attach an image to a surface to create realistic-looking objects.

- Texture coordinates are used to map the texture onto the object.

- OpenGL supports textures of one, two, and three dimensions.

- Texture information is stored in *texture objects*, which can be managed using generated handles called *texture names*.

- Filtering modes alter the way the textures are sampled for display.

- You specify texture data with the glTexImage*() commands.

- A mipmap is a texture consisting of different versions of varying resolutions. These levels are used to improve the texture sampling quality.

Review Questions

1. What is a texture object?

2. If the base texture level is 128×128, what are the dimensions of the mipmaps?

3. Which is the default OpenGL texture wrap mode?

On Your Own

1. Given a pointer to 2D image data, imageData, whose dimensions are 256×256 and type is RGBA, write code to create a texture object, and specify the 2D texture with mipmaps.

PART II

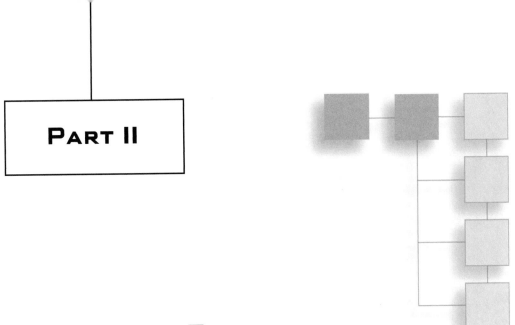

BEYOND THE BASICS

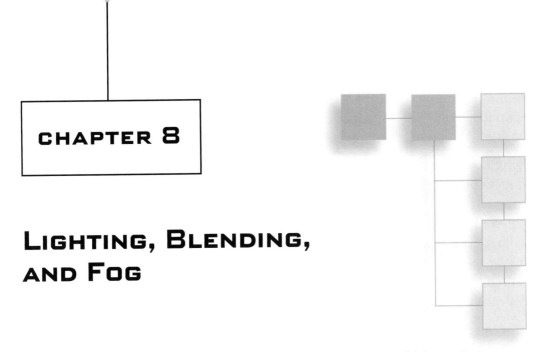

CHAPTER 8

LIGHTING, BLENDING, AND FOG

So far we have covered enough of OpenGL to generate a fairly realistic scene using texture mapping. In this chapter, we will cover three topics that add to the realism of the scene, and which no game should be without, *lighting*, *blending*, and *fog*.

In this chapter, you will learn about:

- Surface normals

- Lighting using GLSL

- Light sources and materials

- Blending and transparency

- Fog

Lighting

After texturing, lighting is probably the most important aspect of creating a realistic scene. If you look around you right now, you will see light everywhere (unless you are reading this in the dark!). Some areas will be brighter than others, depending on how near to a light a surface is, and of course how bright the light source is. It is important to simulate this in your OpenGL applications. In computer graphics, lighting is generally treated separately to shadowing; lighting simply determines how bright any fragment should be regardless of any objects positioned between the fragment and the light source.

Before we begin, let's first discuss how light behaves in the real world. Light sources produce photons of different wavelengths that cover the full spectrum of colors. These photons hit surfaces, and some of them will be absorbed and others reflected depending on reflective properties of the surface. A surface like a mirror will reflect these photons in a fairly uniform way, whereas a rough surface will scatter them. Eventually, the reflected photons will enter our eyes (perhaps after reflecting off more surfaces), which is how we see the object. The color we see depends on which wavelengths of light were absorbed and which were reflected.

Modeling this process precisely in computer graphics is not impossible, but it requires a lot of processing power. Using a totally accurate lighting model is currently a little too expensive for games that would need to perform the calculations in realtime. Instead of providing a perfectly accurate model, it is common to use a simplified lighting model that is faster but less accurate. There is a wide selection of lighting models to choose from, each having its own strengths and weaknesses.

Note

OpenGL has its own built-in lighting functions based on the Blinn-Phong lighting model. However, these API functions have been deprecated because they are part of the fixed-function pipeline. We will produce a similar output as the fixed-function lighting model, but using GLSL shaders instead.

The lighting calculations break down light into four different types, which are combined to generate the output color of a fragment. These terms are as follows:

Ambient light—Ambient light simulates light reflecting off surfaces so many times that the source of the light is no longer apparent. Ambient light is not affected by light positions or the position of the viewer.

Diffuse light—This light comes from a certain direction, but when it hits the surface, it reflects equally in all directions. This type of lighting is affected by the position of the light source, but not the position of the viewer.

Specular light—This light comes from a certain direction and is reflected off a surface in a particular direction. Specular light is affected by the position of the light source and the position of the viewer.

Emissive light—Emissive light is the light that an object emits. It is not easy to show the effect of this light on other objects (a more realistic lighting model could take this into account) so instead the object just appears more intensely lit.

The final result of lighting on an object depends on several factors:

The number of light sources—Each light has its own ambient, diffuse, specular, and emissive contribution. If a surface is affected by a light, it must take this into account.

The orientation of the surface—If the surface is facing the opposite direction of the light, it makes little sense to light it. The lighting calculation is affected by the angle of the light to the surface.

The material of the object—You can provide a number of material properties to a surface; these determine how much light should be reflected, and how shiny the surface is.

The lighting model—Different lighting models produce different output.

Normals

Before we begin looking at how to implement lighting, we should cover some prerequisite knowledge required for the lighting calculation. A normal is a three-dimensional vector that represents the direction a surface is facing. One important thing to note about a normal is that it is a vector with *unit length*; the length of the vector is 1. In the previous list, we mentioned that the orientation of the surface is important to lighting. The surface normal is how we specify which direction the surface is facing for the lighting calculation. Usually, you will specify normals on a per-vertex basis (as a vertex attribute), but when you move on to more accurate lighting techniques (such as bump mapping), you may specify a normal per fragment. Figure 8.1 shows normals on a triangle; all three vertices have identical normals to match the surface normal.

Calculating Normals

Calculating a surface normal is quite simple using some basic vector math, specifically by using the cross-product. Given two vectors, A and B, the cross-product

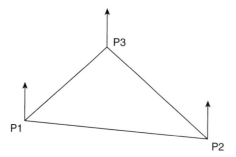

Figure 8.1
A triangle with its associated per-vertex normals.

will return the vector perpendicular to both. The equation for calculating the cross-product is as follows:

$$A \times B = (A_y B_z - A_z B_y, A_z B_x - A_x B_z, A_x B_y - A_y B_x)$$

So, to calculate the normal of a surface, we need two input vectors. These vectors are two edges of the polygon. Given the points on a triangle, P1, P2, and P3, you can calculate these vectors using the following:

```
A = P2 - P1
B = P3 - P1
```

The normal can be discovered by using the cross-product calculation. The order that the vectors are entered into the equation is important. If A and B are swapped, then the calculated normal will point in the opposite direction. The winding of vertices can also affect this. The above example assumes that the triangle is using counterclockwise winding. Figure 8.2 shows how the two input vectors are determined using the three vertices.

Note

One of the reasons that you should primarily use triangles for rendering is that the vertices that make up a triangle will always share the same plane. If you render a surface with four or more vertices, you can't guarantee this will be the case. Because the surface normal will be applied to all vertices, if your vertices aren't on the same plane, the lighting will not work correctly.

Depending on the type of object you are rendering, the method you use to calculate the vertex normals varies slightly. If you are rendering a single polygon, such as a triangle or a multi-faced object with flat sides and angled corners, then calculating a normal for each face (with all vertices sharing the normal) works well. However, if you are rendering a smooth object such as a sphere (where two

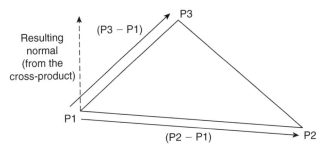

Figure 8.2
Finding the two input vectors for the cross-product.

surfaces may share the same vertex), then the vertex normal should be the average of the normals of the faces that share that vertex. This results in a smooth surface. It gets tricky when lighting more complex meshes that contain both hard edges and smooth curves. There are solutions to this problem such as *smoothing groups* (which identify triangles that can be used together to average the normals).

Giving the Normal Unit Length

Although we can now calculate the vector perpendicular to a surface, we can't reliably use it in lighting calculations until it has been normalized. Normalization is the process of shortening or lengthening a vector to give it a length of 1. The first step in normalization is to find the current length of the vector; this can be done by finding the square root of the sum of the individual components squared, which isn't as complicated as it sounds:

$$|A| = sqrt(A_x^2 + A_y^2 + A_z^2)$$

Once you have the length of the vector, you normalize the vector by dividing each of its components by the length value.

The Lighting Model

The lighting calculations that we will be covering are based on the Blinn-Phong model, which is itself based on the slightly more computationally expensive Phong model. Our lighting will be calculated per-vertex, and the resulting color interpolated across the surface of a polygon. This method of lighting prefers speed over accuracy and quality, but the concept can be extended to the per-pixel level for increased realism.

Materials

The properties of a surface have an effect on the lighting calculation. For example, a silver metallic surface will appear shiny, whereas a brick wall will not. These material properties need to be specified to give a realistic contrast between different surfaces.

The lighting calculation uses material properties to simulate the way a surface would reflect red, green, and blue light. For example, if you have a pure red object, it reflects all red light, but will absorb any green and blue light. If you shine a pure blue light on the object, it will appear black (because there is no red light to reflect and the blue light is absorbed). If you placed the object under a white light, the object will appear red—it would reflect the red light, but absorb the green and blue.

There are five different material properties that we should specify ready for the lighting equation in the vertex shader:

   Diffuse color—The color and intensity that diffuse light is reflected.

   Ambient color—The color and intensity that ambient light is reflected.

   Specular color—The color and intensity that specular light is reflected.

   Emissive color—Light color that this material "emits."

   Shininess—Size of the specular highlight.

The difference between diffuse and specular light can be visualized as the difference between matte and glossy paints. Imagine a wall painted with matte paint. Matte paint reflects light evenly in all directions; the apparent intensity of light reflected doesn't change depending on your viewpoint. In computer graphics, a matte surface would have a high proportion of diffuse light. If the same wall were painted with gloss paint, you would see higher intensities of light depending on the angle between you and the wall, and the angle between the wall and the light. You could simulate this surface using a high proportion of specular light.

The ambient material property defines how well the surface reflects ambient light. A high ambient value means the surface would reflect the surrounding ambient light well. The final material property, shininess, works with the specular value. The higher the shininess value, the larger the specular highlight.

Attenuation

Realistically, lights should illuminate objects less intensely if they are far away from the light source. Eventually, when the object is far enough away, the light should stop illuminating the object altogether. This dimming with distance is known as *light attenuation*. There are times when you don't want your light to suffer from attenuation; for example, light from the sun is so far away, and is so strong a light source, that you may want to represent it without attenuation. Most lights in your scene though will require an attenuation factor for the lighting to appear realistic.

Attenuation is calculated using three editable values: the constant, linear, and quadratic attenuation factors. These three parameters are used to calculate a floating-point attenuation value at each vertex. The diffuse, specular, and source-specific ambient light colors are multiplied by this factor to reduce the intensity of the light depending on the distance from the light source. The attenuation factor is calculated as follows:

$$\frac{1}{k_c + k_l d + k_q d^2}$$

K_c, K_l, and K_q are the constant, linear, and quadratic attenuation, respectively. D is the distance from the light source. Global ambient (see the "Ambient Contribution" section) and emissive light values aren't affected by attenuation.

Lambertian Reflection

Now it's time to move on to the lighting calculations. We'll break down the calculations into component parts before bringing them all together in vertex shaders, beginning with diffuse lighting.

As we have covered, diffuse lighting does not take into account the position of the viewer, only the direction of the light and the surface normal. If a surface is facing away from a light source, then it won't receive any diffuse light, so the intensity of diffuse light on a surface depends on the angle of the surface to the light source. This effect is known as Lambertian reflection. The intensity of the diffuse light can be calculated using the following equation:

$$\max(L \cdot N, 0.0) \times C \times I$$

L is the light direction, N is the surface normal, C is the material's diffuse color, and I is the light's diffuse property; multiplying two vectors (like L and N above) usually means performing the *dot product.* Multiplying colors means a component-wise multiplication.

Note

The *dot product* is a simple calculation that can be performed on two vectors. Provided the vectors are of unit length, the result of the dot product is the cosine of the angle between the two input vectors. The dot product is calculated as:

$$A \cdot B = A_x B_x + A_y B_y + A_z B_z$$

The Specular Term

The specular value is calculated using a lighting equation derived from the Blinn-Phong reflection model. To determine the specular color we must first calculate what is known as the *half vector.* The half vector is the direction halfway between the eye vector and the light vector (see Figure 8.3), which is found by adding together the light and eye vectors.

$$H = L + E$$

L is the direction from the vertex to the light source, and E is the vector from the vertex to the eye position.

Once we have the half vector, the specular contribution to the final color can be found using:

$$\max(N \cdot H, 0)^s \times S_m \times S_l$$

Where N is the vertex normal, H is the half vector, and S is the material's shininess value. S_m and S_l are the material specular and light specular colors, respectively. This value is added to the final fragment color (perhaps after multiplication with

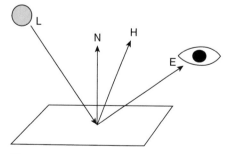

Figure 8.3
Vectors used in Blinn-Phong lighting.

an attenuation factor). We will see an example of the specular value being calculated in the GLSL shaders later in the chapter.

Ambient Contribution

The ambient term represents light that illuminates a surface indirectly by reflecting off other surfaces. There are two types of ambient light that can be modeled: light-specific ambient light, which is found using the ambient values of a light source, and global ambient light, which is a constant that affects the whole scene. Ambient terms are simply multiplied by the material's ambient reflectance and then added to the final color. Global ambient light doesn't suffer from attenuation and so can simply be added at the end of your shader. Light source-specific ambient light is affected by the source's attenuation values and should be multiplied by them before being applied. The examples in this chapter do not use a global ambient value; implementing this is left as an exercise for the reader.

The Normal Matrix

All of the lighting calculations are performed in eye space. As we covered in Chapter 4, we use the modelview matrix to transform a vertex from object space to eye space. Unfortunately, things aren't so simple when it comes to transforming surface normals into eye space. Normals require a special 3×3 matrix known as the *normal matrix* to bring them into eye space. The normal matrix is based on the rotation part of the modelview matrix. Most of the time, the following lines of code will suffice to transform a normal vector into eye space:

```
//a_Normal is the normal vertex attribute,
//normal holds the final transformed normal
mat3x3 normalMatrix = mat3x3(modelview_matrix);
vec3 normal = normalize(normalMatrix * a_Normal);
```

This transformation works fine if your modelview matrix is *orthogonal*. In an orthogonal matrix, the *transpose* matrix (the resulting matrix if all rows and columns are swapped) is the same as the *inverse* of the matrix (multiplying a matrix by its inverse results in the identity matrix). If you only use rotations and translations, then your modelview matrix will be orthogonal and you can use the above code to calculate your normal matrix. If you use any non-uniform scaling when rendering your scene, then the normal matrix should be calculated as:

```
N = transpose(inverse(M))
```

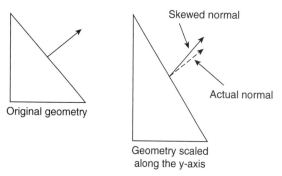

Figure 8.4
Incorrectly transformed normal when using a non-orthogonal modelview matrix.

Where N is the resulting normal matrix, and M is the 3 × 3 matrix formed from the top-left elements of the modelview matrix. Using a non-orthogonal matrix for the transformation can result in a skewed normal like in Figure 8.4.

Note

We can use the top-left 3 × 3 elements of the modelview matrix if the matrix is orthogonal because the transpose and inverse for an orthogonal matrix are the same. In this case, the transpose and inverse cancel each other out, resulting in the original matrix.

Calculating the inverse of a matrix is a complicated process, which we will not cover in detail here. If you would like more information on calculating the inverse of a matrix, there is a commented method that calculates this in the source code examples for this chapter.

Lighting in GLSL

Now that we have covered the basics of lighting, it's time to put that knowledge to use by implementing these concepts in GLSL. In the next sections, you will learn how to light a scene using three different types of light source.

Directional Lighting

We'll begin with the simplest form of lighting: directional light. A directional light comes from a certain direction but has no real source position; the light comes from infinitely far away. Directional lights don't exist in real life, but some light sources such as the sun are far enough away that in your scene you can use a directional light to model them. Directional lights are cheaper to calculate than positional lights because they don't suffer from attenuation and the lighting calculation does not rely on the distance from the light source (which requires a costly square root calculation when using a positional light).

Let's look at how we model a directional light using GLSL. We need to calculate the lighting terms: ambient, diffuse, and specular. The ambient term is simply the material ambient value multiplied by the light's ambient value. Because the ambient term is not affected by distance or direction, it can just be added to the final vertex color. The diffuse and specular contributions use the direction of the light to calculate their value. In a directional light, the light position is the light direction. You should always set the final position component (w) to zero for a directional light to reflect the fact that it is not affected by translation (as it is a direction, not a vertex). Here is a GLSL vertex shader that calculates the effect of a directional light; the uniform and global variables have been left out for brevity.

```
void main(void)
{
    //Transform the normal into eye space using the normal matrix
    vec3 N = normalize(normal_matrix * a_Normal);

    //Calculate the light direction, in a directional light the
    //position is actually a direction vector
    //We transform the position into eyespace before normalizing the vector
    vec3 L = normalize(modelview_matrix *light0.position).xyz;

    //We calculate the angle between the normal and the light direction
    float NdotL = max(dot(N, L), 0.0);

    //The ambient color is fixed, so we add this as the initial color and
    //then build on this with the other lighting contributions
    vec4 finalColor = material_ambient * light0.ambient;

    //Do the standard vertex transformation into eye space
    vec4 pos = modelview_matrix * vec4(a_Vertex, 1.0);

    //Because we are in eye space (everything is relative to the camera)
    //The eye vector is simply the negated position.
    vec3 E = -pos.xyz;

    //If the surface normal is facing towards the light at all
    if (NdotL > 0.0)
```

```
    {
        //Add the diffuse color using Lambertian Reflection
        finalColor += material_diffuse * light0.diffuse *NdotL;

        //Calculate the half vector and make it unit length
        vec3 HV = normalize(L + E);

        //Find the angle between the normal and the half vector
        float NdotHV = max(dot(N, HV), 0.0);

        //Calculate the specular using Blinn-Phong
        finalColor += material_specular * light0.specular *pow(NdotHV,
material_shininess);
    }

    //Output the final color, texture coordinate, and position
    color = finalColor;
    texCoord0 = a_TexCoord0;
    gl_Position = projection_matrix * pos;
}
```

The main lighting calculation is done inside the NdotL if block. This is where
the diffuse and specular terms are calculated. Notice that the ambient term is
calculated near the beginning because this is not affected by the light source
direction. Figure 8.5 is a screenshot of the sample *terrain lighting* application.

Point Lights

There are two main differences between point lights and directional lights:

- Point lights have a position, rather than a direction.

- Point lights suffer from attenuation.

Aside from that, the general algorithm is the same. When specifying the position
for a point light, the w-component should be set to 1.0 because point lights are
affected by translation. Here is a GLSL shader that calculates the effect of a point
light:

```
void main(void)
{
    vec3 N = normalize(normal_matrix * a_Normal);
    vec4 pos = modelview_matrix * vec4(a_Vertex, 1.0);
```

Figure 8.5
Screenshot of the directional light example.

```
//Calculate the light position in eye space by
//multiplying by the modelview matrix
vec3 lightPos = (modelview_matrix *light0.position).xyz;

//Get the light direction vector by finding the
//vector between the vertex and light position
vec3 lightDir = (lightPos - pos.xyz).xyz;

//Find the angle between the normal and the light direction
float NdotL = max(dot(N, lightDir.xyz), 0.0);

//The distance between the vertex and the light is the length
//of the light direction vector
float dist = length(lightDir);

//Find the eye vector (same as a directional light)
vec3 E = -(pos.xyz);

//Assign the ambient color
vec4 finalColor = material_ambient * light0.ambient;
```

```
//The lighting calculation is the same as the directional light
if (NdotL > 0.0)
{
    vec3 HV = normalize(lightPos + E);
    finalColor += material_diffuse * light0.diffuse *NdotL;
  float NdotHV = max(dot(N, HV), 0.0);
    finalColor += material_specular * light0.specular *
                              pow(NdotHV, material_shininess);
}

//Calculate the attenuation factor
float attenuation = 1.0 / (light0.constant_attenuation +
                          light0.linear_attenuation *dist + light0.
quadratic_attenuation * dist * dist);

//The material emissive value isn't affected by
//attenuation so that is added separately
color = material_emissive + (finalColor * attenuation);

texCoord0 = a_TexCoord0;
gl_Position = projection_matrix * pos;
}
```

The only differences of the directional light shader are the calculation of the light direction and the addition of attenuation. Notice that the emissive material value does not suffer from attenuation because it is the surface itself that "emits" this light. Figure 8.6 shows this shader in action.

Spotlights

Spotlights can be thought of as a specialized point light. But unlike a point light, which radiates light in all directions, a spotlight's influence is restricted to a directional cone. A spotlight has a few extra properties to take into account. First, and perhaps most obviously, a spotlight has a direction vector that determines the direction of the cone of light. The second extra property required for the spotlight is the cutoff angle. This is the angle of the spotlight's cone of influence. The final extra property is called the *spotlight exponent*. This value determines how rapidly the light intensity drops from the center of the cone to the walls of the cone. This is effectively attenuation, so in the spotlight GLSL shader it forms part of the attenuation calculation.

Figure 8.6
A screenshot from the point light example.

To determine if a vertex is within the influence of the spotlight, we first find the angle between the surface normal and the vector from the vertex to the light source (the same as the other lighting equations). If the vertex is facing the light source, then we move on to test if it is within the bounds of the cone.

To determine if the vertex should be illuminated, we take the angle between the spotlight direction and the vector from the light to the vertex. If the angle is greater than the cosine of the spotlight cutoff angle, then it can be illuminated. The lighting calculation is the same as the point light except the attenuation takes into account the spotlight exponent. Below is the vertex shader for a single spotlight.

```
void main(void)
{
    vec3 N = normalize(normal_matrix * a_Normal);
    vec3 lightPos = (modelview_matrix *light0.position).xyz;
    vec4 pos = modelview_matrix * vec4(a_Vertex, 1.0);
    vec3 lightDir = (lightPos - pos.xyz).xyz;
```

```
    float NdotL = max(dot(N, lightDir.xyz), 0.0);
    float dist = length(lightDir);
    vec3 E = -(pos.xyz);
    vec4 finalColor = material_ambient * light0.ambient;
    float attenuation = 1.0;

    //If the surface is facing the light source
    if (NdotL > 0.0)
    {
        //Find the angle between the light direction and spotlight direction
        float spotEffect = dot(normalize(light0.spotDirection), normalize
(-lightDir));
        //If it's greater than the cosine of the spotlight cutoff then it should
be illuminated
        if (spotEffect > cos(light0.spotCutOff))
        {
            vec3 HV = normalize(lightPos + E);
            float NdotHV = max(dot(N, HV), 0.0);
            finalColor += material_specular *light0.specular * pow(NdotHV,
material_shininess);

            //Calculate the attenuation using the spot exponent
            spotEffect = pow(spotEffect, light0.spotExponent);
            attenuation = spotEffect /
(light0.constant_attenuation +
light0.linear_attenuation * dist +
light0.quadratic_attenuation * dist * dist);

            finalColor += material_diffuse * light0.diffuse
* NdotL;
        }
    }

    color = material_emissive + (finalColor * attenuation);
    texCoord0 = a_TexCoord0;
    gl_Position = projection_matrix * pos;
}
```

Note how the spotlight cutoff value is used to determine if a vertex should be lit. Figure 8.7 shows a screenshot of the spotlight example, which can be found on the CD.

Figure 8.7
The spotlight example.

Multiple Lights

In this chapter, we have covered lighting a surface with a single light. Most scenes will have several lights, and most surfaces will be lit by more than one of these lights at a time. There are a couple of ways to add multiple lights to your OpenGL applications. You could render the scene multiple times, one for each light. Each rendering pass would blend the scene using additive blending. This method is simple, but will be slow for large complex scenes. Another method would be to write a GLSL shader that loops through a number of light sources passed in via uniform variables.

On the CD, you will find an example called *multiple lights*; the GLSL shader for this example uses the properties of two point lights (passed as uniforms) to light the scene. The shader can easily be extended to include more lights by altering the `lights` array size and passing in the properties (diffuse, specular, etc.) of the new lights.

Improving the Quality

The lighting calculations we have covered in this chapter have been applied inside the vertex shader. Vertex lighting is cheap, and on highly tessellated surfaces can

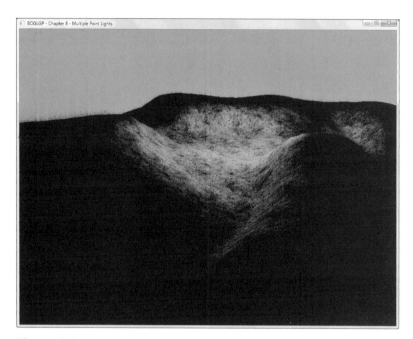

Figure 8.8
The multiple point light example.

provide fairly decent quality lighting. However, many of the surfaces rendered in a 3D scene are not highly tessellated and the resulting lighting may not be very good, especially for spotlights. The quality of the lighting can be drastically improved by moving the lighting calculations into the fragment shader. To do this, simply calculate anything that doesn't depend on distance or direction (e.g., ambient contribution, half vector) in the vertex shader and then pass these values to the fragment shader where the lighting calculation takes place. Remember to renormalize any vectors that should be unit length in the fragment shader. This is because a vector will not necessarily maintain unit length when interpolated for the per-fragment operations.

On the CD, you will find a per-pixel version of the point light example. You'll notice that the vertex shader has become substantially shorter as most of the code has been moved into the fragment shader.

Blending

Blending is a very powerful feature; it is the key to many of the graphical effects that you see in modern computer games. Blending occurs after the fragment processing stage in the pipeline and is used to blend the color of the output

Figure 8.9
The per-fragment point light example.

fragment with the color of the fragment previously rendered to the frame buffer. This technique is normally used to simulate translucent surfaces such as water, glass, etc.

This is where the so far ignored alpha channel comes into play. The alpha value is usually used to represent the opacity of the fragment being rendered. Generally, the fragment that is being rendered is known as the *source*, and the fragment that already exists in the frame buffer is known as the *destination*.

Blending in OpenGL is enabled using `glEnable()` with the parameter `GL_BLEND`; blending then remains enabled until it is later disabled using `glDisable()`.

While blending is enabled, its effects can be controlled by using the `glBlendFunc` function:

```
void glBlendFunc(GLenum sfactor, GLenum dfactor);
```

`glBlendFunc()` specifies the source and destination blending factors, which should be between 0.0 and 1.0. `sfactor` is the source blend factor, and `dfactor` is the destination-blending factor. Blend factors are multiplied by source and destination colors before being combined to create the final fragment color.

Table 8.1 shows the possible values for `glBlendFunc`:

Table 8.1 Blending Factors

Factor	Description
GL_ZERO	Each component is multiplied by zero (i.e., turned to black).
GL_ONE	The color is left unchanged (multiplied by 1.0).
GL_SRC_COLOR	Each color component is multiplied by the corresponding one.
GL_ONE_MINUS_SRC_COLOR	Each component is multiplied by 1.0 – source color component.
GL_DST_COLOR	Each color component is multiplied by the corresponding destination color component.
GL_ONE_MINUS_SRC_ALPHA	Each color component is multiplied by 1.0 – destination color component.
GL_SRC_ALPHA	Each color component is multiplied by the source alpha value.
GL_ONE_MINUS_SRC_ALPHA	Each component is multiplied by 1.0 – source alpha value.
GL_DST_ALPHA	Each color component is multiplied by the destination alpha value.
GL_ONE_MINUS_DST_ALPHA	Each component is multiplied by 1.0 – destination alpha value.
GL_CONSTANT_COLOR	Each color component is multiplied by the corresponding component of the currently set constant color (see "Constant Blend Color").
GL_ONE_MINUS_CONSTANT_COLOR	Each color component is multiplied by 1.0 – constant color component.
GL_CONSTANT_ALPHA	Each color component is multiplied by the alpha component of the current constant color.
GL_ONE_MINUS_CONSTANT_ALPHA	Each color component is multiplied by 1.0 – the constant color alpha value.
GL_SRC_ALPHA_SATURATE	Each color component is multiplied by whichever is lower, the source alpha or 1.0 – destination alpha. The alpha value is not modified. This is only valid as a source factor.

The default blend factors are GL_ONE for the source and GL_ZERO for the destination, which essentially means that no blending is used because the destination color is multiplied by zero (so has no influence) and the source color maintains its full intensity.

Different combinations of blending factors can be used to create different effects. The most common effect that blending is used for is translucency, more commonly referred to as transparency. Usually transparency effects use GL_SRC_ALPHA as the source blending factor and GL_ONE_MINUS_SRC_ALPHA as the destination factor. This combination allows the contribution of a fragment color to be determined by its alpha channel. A high alpha value will result in more influence being given to the source color, resulting in a more opaque looking surface. A low alpha value results in the destination color having more influence, making the surface being rendered appear more translucent. The following code would set up blending for transparency:

```
glEnable(GL_BLEND);
glBlendFunc(GL_SRC_ALPHA, GL_ONE_MINUS_SRC_ALPHA);
```

Let's look at a concrete example. Say that you draw a triangle in red (1.0, 0.0, 0.0, 1.0) and then in front you render a triangle in blue (0.0, 0.0, 1.0, 0.5). As it is the source alpha channel that is being used as a combination factor, the blue triangle will be rendered at 50% transparency. The resulting colors before combination would be calculated as follows:

$$Source.R = 0.0 \times 0.5 = 0.0$$
$$Source.G = 0.0 \times 0.5 = 0.0$$
$$Source.B = 1.0 \times 0.5 = 0.5$$
$$Source.A = 0.5 \times 0.5 = 0.25$$

$$Dest.R = 1.0 \times 0.5 = 0.5$$
$$Dest.G = 0.0 \times 0.5 = 0.0$$
$$Dest.B = 0.0 \times 0.5 = 0.0$$
$$Dest.A = 1.0 \times 0.5 = 0.5$$

The final color of the fragment is determined by adding these two colors together to get the resulting color (0.5, 0.0, 0.5, 0.75).

Things, unfortunately, aren't quite this simple as scenes get more complex. When rendering without any kind of translucency, you can render the polygons that make your scene and the z-buffer (depth buffer) will take care of determining whether a fragment is visible or hidden behind another surface. The order of rendering doesn't really matter with opaque surfaces, but when rendering transparent surfaces, it does. When rendering a scene containing transparent surfaces, you should render opaque objects first, and then transparent objects, in order of depth from the camera, from back to front. This is because if you render a transparent polygon and then render another polygon behind it, the second polygon will fail the depth test and will not be rendered, and so will not been seen behind your transparent polygon.

Figure 8.10
Screenshot of the blending example.

The example application for this chapter adds translucent water to our terrain application.

Separate Blend Functions

As you saw in the sample color calculation in the last section, the alpha channel of a blended fragment is also affected by the blend factors specified using glBlendFunc(). In the example, the alpha value supplied for the source fragment was 0.5, but after blending with the destination fragment, the final alpha was 0.75. Sometimes you will not always want the alpha component to be affected by the same blend factors as the red, green, and blue color components. Fortunately, OpenGL provides a function that is similar to glBlendFunc() but allows the source and destination factors for the alpha channel to be specified separately. This function is called glBlendFuncSeparate():

```
void glBlendFuncSeparate(GLenum sfactorRGB, GLenum dfactorRGB, GLenum sfactor-
Alpha, GLenum dfactorAlpha);
```

sfactorRGB and dfactorRGB specify the source and destination factors for the red, green, and blue color components. sfactorAlpha and dfactorAlpha specify the blend factors for the alpha component.

Constant Blend Color

Some of the blending factors listed in Table 8.1 refer to a constant blend color. This is usually used to blend RGB images that don't specify an alpha value. You can specify the constant blend color by using the `glBlendColor()` function:

```
void glBlendColor(GLclampf red, GLclampf green, GLclampf blue, GLclampf alpha)
```

The parameters are fairly self-explanatory; they define red, green, blue, and alpha components of the constant color. The `GLclampf` type indicates a floating-point value between 0.0 and 1.0. The default blending color is (0, 0, 0, 0). The current value of the blend color can be retrieved by passing `GL_BLEND_COLOR` to `glGet()`.

Fog

Fog is a very easy effect to add to a scene. It not only adds realism, but can also be used to prevent geometry that has been culled in the distance from suddenly popping into existence as you move closer. Fog can be specified as any color, although in most cases it will be some shade of gray. Fog is simulated by mixing the fog color with the color of the fragment being rendered. The contribution of fog color versus fragment color is commonly determined using one of three different fog calculations: *linear*, *exponential*, and *squared exponential.*

Using the linear calculation, the intensity of the fog increases linearly with the distance the fragment is from the camera; the further away something is, the more influence the fog color has on the final output color. The affected area of the fog can be controlled by using two values that limit the range of the fog. We'll call these parameters *fog start* and *fog end*, which define the start and end z-distance of the fog, respectively. The *blend factor* (the contribution of the fog color to the final fragment color) can be calculated using the following formula:

```
blendFactor = (fogEnd - fragDistance) / (fogEnd - fogStart)
```

To calculate the final color in GLSL, you can use the `mix` function in the fragment shader. The `mix` function has the following prototype:

```
genType mix(genType x, genType y, genType a)
genType mix(genType x, genType y, float a)
```

The `mix` function performs the following calculation on x and y and returns the result:

$$result = x \times (1 - a) + (y \times a)$$

Passing the fog color as the first parameter, the fragment color as the second parameter, and the blend factor as the final parameter will give the resulting fog color, like so:

```
outColor = mix(fogColor, fragColor, blendFactor);
```

The remaining two fog modes aren't limited by start and end values. Instead, all fragments are affected by fog; the distance from the camera determines how much influence the fog color has on the fragment. With exponential fog, the fog intensity increases exponentially with the distance from the camera. Although there is no range defined with these fog modes, you can use a density factor to control the intensity of the fog. The blend factor for exponential fog is calculated as:

```
blendFactor = exp(-fogDensity * fragDistance);
```

The exp function returns the natural exponentiation of its only parameter. Squared exponential fog gives better quality fog to regular exponential fog. The blend factor can be calculated by:

```
blendFactor = exp2(-fogDensity * fragDistance);
```

Fog Example

The fog example included on the CD shows all three fog modes in action. Pressing the space bar will allow you to cycle through the different modes.

Summary

There has been a lot to learn in this chapter. We have covered a basic lighting model based on the Blinn-Phong model, and you have learned how to implement it on a per-vertex level. You have learned how to simulate translucent surfaces blending. Finally, we covered implementing fog into your scene and using different fog modes to achieve different fog effects.

What You Have Learned

- Surface normals are used to define the direction a surface faces and are required for lighting calculations.

- Lighting is calculated by combining the contributions of different kinds of light: *diffuse, ambient, specular,* and *emission.*

Figure 8.11
The terrain with fog enabled.

- Material properties are considered while calculating lighting to determine the final color.

- Attenuation is the fading of light over distance.

- You can model three different kinds of lights in OpenGL: *directional, point,* and *spot* lights.

- Directional lights don't suffer from attenuation.

- Lighting can be calculated at the vertex level, or per-pixel for higher quality.

- Blending combines the color of a new fragment with that of one already in the frame buffer.

- Blending can be controlled using *blend factors*, which are specified using `glBlendFunc()`.

- Fog is simulated by combining a fog color with a fragment based on its distance from the camera.

Review Questions

1. What does the ambient contribution to lighting represent?

2. What are the two main differences between point and directional lights?

3. What does the shininess material property do?

On Your Own

1. Write a per-pixel directional light implementation.

2. Extend the multiple light example and add a third point light with a yellow diffuse color.

CHAPTER 9

MORE ON TEXTURE MAPPING

Texture mapping is a massive subject, and what was covered in Chapter 7 is just the tip of the texture-mapping iceberg.

In this chapter, we will cover:

- Using OpenGL to update portions of an existing texture

- Copying data from the frame buffer into a texture

- Using alpha testing to make parts of your textured surfaces completely transparent

- Using multitexturing to apply more than one texture to a surface

Subimages

Creating a new texture is quite an expensive process in OpenGL. Each time glTexImage() is called, OpenGL has to allocate memory to hold the texture and perform other operations to get the texture into a usable state. This isn't really a problem if it is happening once per texture during the application's loading stage. But sometimes you may want to update a texture (or even several!) each frame. This repeated texture creation can quite quickly eat up your frame rate.

Fortunately, OpenGL provides a way to update an already existing texture, either wholly or partially, with new data. This is far more efficient than reallocating the memory each time. Given an existing texture, you can update the image data with one of the following functions:

```
void glTexSubImage1D(GLenum target, GLint level, GLint xoffset, GLsizei width,
GLenum format, GLenum type, const GLvoid* pixels);
void glTexSubImage2D(GLenum target, GLint level, GLint xoffset, GLint yoffset,
GLsizei width, GLsizei height, GLenum format, GLenum type, const GLvoid *pixels);
void glTexSubImage3D(GLenum target, GLint level, GLint xoffset, GLint yoffset,
GLint zoffset, GLsizei width, GLsizei height, GLsizei depth, GLenum format,
GLenum type, const GLvoid* pixels);
```

Most of the parameters are the same as the glTexImage*() functions. xoffset, yoffset, and zoffset are the left, bottom, and front (for 3D textures) coordinates of the area to be replaced with the new data. width, height, and depth define the size of the area. The defined area must fit within the bounds of the texture.

Copying from the Color Buffer

Imagine that in a game your character visits a security camera control room. Inside the room is a TV screen showing the view from the camera in the corridor outside. To achieve this type of effect, the image on the screen would be a mapped texture that is updated dynamically. There are several ways to do this, including:

- Rendering the scene to the frame buffer from the camera's point of view and reading back the pixels that were rendered and storing them in a texture.

- Rendering the scene from the camera directly to a texture using frame buffer objects.

The latter of those two options is more efficient, but more complex and beyond the scope of this book. The simpler method, which we will be covering, is just as effective, although slightly slower. OpenGL provides several functions for reading the frame buffer into a texture depending on the dimensionality of the destination texture:

```
void glCopyTexImage1D(GLenum target, GLint level, GLint internalformat, GLint x,
GLint y, GLsizei width, GLint border);
void glCopyTexImage2D(GLenum target, GLint level, GLint internalformat, GLint x,
GLint y, GLsizei width, GLsizei height, GLint border);
```

These functions create a brand new texture with the designated area of the frame buffer as the source data. The `target`, `level`, and `internalformat` parameters are the same as the `glTexImage()` functions. `border` has been deprecated and should always be zero. `x`, `y`, `width`, and `height` define a rectangle in the frame buffer to copy the texture data from, with `x` and `y` specifying the bottom-left corner of the rectangle. There is no 3D version of the `glCopyTexImage()` function; this is because it is not possible to create a 3D texture from a 2D frame buffer.

Sometimes it is useful to only update part of a texture using the frame buffer. OpenGL provides the `glCopyTexSubImage()` functions for this purpose:

```
void glCopyTexSubImage1D(GLenum target, GLint level, GLint xoffset, GLint x,
GLint y, GLsizei width);
void glCopyTexSubImage2D(GLenum target, GLint level, GLint xoffset, GLint yoffset,
GLint x, GLint y, GLsizei width, GLsizei height);
void glCopyTexSubImage3D(GLenum target, GLint level, GLint xoffset, GLint yoffset,
GLint zoffset, GLint x, GLint y, GLsizei width, GLsizei height);
```

Unlike the functions that create a new texture, there is a 3D version of the `glCopyTexSubImage()` function that can copy frame buffer data into an existing 3D texture. The extra parameters to these functions `xoffset`, `yoffset`, and `zoffset` are used to specify the bottom-left-front corner of the rectangular region of the destination texture to update. You will see these functions in use in the environment-mapping demo in the next section.

Environment Mapping

Environment mapping is a process that allows you to simulate reflective surfaces by mapping the surrounding environment to a texture (hence the name). The object then applies dynamically calculated texture coordinates to give an illusion of reflection. We will cover two types of environment mapping: sphere mapping and cube mapping.

Sphere Mapping

Sphere mapping is a very simplistic method of providing the effect of a reflection. When using sphere mapping, texture coordinates are generated by taking the vector from the eye to a surface and reflecting it across the surface normal. This reflected vector is then used to generate the *s* and *t* coordinates to look up the texel color in a special texture. A sphere map texture is an image that has been passed through a fisheye-style filter. The resulting image looks like a sphere with the surroundings warped to the side of it. Sphere maps have several drawbacks. First, they are view dependant, so unless you are viewing the object at a specific angle, the reflection doesn't look realistic. Second, because they are modeled on a sphere, applying a sphere map to an object that is not spherical doesn't look right. Finally (and probably most importantly), the image usually must be generated manually and remains static so the reflection will not show any objects moving around your scene. Fortunately, cube mapping fixes all of these problems and is actually easier to implement in GLSL than sphere mapping.

Reflective Cube Mapping

Reflective cube mapping can provide more realistic reflection than a sphere map. In the cube mapping method, the scene is rendered to six textures at 90-degree angles (north, east, south, west, up, down). These textures are used to form a cube map. The texture coordinates are generated in a similar fashion to the sphere mapping method, but instead of only generating two-component texture coordinates (s and t), we generate three-component texture coordinates (s, t, and r). These coordinates then access the correct image of the cube map for the texel color; this allows the reflection to accurately draw the surroundings. See Figure 9.1 to see how the texture lookup works.

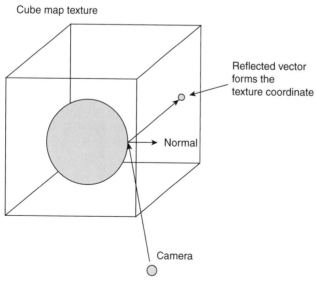

Figure 9.1
Cube map coordinates are generated by reflecting the eye vector over the normal.

Figure 9.2
A screenshot of the cube mapping example.

The cube mapping sample application contains a GLSL shader that generates the texture coordinates for cube mapping and uses them to reflect rotating orbs into the surface of a sphere.

Alpha Testing

In the last chapter, we looked at how blending can simulate translucent surfaces by using the alpha channel to represent opacity. But, what if we want part of a surface to be completely transparent, like the gaps in a wire mesh fence? In this situation, we can discard certain fragments if the alpha channel is a certain value, resulting in transparent areas of a polygon. Specifying the alpha component for a fragment can be done using a texture map with an alpha channel; the texture map can be sampled in the fragment shader and then compared with a threshold value to determine whether the fragment should be discarded.

Figure 9.3
Simple tree rendered using two quads

Let's look at an example. A simple and cheap way of rendering trees in a scene is to render a 2D tree texture onto two quads that cross over like in Figure 9.3.

Obviously, we don't want the background of the texture to be displayed on the polygons; only the tree itself. If the texture image, for example, stores an alpha channel value of 0 for all the transparent parts of the image, and an alpha value of 1 for all the visible parts of the image, then you can discard the "invisible" fragments in the fragment shader like so:

```
#version 130
uniform sampler2D texture0;
in vec2 texCoord0;
out vec4 outColor;
void main(void) {
```

Figure 9.4
Trees implemented using alpha testing.

```
//Sample the texture
outColor = texture(texture0, texCoord0.st);

//If the alpha component is too low then discard
//this fragment
if (outColor.a < 0.1) {
    discard;
}
}
```

The discard keyword simply prevents the fragment from being processed any further. Figure 9.4 shows an updated version of the terrain application showing trees mapped with a texture that has transparent areas.

Multitexturing

Put simply, multitexturing is the process of using more than one texture map on a single surface. In the examples so far, we have used a single texture to set the diffuse color of each fragment. This type of texture is called a *diffuse map*;

however, there are many other uses for textures besides setting the diffuse color. Many games use a grayscale texture map, which is combined with the diffuse map to give the illusion of static lighting on a surface. This technique is known as *light mapping*. Textures might contain other information than just color. As an RGB texture is made up of three components per texel, it is possible to use the texture map to store a compressed three-component normal vector for each texel. This allows for a technique known as *bump mapping*, which allows bumpy surfaces to be modeled by using per-pixel lighting that uses the normal passed from the bump map. These are just some of the ways that multitexturing is commonly used but there are many others, and textures are used in innovative new ways all the time.

So far when using texturing we have used a sampler uniform in the fragment shader to access the texture data. In the application, this uniform has been given the value of 0. This value represents the texture unit that the sampler provides access to.

Texture Units

When a call is made to `glBindTexture()`, the texture object is bound to the "currently active texture unit," which up until now has been unit zero. We can change the active texture unit by using the `glActiveTexture()` function, which has the following prototype:

```
void glActiveTexture(GLenum texture)
```

The `texture` argument takes the form `GL_TEXTURE`*n* where *n* is a value between 0 and `GL_MAX_TEXTURE_UNITS` - 1. You can find the maximum number of supported texture units by using the `glGetIntegerv()` function:

```
int maxTexUnits; //Holds the max number of units
glGetIntegerv(GL_MAX_TEXTURE_UNITS, &maxTexUnits);
```

A `GL_INVALID_ENUM` error is generated if the value passed to `glActiveTexture()` is outside the valid range. Each texture unit holds its own current texture environment, filtering parameters, and image data; also, texture targets (`GL_TEXTURE_2D`, `GL_TEXTURE_3D`, etc.) are enabled on a per-texture unit basis.

The following example shows how to bind different textures to texture units 0 and 1:

```
glActiveTexture(GL_TEXTURE0);
glBindTexture(GL_TEXTURE_2D, texture1);
```

```
glActiveTexture(GL_TEXTURE1);
glBindTexture(GL_TEXTURE_2D, texture2);
```

Note

If you are using the fixed function pipeline, you are required to call `glEnable()` with the texture target you require for each texture unit. So, in the above example, you would need to call `glEnable(GL_TEXTURE_2D)` after each call to `glActiveTexture()`. When using GLSL you are not required to do this.

Multitexturing in GLSL

Once you have bound your texture objects to the texture units you want to use, you need to associate a sampler with each one by setting the value of the sampler uniforms to the respective texture units. You will then be able to access the bound textures using the GLSL `texture()` function. You can use the sampled values as you wish, depending on your purposes. The most common cases of multi-texturing combine the texel colors, which can be done by multiplying the colors together, or using the GLSL `mix()` function, which takes a blending value to determine how much of each color contributes to the final value.

Multiple Texture Coordinates

You can specify texture coordinates for different texture units by passing them as vertex attributes in the same way as the texture coordinates for the first texture unit. You would then use the respective coordinate attribute as the second parameter to the `texture()` function to look up the texel color. Like the first set of texture coordinates, you must forward the attribute to an `out` variable in the vertex shader so that it is interpolated for the fragment shader.

The Multitexturing Example

On the CD is an updated version of the terrain sample. This sample uses two textures; a 1D texture, which is used to color the terrain based on the height, and a 2D grayscale texture, which is tiled to add grass detail. When these textures are combined, the result is a much more varied and realistic terrain. The single texture coordinate for the 1D texture is generated by taking the height of the terrain and normalizing it into the range 0.0–1.0. The highest point in the terrain gets a coordinate of 1.0 and the lowest point gets a coordinate of 0.0. The resulting terrain can be seen in Figure 9.5.

Figure 9.5
Screenshot of the multitextured terrain.

Summary

In this chapter, you learned that parts of an existing texture can be updated dynamically, which can be far more efficient than replacing the texture with a new one. You learned that the glTexSubImage*() set of functions provide this functionality. You discovered that environment mapping provides a simple way of simulating reflective surfaces and that the reflected images can be updated dynamically by copying data from the color buffer. You learned that parts of a polygon can be made completely transparent by using alpha testing to discard the unwanted fragments in the fragment shader. You also learned that multi-texturing can allow for effects such as light mapping.

What You Have Learned

- You can update part or all of a texture using the glTexSubImage*() family of functions.

■ Data can be read back from the color buffer after rendering and then used for effects such as environment mapping.

■ Environment mapping allows you to simulate reflections by using dynamically generated texture coordinates.

■ By checking the alpha value of a fragment and using the `discard` keyword, you can make parts of a polygon transparent.

■ More than one texture can be applied to a single surface using multi-texturing.

Review Questions

1. What does the `discard` fragment shader keyword do?

2. What are the drawbacks of sphere mapping?

3. Which OpenGL command sets the active texture unit?

On Your Own

1. Adapt the multitexture example to use a third texture that adds shading to the terrain.

CHAPTER 10

IMPROVING YOUR PERFORMANCE

The examples we have seen so far have not been too GPU intensive (by modern standards); the polygon count has been quite low. Complex games, however, have hundreds of thousands of polygons to render each frame, sometimes made up of millions of vertices. Processing, transforming, lighting, and rendering all of these polygons without any kind of culling will drastically affect performance. The most important way to improve performance is to not render polygons that the player won't see. There are many methods of culling unseen geometry. In this chapter, we will cover a simple method of culling groups of polygons known as *frustum culling.*

Frustum Culling

Frustum culling is a quick and effective way to prevent the rendering of large numbers of polygons that will not be seen because they are outside the view of the camera. As you learned in Chapter 4, "Transformations and Matrices," the scene that is viewed in OpenGL is contained within what is known as a *frustum.* The viewing frustum for a perspective projection is the shape of a pyramid rotated so that it is horizontal, with the camera positioned at the point (see Figure 10.1).

Only objects partially or completely inside the viewing frustum will be rendered to the frame buffer; anything else is clipped by OpenGL, but not before a large amount of processing has been done on objects that will never make it to the screen. Frustum culling is a method for checking that objects are contained

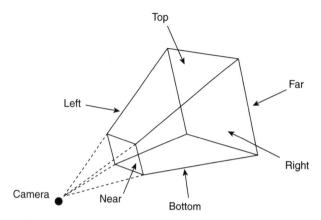

Figure 10.1
The view frustum for a perspective projected scene.

within the frustum before they are rendered. If an object is outside the frustum it can be skipped altogether.

You may be thinking that the term "object" is a little vague. Frustum culling works best when applied to associated groups of polygons. For example, a 3D character model would be suitable for culling as a whole; if the entire model is outside the frustum then none of its polygons will be rendered. So it is up to you to logically group polygons so they can be culled together. Normally, this will involve giving a set of polygons a bounding primitive (for example, a sphere), which is tested against the frustum. The bounding primitive should encompass all of the polygons that make up your object.

The Plane Equation

A *plane* can be visualized as being like a flat piece of paper that stretches infinitely in all directions. A plane is defined by the *plane equation*, which is:

ax + by + cz + d = 0

a, b, and c are the three components of the plane's normal. d is the distance of the plane from the origin. x, y, and z define any point on the plane. Any 3D world coordinate can be used as the x, y, and z arguments, and if the result is 0 then the point is on the plane. If the result is positive, then the point is in front of the plane; if the result is negative, the point is behind the plane. If the plane's normal is unit-length, then the result is the distance in units that the point is from the plane. This is exceptionally useful for collision detection, and indeed for frustum culling as the viewing frustum can be defined by six planes (top, bottom, left, right, near, and far).

Defining Your Frustum

The first step to frustum culling is to calculate the planes that make up your viewing frustum. The planes that make up the frustum are stored in the modelview-projection matrix. If you refer back to Chapter 4, you will remember that this matrix transforms the vertex data to clip space and is found by multiplying the modelview matrix by the projection matrix (something that we have been doing in the vertex shaders in all the examples). Manual matrix multiplication involves quite a bit of code, but fortunately there is a neat trick that makes the OpenGL matrix stack do all the work. Remember, however, that the OpenGL matrix stack has been deprecated, so future OpenGL implementations may require manual matrix multiplication. Rather than multiply the matrix in our own code, we can perform the following steps:

1. Grab the current modelview and projection matrices (glGetFloatv())

2. Push the current modelview matrix (glPushMatrix())

3. Load the stored projection matrix (glLoadMatrixf())

4. Multiply the stored modelview matrix (glMultMatrixf())

5. Grab the current state of the modelview matrix (glGetFloatv())

6. Restore the original modelview matrix (glPopMatrix())

The following code does exactly that:

```
GLfloat projection[16];
GLfloat modelview[16];
GLfloat mvp[16];
/* Get the current PROJECTION and MODELVIEW matrices from OpenGL */
glGetFloatv(GL_PROJECTION_MATRIX, projection);
glGetFloatv(GL_MODELVIEW_MATRIX, modelview);

glPushMatrix();
    //Load the stored projection matrix
    glLoadMatrixf(projection);
    //multiply the stored MODELVIEW matrix with the projection matrix
    glMultMatrixf(modelview);
```

```
    //we read the result of the multiplication
    glGetFloatv(GL_MODELVIEW_MATRIX, mvp);
    //and restore the former MODELVIEW_MATRIX
glPopMatrix();
```

After this code has run, mvp will contain the modelview-projection matrix. Using this matrix, the six planes that make up the frustum can be extracted by either adding one of the first three rows of the matrix to the fourth row, or subtracting one of the first three rows from the fourth row. Table 10.1 shows which rows are added to, or subtracted from, the fourth row to get each plane.

As an example, to obtain the, a, b, c, and d values for the near plane, you would do the following:

```
a = mvp[3] + mvp[2];
b = mvp[7] + mvp[6];
c = mvp[11] + mvp[10];
d = mvp[15] + mvp[14];
```

The same can be done for the other planes by changing the indices of the elements being added/subtracted and using the correct operation from Table 10.1. Once you have obtained the plane values, you must normalize the plane (not just the normal part) by dividing a, b, c, and d by the length of the plane's normal (a, b, c). The following code will normalize a plane when given the values of a, b, c, and d:

```
Plane p; //A simple structure to hold our result
float t = sqrt(a * a + b * b + c * c);
p.a = a / t;
p.b = b / t;
p.c = c / t;
p.d = d / t;
```

Table 10.1 Source Rows to Extract the Frustum Planes

Plane	Row	Add/Subtract
Left	1st	Add
Right	1st	Subtract
Bottom	2nd	Add
Top	2nd	Subtract
Near	3rd	Add
Far	3rd	Subtract

Once this is repeated for all six planes, you will have a valid frustum representation against which to begin testing objects.

Testing a Point

Checking to see if a point is contained within the viewing frustum is a simple operation and the basis for checking more complex objects such as spheres. If the point is behind any of the planes that make up the frustum, then the point is outside of the frustum. As we have already covered, plugging a point into the plane equation will tell us if it is in front of, behind, or on the plane. We simply have to loop through all six planes, checking the point against each one. If the point is behind any of the planes then it is deemed outside the frustum. Assuming the array m_planes stores the six planes that make up the frustum, the following function will return true if the specified point is inside the frustum, or false otherwise.

```
bool PointInFrustum(float x, float y, float z)
{
    for (int p = 0; p < 6; p++ )
    {
        if (m_planes[p].a * x + m_planes[p].b * y +
            m_planes[p].c * z + m_planes[p].d < 0)
        {
            return false;
        }
    }
    return true;
}
```

Testing a Sphere

Checking if a sphere is inside the frustum is just an extension of the point test. We know that the result of using a point in the plane equation returns the distance between the point and the plane. Given a sphere with a radius of R and a center point P, we can determine if a sphere is contained within a frustum if the distance from the plane to P is greater than or equal to R. The following code will return true if the sphere is at least partially inside the frustum, or false otherwise.

```
bool sphereInFrustum(float x, float y, float z, float radius)
{
    for (int p = 0; p < 6; p++)
```

```
    {
        if (m_planes[p].a * x + m_planes[p].b * y +
            m_planes[p].c * z + m_planes[p].d <= -radius)
        {
            return false;
        }
    }
    return true;
}
```

Frustum Culling Applied

On the CD is a sample application that displays a number of Quake 2 models in MD2 format on a terrain. Frustum culling can be toggled on and off using the

Figure 10.2
Screenshot of the frustum culling application.

spacebar, and the camera can be rotated on the spot using the left and right arrow keys. Each MD2 model has a bounding sphere associated with it when it is loaded. It is this sphere that is tested against the frustum. If the sphere is totally outside of the viewing frustum then the model will not be rendered. A "frames per second" counter is displayed in the title bar of the window so you can observe the change in frame rate when frustum culling is enabled and disabled. You should pay special attention to the `Frustum` class, which contains the code to calculate the viewing frustum, and test if objects are visible. Figure 10.2 shows a screenshot of the frustum culling application in action.

Summary

In this chapter, we looked at a simple method of preventing the rendering of polygons that lay outside the viewing frustum. Culling what you can't see is a vital part of writing an efficient game engine. You have learned that grouping geometry for culling can greatly increase the frame rate of your applications. You have learned that planes can be represented using the plane equation, and the viewing frustum can be defined using six planes. You have also learned that plugging a point into the plane equation allows us to determine the distance between the point and the plane; this knowledge allows us to determine if a point is inside or outside of the viewing frustum.

What You Have Learned

- Culling unseen geometry is vitally important to achieve high frame rates.

- Frustum culling is just one way in which we can cull unseen geometry.

- A plane is represented by the plane equation.

- The plane equation can tell us how far away a point is from a plane.

- The viewing frustum is made up of six planes.

- The viewing frustum can be extracted from the modelview-projection matrix.

Review Questions

1. How do you extract the left plane from the modelview-projection matrix?

2. How do you normalize a plane?

3. What is the plane equation?

On Your Own

1. Research the Octree culling algorithm, which makes use of frustum culling.

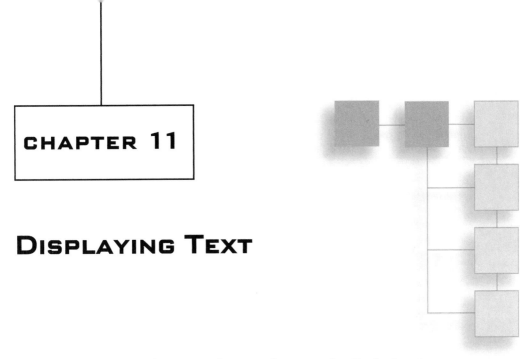

CHAPTER 11

DISPLAYING TEXT

Most games must display text to the user, for example, displaying the current score, the time remaining, or even messages from other team members in multiplayer games. Unfortunately, OpenGL does not concern itself with providing text output functionality in its API, so displaying text is not a simple task.

In this chapter, we will cover:

- Using 2D texture-mapped fonts
- The FreeType library
- Using the FreeType library to output anti-aliased text

2D Texture-Mapped Fonts

2D texture-mapped fonts are one of the simplest ways to display text in OpenGL. A *font texture* is created separately (normally generated using a font building application); this texture usually contains a grid of 256 characters (16 rows of 16 characters) and is loaded just like any other texture into your application. Figure 11.1 shows an example font texture. Each character in a string is displayed as a quadrilateral (made of two triangles) with the part of the texture containing the character mapped to it. The texture coordinates are manipulated for each character to render a whole string.

Figure 11.1
A sample font texture.

Generating the Texture Coordinates

Generating the texture coordinates based on the character is the trickiest part of using texture-mapped fonts. As the texture holds 16 characters in each direction, the width of each character is $1/16^{th}$ of the total width. As texture coordinates normally range between 0.0 and 1.0, the width and height of a character in texture coordinates is 1.0/16.0.

The dimensions of each character are the same, but the position of each character must be determined dynamically. Finding the X position of the character can be found by using the remainder of the integer division of the character's ASCII value by 16. Similarly, the Y position can be found by dividing the character's value by 16. The resulting X and Y positions should be multiplied by the character width/height to find the final position. The resulting code for finding the position for a character (ch) is as follows:

```
const float oneOverSixteen = 1.0f / 16.0f;
float xPos = float(ch % 16) * oneOverSixteen;
float yPos = float(ch / 16) * oneOverSixteen;
```

Using these positions and the character dimensions, you can find the texture coordinates for all four corners of the character, like so:

```
texCoords[0] = xPos;
texCoords[1] = 1.0f - yPos - oneOverSixteen;

texCoords[2] = xPos + oneOverSixteen;
texCoords[3] = 1.0f - yPos - oneOverSixteen;

texCoords[4] = xPos + oneOverSixteen;
texCoords[5] = 1.0f - yPos;

texCoords[6] = xPos;
texCoords[7] = 1.0f - yPos;
```

Notice that the y-axis position is subtracted from 1.0. This is so that the texture coordinates range from 0.0 at the bottom to 1.0 at the top; without the subtraction the textures would be flipped.

The Texture-Mapped Fonts Example

On the CD is a sample application that loads a font texture and prints a string to the screen. The fragment shader in the example discards any black pixels; this means that if text overlaps other objects, you will see them through the non-white parts of the font.

2D Fonts with FreeType

Although texture-mapped fonts are simple, they suffer from many drawbacks. A font texture must be generated separately, which can be time consuming if you are using several textures. Texture-mapped fonts also suffer from aliasing, and lose their sharpness when scaled. Finally, each texture-mapped character is displayed at the same width. Unless you are using a mono-spaced font, the spacing between characters can be too wide. Despite these drawbacks, they can be useful for small standalone demos where depending on a library is not ideal. Some of the drawbacks of texture-mapped fonts can be worked around (e.g., by storing the widths of each character) but not all.

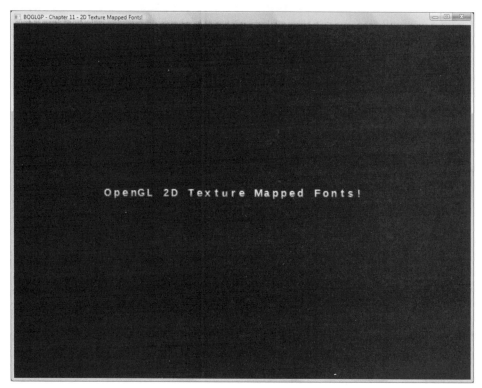

Figure 11.2
A screenshot of the 2D texture-mapped font example.

The FreeType Library

The FreeType library is an open-source font engine that can load many different file formats and provide applications with an API for accessing their content. The latest version of the FreeType library can be found at http://www.freetype.org/, but the version current at the time of writing is included on the CD. What the FreeType library can provide us is a means to load a font file and render each character to a texture complete with anti-aliasing. We can then use these textures to render our text. FreeType also gives us access to font information such as character widths, and also the position of the character for those letters such as "p," which may extend below the other characters on the line.

To use FreeType to print 2D fonts in OpenGL, the following steps must be taken:

■ Initialize the FreeType library

■ Load the chosen font file

■ Set the chosen font size using the FreeType API

- Load a glyph (character shape) for each character

- Generate a texture from the loaded glyph

- Unload the font and the library

- Use the generated textures to render the characters

Initializing FreeType and Loading a Font

To initialize the FreeType library, you must use the `FT_Init_FreeType()` function, which has the following prototype:

```
FT_Error FT_Init_FreeType(FT_Library* alibrary);
```

The `alibrary` parameter is a pointer to an `FT_Library` object, which is used later to load the font. `FT_Error` is a typedef for an integer. `FT_Init_FreeType`, like most FreeType API functions, will return 0 if successful.

Once the FreeType library is initialized, then it is possible to load a font (also known as a *face*). A font file is loaded by passing its file path to the `FT_New_Face()` function:

```
FT_Error FT_New_Face(FT_Library library, const char*
filepathname, FT_Long face_index, FT_Face* aface);
```

`library` is the `FT_Library` object, which was initialized previously. `filepathname` is the location on the file system of the font file. Some font files may contain several faces; `face_index` is used to specify the one you want to load. The final parameter is a pointer to an `FT_Face` object, which is used to provide access to all the information related to the loaded face. Again, if there is a failure while loading the font face, this function will return a non-zero value.

Once these two functions have completed successfully, the library will be initialized and the font face will have been loaded ready to access the font information. The following code demonstrates this:

```
FT_Library library; //Create a freetype library instance

if (FT_Init_FreeType(&library))
{
    std::cerr << "Could not initialize the freetype library" << std::endl;
    return false;
}
```

```
FT_Face fontInfo;   //Stores information on the loaded font

//Now we attempt to load the font information
if(FT_New_Face(library, fontName.c_str(), 0, &fontInfo))
{
    std::cerr << "Could not load the specified font" << std::endl;
    return false;
}
```

In the above example, `fontName` is a `std::string` object, which contains the path to the font file.

Setting the Font Size

Once the face has been loaded, the next step is to specify the size of the font that should be used. The font size is set using the `FT_Set_Char_Size()` function:

```
FT_Error FT_Set_Char_Size(FT_Face face, FT_F26Dot6
char_width, FT_F26Dot6 char_height, FT_UInt
horizontal_resolution, FT_UInt vertical_resolution);
```

`face` is the `FT_Face` object that stores the font face information. `char_width` and `char_height` are the requested width and height of the character, respectively. `FreeType` stores dimensions in units, which are the equivalent of one 64th of a pixel. This means that the values passed to `char_width` and `char_height` must be the required pixel height multiplied by 64. The final two parameters are the horizontal and vertical resolution in dots per inch (DPI). Passing zero to these parameters will use the default, which is 72dpi.

Generating Glyph Textures

Once the font size has been specified, you can begin generating textures from the font face. The first step is to get an index to the glyph we want to generate a texture for. There is a FreeType API function called `FT_Get_Char_Index()` to do this:

```
FT_Uint FT_Get_Char_Index(FT_Face face, FT_ULong charcode);
```

This function will return an index for the specified character by using the currently selected *charmap*. Each font face contains charmaps, which map characters to glyphs. FreeType by default uses the Unicode charmap contained in the font. If the font doesn't contain a Unicode charmap, FreeType will fall back to try emulating a charmap by performing comparisons on the glyph names.

The returned index is then passed to the FT_Load_Glyph() function, which loads the glyph from the font face.

```
FT_Error FT_Load_Glyph(FT_Face face, FT_UInt glyph_index,
FT_Int32 load_flags);
```

Again, face is the font face object, glyph_index is the index returned from FT_Get_Char_Index(), and load_flags is a bitmask of options used to load the glyph. The default option is FT_LOAD_DEFAULT. Table 11.1 shows some useful possible load flags. The full listing can be found in the FreeType documentation. The loaded glyph is stored in the "glyph" attribute of the font face.

Once the glyph is loaded, we can retrieve it and store it in a local variable using the FT_Get_Glyph() function:

```
FT_Error FT_Get_Glyph(FT_GlyphSlot slot, FT_Glyph* aglyph);
```

slot is the glyph attribute of the FT_Face object and aglyph is a pointer to the FT_Glyph object, which we want to store the glyph in. The next step is to tell FreeType to render the glyph to a bitmap for us, which we can then load into a texture. This is done with the aptly named FT_Glyph_To_Bitmap() function:

```
FT_Error FT_Glyph_To_Bitmap(FT_Glyph* the_glyph,
FT_Render_Mode* render_mode, FT_Vector* origin, FT_Bool destroy);
```

the_glyph is the glyph to render. render_mode can be any of the parameters from Table 11.2 and alters the way the glyph is rendered. The origin parameter is a pointer to a vector that will translate the glyph before rendering; passing 0 (or

Table 11.1 Useful FreeType Load Flags

Option	Behavior
FT_LOAD_DEFAULT	Returns a bitmap for the glyph; if no bitmap is found, then FreeType uses the glyph's scalable font outline instead.
FT_LOAD_NO_HINTING	Disables font hinting.
FT_LOAD_RENDER	After the glyph is loaded, a call to the FT_Render_Glyph function is made automatically.
FT_LOAD_NO_AUTOHINT	Disable the auto-hinter.

Table 11.2 FreeType Render Modes

Mode	Behavior
FT_RENDER_MODE_NORMAL	Generate 8-bit anti-aliased grayscale bitmaps.
FT_RENDER_MODE_LIGHT	Same as FT_RENDER_MODE_NORMAL.
FT_RENDER_MODE_MONO	Generate 1-bit bitmaps.
FT_RENDER_MODE_LCD	Generate 8-bit bitmaps 3x the width of the original glyph.
FT_RENDER_MODE_LCD_V	Generate 8-bit bitmaps 3x the height of the original glyph.

NULL) will result in no translation. The final parameter is a flag indicating whether the original glyph should be destroyed after converting it to a bitmap. Once this call is complete, the glyph should be cast to an FT_BitmapGlyph object.

Generating a texture from the loaded bitmap is just a case of iterating through the bitmap pixels and assigning them to an image-data array which is then loaded using glTexImage2D(). The image data can be accessed through the bitmap attribute of the glyph and is in turn stored in the buffer attribute of bitmap.

When loading each glyph, take care to store additional attributes of the glyph that may be required for rendering. These include the dimensions of the glyph in pixels, the position of the glyph (for low hanging letters such as "p" or "y"), and also the advance of the glyph (how far to translate for the following character). The use of these attributes can be seen in the sample application on the CD.

Freeing FreeType Resources

Once your glyph characters have been rendered to textures, you no longer need the FreeType library and font face loaded. You can release these resources using the FT_Done_Face and FT_Done_FreeType() functions for the face and the library, respectively:

```
FT_Error FT_Done_Face(FT_Face face);
FT_Error FT_Done_FreeType(FT_Library library);
```

The FreeType Example

On the CD is a sample application with a FreeTypeFont class that takes care of loading a font file such as a TrueType Font (.ttf) and generating textures for the ASCII character set. Extending the application for Unicode characters is left as an exercise for the reader.

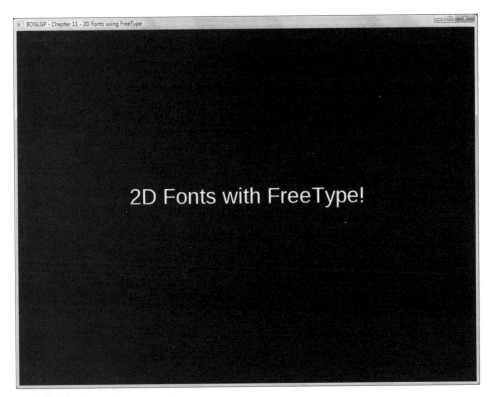

Figure 11.3
A screenshot of the FreeType example.

Generating a texture for each character is far less efficient than generating a single texture containing many characters and manipulating the texture coordinates to display them. The action of rebinding the texture for each character can be quite slow when rendering a lot of text. The multiple texture approach is used in the example for simplicity.

A Note on 3D Fonts

In this chapter, we have covered two methods of rendering 2D fonts. It is also possible to render text that has been extruded into three dimensions. This text can then be rotated and translated like any other 3D object. We will not be covering three-dimensional fonts in this book for several reasons. Specifically:

- The most common methods for rendering 3D text are platform specific.

- Many methods make heavy use of display lists, which are now deprecated.

- At the time of writing, the available 3D font libraries have not been updated to remove the use of deprecated functionality.

- Generating 3D fonts using the information from FreeType is a complicated process, which is beyond the scope of this book.

If you are on the Windows platform and you want to use 3D fonts (and you are happy to use the deprecated display lists) the `wglUseFontOutlines()` function will generate 3D characters and store them as display lists. There are many tutorials and articles on the usage of *outline fonts* on the web. A more portable method of rendering 3D fonts is to use the metrics provided by the FreeType library to manually generate the 3D polygons that make up the characters; although this is a complicated procedure there are many examples available online.

Summary

In this chapter, you have learned two different methods of printing text to the screen. You have learned how to use 2D texture-mapped fonts to provide a portable means to render basic text. You also learned about the FreeType library, and how to use it to load fonts from a font file. Finally, you discovered one method of using the FreeType library to generate textures and render them to polygons to print text.

What You Have Learned

- OpenGL does not have built-in text-rendering functionality.

- 2D texture-mapped fonts provide a quick and portable way to render text.

- 2D texture-mapped fonts suffer from several drawbacks, including poor quality and aliasing.

- The FreeType library is an open source, portable font engine.

- FreeType can load many font formats and provide access to the font information.

- You can use FreeType to generate anti-aliased textures at runtime, which provides better quality output than texture-mapped fonts.

Review Questions

1. What are the inherent problems with texture-mapped fonts?

2. What is the FreeType library?

3. How do you set the size of the font with FreeType?

On Your Own

1. Extend the FreeType application to work with Unicode characters.

2. Alter the FreeType application so that character textures are rendered to a single texture rather than multiple textures.

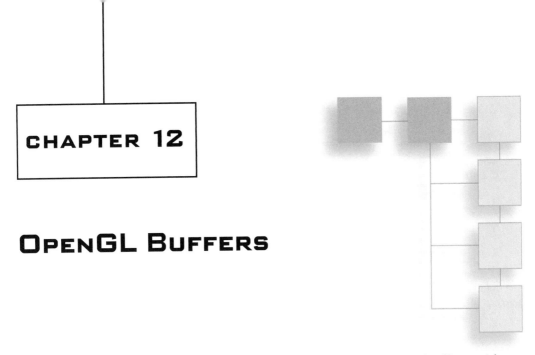

CHAPTER 12

OpenGL Buffers

Throughout the book, we have been using several OpenGL buffers without actually looking at them in detail.

In this chapter, we will take a closer look at the following:

- General buffer operations
- The color buffer
- The depth buffer
- The stencil buffer

What Is An OpenGL Buffer?

A buffer in OpenGL is a consecutive area of memory that is used to temporarily hold data that is related to pixels or vertices. There are several different types of buffers that store pixel-related data, which when combined form a single *framebuffer*. The main types of buffers that are combined to create the framebuffer are the depth, stencil, and color buffers. In current versions of OpenGL, there is a fourth buffer known as the accumulation buffer; however, usage of this buffer is deprecated. For this reason, we won't be covering the accumulation buffer in this chapter.

Table 12.1 Valid Mask Values

Value	Buffer
GL_COLOR_BUFFER_BIT	Clear currently enabled color buffers
GL_DEPTH_BUFFER_BIT	Clear the depth buffer
GL_STENCIL_BUFFER_BIT	Clear the stencil buffer
GL_ACCUM_BUFFER_BIT	Clear the accumulation buffer (deprecated)

Vertex buffers have been used throughout this book in the form of vertex buffer objects. This chapter will focus on OpenGL pixel buffers relating to the frame-buffer.

Clearing Buffers

Before using a buffer, it should be cleared, ready for storing a fresh set of data. Normally the buffers should be cleared at the start of each frame. If the buffers are not cleared, then any part of the buffer that isn't rendered to in a frame will still contain the data from the previous frame, which can cause problems with the rendering. OpenGL buffers are cleared using the glClear() function:

```
void glClear(GLbitfield mask)
```

The mask parameter is a bitwise OR of values that determines which buffers will be cleared. We have used glClear() in the examples so far to clear both the depth and color buffers at the same time using the following command:

```
glClear(GL_COLOR_BUFFER_BIT | GL_DEPTH_BUFFER_BIT);
```

Any combination of the values in Table 12.1 can be used to select the buffers to be cleared.

The Scissor Test

Scissor testing is a very powerful feature that is sometimes overlooked. OpenGL allows you to define a rectangular area on the screen called the scissor box. Once defined, all rendering commands can only affect the area of the framebuffer inside the scissor box. If you attempt to draw anything outside of the scissor box, it will not be rendered. The scissor test can be enabled by passing GL_SCIS-SOR_TEST to glEnable() and disabled with a corresponding call to glDisable(). Initially, the scissor box is defined as the same size as the window when the

OpenGL context was created. If the window hasn't been resized since that time, then enabling the scissor test will have no effect. To set the dimensions of the scissor box, you call glScissor():

```
void glScissor(GLint x, GLint y, GLsizei width, GLsizei height);
```

x and y specify the lower-left corner of the scissor box in window coordinates. width and height are the dimensions of the box also in window coordinates. Remember all rendering commands will only affect the area inside the scissor box; this includes glClear().

The Color Buffers

A color buffer stores a color for each pixel on the screen. An OpenGL context may actually contain several color buffers, but most applications are double-buffered and make use of two: the front buffer and back buffer. We have been using a double-buffered context in all of the examples. In a double-buffered context, every rendering operation that isn't clipped in some way is rendered to the off-screen back buffer. At the end of the frame the buffers are swapped, so the back buffer becomes the visible on-screen front buffer. The rendering for the next frame affects the new back buffer until the buffers are swapped again. This process prevents an artifact called *tearing*, which can occur in a single buffered context. Generally speaking, any mention of the *color buffer* refers to the buffer, which is the current target of rendering (usually the back buffer).

Color Masking

For some rendering effects, you might not want to render all of the color channels. For example, you may choose to render only to the green color channel to get a night-vision goggle-style effect. In some cases, you might want to disable writing to the color buffer altogether. This is useful when you plan to write to the depth or stencil buffers only. OpenGL provides a function, glColorMask():, that can enable or disable individual color channels.

```
void glColorMask(GLboolean r, GLboolean g, GLboolean b, GLboolean a);
void glColorMask(GLuint buf, GLboolean r, GLboolean g, GLboolean b, GLboolean a);
```

The first version of this function enables or disables the individual channels of the color buffer of the default framebuffer. Passing GL_FALSE as one of the arguments will disable color writes to that channel; passing GL_TRUE will enable color writes.

By default, all color channels are enabled. The second version of `glColorMask()` is used along with framebuffer objects, which are briefly discussed later in this chapter. The enabled channels affect all operations that alter the color buffer, including `glClear()`.

Setting the Clear Color

When `glClear()` is called with `GL_COLOR_BUFFER_BIT` as one of the mask values, the color buffer is cleared to the clear color. The clear color is set using the `glClearColor()` function:

```
void glClearColor(GLclampf r, GLclampf g, GLclampf b, GLclampf a);
```

The arguments r, g, b, and a are the red, green, blue, and alpha components of the clear color, respectively. The default clear color is black with zero alpha (all components are 0.0).

The Depth Buffer

The depth buffer (which is also commonly known as the z-buffer) records the depth value of pixels that are rendered to the screen. When depth testing is enabled, the distance between a pixel being rendered and the viewpoint (the z-component) is compared with the corresponding value (i.e., the one in the same x/y location) currently stored in the depth buffer. If the distance is greater (i.e., the pixel is farther away) than the currently stored value then (traditionally) the pixel is not drawn. Otherwise, the pixel is drawn and the value in the depth buffer is updated. This *depth testing* prevents objects that are farther from the camera from being rendered over objects that are nearer. The depth comparison must be enabled by passing `GL_DEPTH_TEST` to `glEnable()` and can be disabled using `glDisable()`. By default, depth testing is disabled.

Controlling Depth Testing

Although the usual behavior of the depth test is for a pixel only to be rendered if it passes the test (i.e., the incoming z-value is less than or equal to the corresponding depth buffer value), the behavior can be controlled by changing the comparison function that determines if the depth test passes or fails. The comparison function can be controlled by using the `glDepthFunc()` function:

```
void glDepthFunc(GLenum func);
```

Table 12.2 Depth-Comparison Functions

Value	Behavior
GL_NEVER	The incoming fragment never passes the depth test and is discarded.
GL_ALWAYS	The incoming fragment always passes the depth test.
GL_LESS	If the incoming z-value is less than the stored value, the fragment passes.
GL_EQUAL	If the incoming z-value is equal to the stored value, the fragment passes.
GL_LEQUAL	If the incoming z-value is less than or equal to the stored value, the fragment passes.
GL_GREATER	If the incoming z-value is greater than the stored value, the fragment passes.
GL_GEQUAL	If the incoming z-value is greater than or equal to the stored value, then the fragment passes.
GL_NOTEQUAL	If the incoming z-value is not equal to the stored value, the fragment passes.

The func parameter can be any of the values in Table 12.2.

Although passing GL_ALWAYS may seem to provide the same behavior as disabling depth testing altogether, there is a difference. When using GL_ALWAYS, the depth buffer will be updated with the incoming depth values. If depth testing is disabled, then the depth buffer isn't updated at all.

Disabling Depth Buffer Writes

Similarly to the way that writing to the color buffer can be disabled with glColorMask(), writing to the depth buffer can be disabled using glDepthMask():

```
void glDepthMask(GLboolean mask);
```

Passing GL_FALSE will disable writing to the depth buffer, and GL_TRUE will re-enable it. Disabling writing to the depth buffer is particularly useful when using a particle system (see Chapter 13, "The Endgame"). A particle system is made up of many individual polygons that should be depth tested against existing geometry but not against each other. One approach would be to sort the particles from back-to-front (farthest to nearest) before rendering, but that would be incredibly inefficient, especially for systems with a large number of particles. A better and more efficient approach is to render the particle system last and to disable depth buffer writes before rendering the particles. This is how the explosions are handled in the game covered in the next chapter.

Potential Issues

There are a couple of things related to the depth buffer to watch out for when rendering. Two quite common issues are z-fighting and incorrect rendering of translucent surfaces.

Z-Fighting

The depth buffer has a limited amount of precision. When the pixel format for an OpenGL window is determined, one of the options is the number of bits per-pixel reserved for the depth buffer; the more bits available, the higher the precision. Z-fighting occurs when two polygons overlap each other at a similar depth. Due to a lack of precision, some fragments that should fail the depth test may pass it, which can then cause visual artifacts. Usually, increasing the number of bits allocated to the depth buffer will help solve the problem. The other (and better) option is to shorten the distance between the near and far planes that makes the z-buffer more precise. Another factor is the z-buffer has a higher precision closer to the near plane, which degrades towards the far plane. This means that moving the near plane farther away will improve the precision much more than moving the far plane closer.

These are possible ways to reduce the likelihood of z-fighting; however, there are occasions where z-fighting is unavoidable and the only solution is to prevent the situation where overlapping polygons share the same plane.

Rendering Translucent Surfaces

We covered this problem briefly in Chapter 8 when discussing blending, but now that the depth buffer has been covered in detail, it is probably worth a recap.

Depth testing is an excellent way to prevent rendering fragments that will be hidden behind other, previously rendered, fragments. This becomes a problem with translucent polygons, because in this case the viewer *needs* to see polygons that are behind other polygons. If a translucent polygon is drawn before the polygons behind it, they will fail the depth test and will not be rendered. Of course, depth masking allows us to disable writes to the depth buffer, so one common (but misguided) approach is to disable depth writes for translucent polygons. This will allow fragments behind the translucent surface to be rendered, but the translucency will not be rendered correctly. As we covered in Chapter 8, translucency is achieved by blending the incoming fragment with the value in the color buffer. This assumes, of course, that the polygons that will appear behind the translucent surface have already been rendered; disabling depth writes will not help because the order that the polygons are rendered matters, and translucent surfaces must be rendered after the ones behind it.

The usual approach is to render all of the opaque surfaces in the scene first, then render the translucent surfaces in back-to-front order (farthest-to-nearest). This will give good results most of the time, but there are situations where determining the correct back-to-front order for polygons is not always possible.

The Stencil Buffer

The stencil buffer is a general-purpose buffer, which, when combined with stencil testing, can be used to achieve various different effects. It is commonly used to limit rendering to certain parts of the screen and is used for effects such as reflections where the reflected objects should only be rendered on the reflective surface. The stencil buffer is also commonly used for shadow techniques.

The stencil buffer must be enabled during context creation. On Windows this is done by setting the `cStencilBits` parameter of the `PIXELFORMATDESCRIPTOR` like so:

```
pfd.cStencilBits = 8;
```

This allocates eight bits to each pixel in the stencil buffer. To enable stencil testing, you pass `GL_STENCIL_TEST` to `glEnable()`. When the stencil test is enabled, its behavior is controlled by the stencil function and the stencil operation. The stencil function defines a comparison function that determines which fragments pass or fail the test. The stencil operation specifies what happens when a fragment passes or fails. The stencil test function requires a reference value and a mask. When a fragment is processed, the bitwise AND of the reference value is compared to the bitwise AND of the stencil value for the pixel and the mask. The stencil function, reference value, and mask are all specified with the `glStencilFunc()` function:

```
void glStencilFunc(GLenum func, GLint ref, GLuint mask);
```

The possible values for `func` are listed in Table 12.3.

If a fragment is processed, what happens to the stencil buffer is determined by the stencil operation, which can be specified using the `glStencilOp()` function.

Table 12.3 Stencil Functions

Function	Description
GL_NEVER	Always fails.
GL_ALWAYS	Always passes.
GL_LESS	Fragment passes if (ref & mask) < (stencil & mask).
GL_LEQUAL	Fragment passes if (ref & mask) <= (stencil & mask).
GL_GREATER	Fragment passes if (ref & mask) > (stencil & mask).
GL_GEQUAL	Fragment passes if (ref & mask) >= (stencil & mask).
GL_EQUAL	Fragment passes if (ref & mask) == (stencil & mask).
GL_NOTEQUAL	Fragment passes if (ref & mask) / (stencil & mask).

When calling glStencilOp(), you specify what happens in three different situations:

1. The stencil test fails (fail).

2. The stencil test fails, but the depth test passes (zfail).

3. The stencil test and depth test pass (or the stencil test passes but depth testing is disabled) (zpass).

The glStencilOp() function has the following definition:

```
void glStencilOp(GLenum fail, GLenum zfail, GLenum zpass);
```

The three parameters determine what happens in each of the three situations listed above. Each argument can be any value from Table 12.4.

Table 12.4 Stencil Operations

Function	Description
GL_KEEP	Keeps the current stencil value.
GL_ZERO	Sets the stencil value to zero.
GL_REPLACE	Sets the stencil value to the reference value.
GL_INCR	Increments the stencil value.
GL_DECR	Decrements the stencil value.
GL_INVERT	Bitwise inverts the stencil value.
GL_INCR_WRAP	Same as GL_INCR, but wraps the stencil value to zero when the maximum representable value is reached.
GL_DECR_WRAP	Same as GL_DECR, but the value wraps around to the maximum representable value if applied to a stencil value of zero.

As mentioned earlier, stencil buffers are regularly used to restrict the rendering of reflected objects to the reflective surface. For example, imagine a scene with a mirror on the floor. The reflection can be simulated by rendering the scene twice, once normally and the second time flipped vertically with the rendering restricted to the mirror. The stencil buffer can be used to restrict the rendering to the mirror like so:

```
glEnable(GL_STENCIL_TEST); //Enable stenciling
glDepthMask(GL_FALSE); //Disable depth writes

//Always replace the stencil value whether it passes or fails
glStencilOp(GL_REPLACE, GL_REPLACE, GL_REPLACE);

//Make the test always pass
glStencilFunc(GL_ALWAYS, 1, 0xFFFFFFFF);

drawMirror(); //Render the reflective surface

//Re-enable depth writes
glDepthMask(GL_TRUE);
//Only render where the stencil value is 1
glStencilFunc(GL_EQUAL, 1, 0xFFFFFFFF);
//Don't change the stencil values any more
glStencilOp(GL_KEEP, GL_KEEP, GL_KEEP);

drawFlippedScene(); //Render the flipped scene

//Disable the stencil test
glDisable(GL_STENCIL_TEST);

//. . .

drawScene();
```

Let's step through the above semi-pseudo code. First, depth testing is disabled. The mirror shouldn't affect the depth buffer; otherwise, it might obscure the reflected objects and they might not be rendered. Next, stencil testing is disabled; the stencil operation is set to always replace the stencil value (whether the test passes or fails). The stencil function is set to always pass. Once the mirror is rendered, the whole stencil buffer will be full of zeros, except for the pixels that make up the mirror, which are instead set to 1.

Depth writes are re-enabled to actually render the reflected scene; this time the fragments will pass the stencil test *only* where the stencil buffer is equal to 1 (i.e., where the mirror was). Once the reflections have been drawn, the stencil test can be disabled ready to render the normal (non-flipped) scene.

That's about it for the stencil buffer. The last thing to mention is that when using the stencil buffer, do not forget to clear it each frame along with the other buffers (color and depth).

A Note on Framebuffer Objects

The buffers discussed in this chapter are combined to form the default framebuffer. However, OpenGL allows the creation of *framebuffer objects*, which can be thought of as other framebuffers that you can render to and then read the rendering back (into a texture for example) for display in your application. Framebuffer objects are an advanced topic that we won't be covering in detail, but they are a very powerful feature worth researching when you are comfortable using OpenGL.

On the CD is an application called *stencil testing*, which shows a sphere reflected onto a checkerboard surface. Figure 12.1 shows a screenshot of the application.

Figure 12.1
A sphere reflected on a checkerboard surface.

Summary

The framebuffer is comprised of four buffers: color, depth, stencil, and accumulation. The accumulation buffer is deprecated and should no longer be used. Of the remaining three buffers, the most obvious is the color buffer, which is what is finally displayed on the screen; however, the depth and stencil buffers both contribute to what finally ends up in the color buffer.

What You Have Learned

- The framebuffer is made up of the color, depth, stencil, and accumulation buffers.

- `glClear()` sets all of the elements in a buffer to a set value. In the case of the color buffer, this is the color set by `glClearColor()`; other buffers have their elements set to zero.

- A scissor box defines an area of the window that will be affected by OpenGL commands. While the scissor test is enabled, all other parts of the window will not be affected by any rendering commands.

- The depth buffer is used in the depth test to discard fragments that would be hidden behind other, previously rendered fragments.

- The stencil buffer allows you to finely control which parts of the screen are rendered. It can be used to limit the rendering of reflections to the reflective surface.

Review Questions

1. What function is used to clear an OpenGL buffer?

2. What does the `glScissor()` command do?

3. How do you disable writes to the depth buffer?

4. How do you enable stencil testing?

On Your Own

1. Using the stenciled reflection pseudo code as a base, write an application that renders a spinning cube that is reflected into a square mirror on the floor.

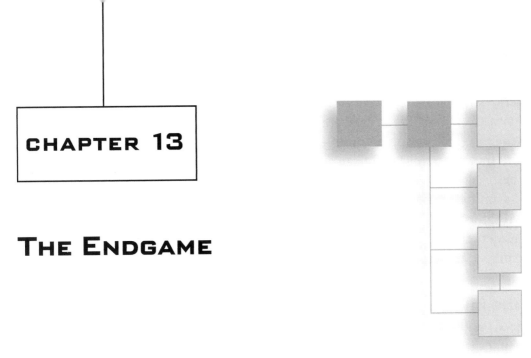

CHAPTER 13

THE ENDGAME

Now it's time to put together all the OpenGL information we have covered to create a game called *Ogro Invasion!* In this chapter, we will briefly cover the design of the game and any last bits of knowledge needed to understand the code.

Specifically, we will cover:

- Loading and animating MD2 models

- Particles and point sprites

- An overview of the game design

The MD2 Model Format

Storing model vertex data in a file is far more flexible than storing it statically in the source code. The models can be created in a 3D modeling application and saved to a file that can then be read into the application. There are many different model formats, but the one we will be covering is the MD2 format. The MD2 format is an animated model format that is very popular among amateur game developers as it is easy to parse and animate, many free modeling tools support it, and there are plenty of free models available on the Internet.

The MD2 model format was originally created to store the animated characters for the game *Quake 2* by iD Software. MD2 files store animated models as a series of *keyframes*. Each keyframe stores the vertex data for a single frame of animation. The keyframes are organized in the file in different animation sequences; for example, frames 40 to 45 define a character's running animation, and frames 46 to 53 define an animation of a character attacking. The vertices in these keyframes are linearly interpolated based on the animation time to create dynamic frames between the keyframes, which creates a smooth animation. The MD2 format is logically split into two distinct sections. The first section is the file header; the header stores information needed to read the rest of the file that contains the keyframe data.

The MD2 Header

The MD2 header can be read into a simple structure that has the following definition:

```
struct MD2Header {
    char ident[4];          // Must be equal to "IDP2"
    int version;            // MD2 version
    int skinWidth;          // texture width
    int skinHeight;         // height of the texture
    int frameSize;          // size of one frame in bytes
    int numSkins;           // number of textures
    int numVertices;        // number of vertices
    int numTextureCoords;   // number of texture coordinates
    int numTriangles;       // number of triangles
    int numGLCmds;          // number of opengl commands
    int numFrames;          // total number of frames
    int skinOffset;         // offset to skin names (64 bytes each)
    int texCoordOffset;     // offset to s-t texture coordinates
    int triangleOffset;     // offset to triangles
    int frameOffset;        // offset to frame data
    int GLCmdOffset;        // offset to opengl commands
    int eofOffset;          // offset to end of file
};
```

ident is a four-character string that identifies this file as an MD2 model. The version number should always be equal to 8. skinWidth and skinHeight are the dimensions of the model's texture map(s). frameSize is the size of each keyframe in bytes.

numVertices, numTexCoords, and numTriangles are fairly self-explanatory. It is worth noting though that numVertices is the number of vertices per frame,

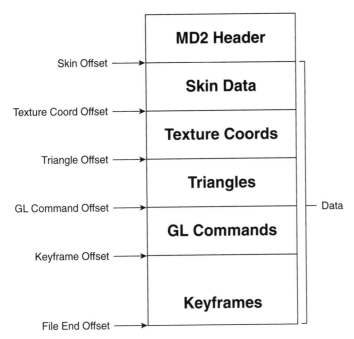

Figure 13.1
MD2 file layout.

whereas triangles and texture coordinates are shared between all frames. numGLCmds needs a little more explanation; the last part of an MD2 file stores the triangle index data as a list of triangle fans and triangle strips. When rendering with immediate mode, using the GL command list to render the model is much faster than rendering with plain triangles. However, when using VBOs, it is far easier and likely more efficient to send the indexed triangles all at once rather than using the GL command list to differentiate between triangle lists and triangle fans. numGLCmds is the number of commands in the command list. numFrames is the number of keyframes in the model. The rest of the header is made up of offsets. Each offset represents where in the file each set of data is located. In the MD2 loader on the disk, these offsets are used to move to the correct location in the file to read the data. Figure 13.1 shows the layout of the MD2 model file.

Loading the Model Data

The header provides enough information to allocate memory to store the model data and the offsets needed to navigate the file. The rest of the model data is stored in sequential chunks. Each chunk stores a certain type of data. The first set of data in the file is the skin information (a skin is a model texture). An MD2 model may have several different skins associated with it. The data for each skin can be read into the following structure:

```
struct Skin {
    char name[64];  //texture file name
};
```

Each skin stores the file path of the texture. The path is normally relative to the directory structure of *Quake 2* so to make it usable for your own games, you will likely want to strip out the directory path and leave the filename. Although our simple model loader will load the skin data, the model rendering simply uses the currently bound texture.

Following the skin data is the list of texture coordinates. MD2 texture coordinates are stored as `shorts` rather than floats:

```
struct TexCoord {
    short s;
    short t;
};
```

The textures need to undergo a little manipulation before they can be used in our applications. First, they must be scaled to between 0.0 and 1.0 by dividing both the s and t components by the `skinWidth` and `skinHeight`, respectively. Second, the t coordinate is flipped so it must be converted to $1.0 - t$. The following code will convert the texture coordinates to a form that we can handle:

```
float s = (float(md2TexCoords[i].s) / (float)header.skinWidth);
float t = 1.0f - (float(md2TexCoords[i].t) / (float)header.skinHeight);
```

where i is an index to the current texture coordinate in the texture coordinate array.

Following the texture coordinates is the triangle data. Each triangle stores three indices into the keyframe vertices and three indices into the texture coordinates that we loaded previously. The MD2 triangle structure is as follows:

```
struct Triangle {
    short vertexIndex[3];
    short texCoordIndex[3];
};
```

The next step is to load the actual keyframe data. Each keyframe has the following structure:

```
struct KeyFrame {
    float scale[3];
    float translate[3];
    char name[16];
    Vertex vertices[numVertices];
};
```

The name field is used during model creation; it is simply a unique identifier for the keyframe. The vertices in each keyframe are stored in a compressed form. To decompress them you need to multiply each vertex by the scale factor and then add the translate vector. The MD2 vertex structure has the following definition:

```
struct Vertex {
    unsigned char v[3];
    unsigned char lightNormalIndex;
};
```

The vertex x, y, and z components are stored as an array of chars. The light-NormalIndex is specific to *Quake 2* and is an index into an array of vertex normals. One final thing to note about the vertices is that in *Quake 2* the z and y axes are swapped, so when loading your MD2 model you should swap these coordinates so that the model is the correct orientation. The following code will decompress a keyframe vertex where frame is an iterator pointing to the current keyframe, and k is an index to the vertex being decompressed:

```
x = ((*frame).scale[0] * (*frame).vertices[k].v[0] + (*frame).translate[0]);
z = ((*frame).scale[1] * (*frame).vertices[k].v[1] + (*frame).translate[1]);
y = ((*frame).scale[2] * (*frame).vertices[k].v[2] + (*frame).translate[2]);
```

Animating the MD2 Model

Animating the MD2 model is quite simple. The keyframes in an MD2 model are separated at distinct time intervals. If you simply rendered them one after the other, the animation would be jumpy and not very realistic. Vertices would simply jump from one position to the next. To make the animation run smoothly, we must generate frames between the keyframes using *interpolation*. To help you visualize interpolation, imagine a piece of paper with two black dots some distance apart. We'll refer to these points as v1 and v2. Each of these points represents a keyframe of animation. If you draw a line from v1 to v2, you are tracing the path of an interpolated point. Given a time value between 0.0 and 1.0, you can see that a point can be generated along the line. For example, at time 0.0, the interpolated point will be the same as v1, and at time 1.0 the interpolated point will be the same as v2. So at time 0.5 the interpolated point will be exactly halfway between v1 and v2. This linear interpolation between two points can be achieved with the following calculation:

$$v_i = v_1 + t \times (v_2 - v_1)$$

where v_i is the interpolated vertex. v_1 and v_2 are the current and next vertices, respectively, and t is the interpolation time (between 0.0 and 1.0).

In the MD2 model class we keep track of the following five important variables:

- m_startFrame—An integer. The frame number that is the start of the current animation sequence.

- m_endFrame—An integer. The ending frame of the current animation.

- m_currentFrame—An integer. The current keyframe in the animation.

- m_nextFrame—An integer. This is normally (m_startFrame + 1), except for when the model reaches the end of its animation sequence, in which case m_nextFrame is equal to m_startFrame.

- m_interpolation—A float. This is a value between 0.0 and 1.0 and is used to calculate an interpolated frame between the current keyframe and the next keyframe. The interpolation is increased with time; when it reaches 1.0, the current and next keyframes are incremented, and m_interpolation is reset to 0.0.

You should now be able to visualize how the animation works. For every point in the model, a new vertex is calculated each frame. Using the interpolation factor, this point gradually moves from the current keyframe position to the next keyframe position. When the interpolation factor is 0.0, then the generated vertex is the same as the *current* keyframe. When the interpolation factor reaches 1.0, the vertex is the same as the *next* keyframe. When the interpolation factor is 1.0, the current frame and next frame are incremented, the interpolation factor is reset to 0.0, and the whole process is repeated.

The following code generates an interpolated keyframe using linear interpolation:

```
float t = m_interpolation;
int i = 0;
for (vector<Vertex>::iterator vertex = m_interpolatedFrame.vertices.begin();
     vertex != m_interpolatedFrame.vertices.end(); ++vertex) {

    float x1 = m_keyFrames[m_currentFrame].vertices[i].x;
    float x2 = m_keyFrames[m_nextFrame].vertices[i].x;
    (*vertex).x = x1 + t * (x2 - x1); //Calculate the interpolated X component

    float y1 = m_keyFrames[m_currentFrame].vertices[i].y;
    float y2 = m_keyFrames[m_nextFrame].vertices[i].y;
    (*vertex).y = y1 + t * (y2 - y1); //Calculate the interpolated Y component

    float z1 = m_keyFrames[m_currentFrame].vertices[i].z;
    float z2 = m_keyFrames[m_nextFrame].vertices[i].z;
    (*vertex).z = z1 + t * (z2 - z1); //Calculate the interpolated Z component
    ++i;
}
```

The logic for increasing the interpolation time and moving through the animation is quite simple. The following code takes care of calculating the interpolation and the current and next frame indexes:

```
//Increase the interpolation based on the time passed and the frame rate
m_interpolation += dt * FRAMES_PER_SECOND;
if (m_interpolation >= 1.0f)
{
    //Make the current frame the same as the next frame
    m_currentFrame = m_nextFrame;
    m_nextFrame++; //Increment the next frame
    //If we just passed the end of the animation
    if (m_nextFrame > m_endFrame)
    {
        //Set the next frame to the start frame and reset the interpolation
        m_nextFrame = m_startFrame;
        m_interpolation = 0.0f;
    }
}
```

Rendering the Model

The interpolated frame is best calculated before being rendered as a whole so that the model's vertices can be sent for rendering altogether. Rendering an *untextured* frame of the model is simple because the MD2 file provides a list of indexed triangles that can be passed to glDrawElements(). However, rendering a textured frame isn't so simple. If you look back at the Triangle structure from the MD2 file, you will notice that it contains three indexes into the vertex array, and three indexes into the texture coordinate array. This presents a problem because glDrawElements() only takes one set of indexes and will use the vertex index to also look up the texture coordinate, which will likely result in the wrong texture coordinate being applied. To fix this problem we can forgo the use of the MD2 triangle data during rendering and instead use it to duplicate some of the vertices and texture coordinates so that they are arranged into sequential triangles in a way that glDrawArrays() can handle. In the game source code on the CD there is a method that performs this task called reorganizeVertices(), which can be found in the MD2 model loader source file (md2model.cpp).

Once the vertices are arranged appropriately, rendering the interpolated key-frame is just a case of calling glDrawArrays().

```
//Enable the vertex and texture coordinate attributes
glEnableVertexAttribArray(0);
glEnableVertexAttribArray(1);

//Bind the vertex buffer for rendering
glBindBuffer(GL_ARRAY_BUFFER, m_vertexBuffer);
glVertexAttribPointer((GLint)0, 3, GL_FLOAT, GL_FALSE, 0, 0);

//Bind the texture coordinate buffer for rendering
glBindBuffer(GL_ARRAY_BUFFER, m_texCoordBuffer);
glVertexAttribPointer((GLint)1, 2, GL_FLOAT, GL_FALSE, 0, 0);

//Draw the triangles that make up the interpolated frame
glDrawArrays(GL_TRIANGLES, 0, m_interpolatedFrame.vertices.size());

//Disable the vertex attribute arrays
glDisableVertexAttribArray(1);
glDisableVertexAttribArray(0);
```

The information we have covered should give you a basic understanding of how MD2 models are loaded and animated. The best way to fully understand the format is to study the accompanying source code.

Creating Explosions

The game (being of the shoot and kill type) requires some explosions. An explosion effect is created by using what is known as a *particle system*. Particle systems are used for all different kinds of effects, such as smoke, fire, water, and sparks—any entity that is made up of many particles of matter. A particle system may contain many hundreds or thousands of particles, each one with its own position, size, color, and velocity. These particles are moved and animated each frame before being rendered.

The explosion particle system is very simple. The particles that make up the explosion all start at the same center point and each is given a random velocity at the point the explosion is created. Each particle has a *life* variable associated with it; this variable is initialized to 1.0 and decreased each frame until it reaches 0.0. At that point, the particle is classed as dead; once all the particles are dead, the explosion has finished, and its memory can be freed. The particle structure is made up of four variables:

```
struct Particle
{
    float life;
    Vector3 position;
    Vector3 velocity;
    Color color;
};
```

We've already discussed how the life value determines when the particle dies, but we also use it as the alpha component of the particle's color. When combined with blending, this creates a fading effect as the particle moves outwards from the center of the explosion. The position is the location of the particle in world coordinates; this is set to the center of the explosion initially and each frame the velocity is added to it to move the particle outwards. The color is set to red, orange, or yellow, again at random.

In the game, the Explosion class holds an array of particles. Each frame the code updates each particle in the array with the following code:

```
particle.life -= 1.0f * dT; //Decrease the life of the particle (based on time)
particle.position += particle.velocity * dT; //Update the particle's position
```

The particles are then rendered using *point sprites*, which we will discuss in the following section. To see in detail how the explosions are rendered, look at the `explosion.cpp` and `explosion.h` source files in the *Ogro Invasion!* game demo on the CD.

Point Sprites

Normally particles are textured when they are rendered and then blended so that they appear as a suitable shape. Although you could render the particles as points, points can't be textured correctly (because you can't specify corner texture coordinates) and may not appear realistic. The traditional way to circumvent this is to render each particle as a quad. This is a lot more expensive than it should be; not only does it mean sending four vertices per particle to the graphics card (rather than just 1), but also each quad needs to be rotated to face the camera so that the viewer doesn't see the particle side-on, which would ruin the effect. Fortunately, graphics card vendors developed an extension (`GL_ARB_POINT_-SPRITE`), which combines the advantages of rendering points with the ability to properly texture them. The `GL_ARB_POINT_SPRITE` extension was promoted to core in OpenGL 2.1 and so will be available under an OpenGL 3.0 context.

Using Point Sprites

Point sprite rendering is enabled and disabled by passing `GL_POINT_SPRITE` to `glEnable()` or `glDisable()`, respectively. While point sprite rendering is enabled, any rendering performed using `GL_POINTS` will be rendered as point sprites. Point sprite texture coordinates are generated automatically. By default, a single texture coordinate is specified for the entire sprite, which is rarely what you want. The traditional texture coordinate generation for point sprites can be enabled on a per-texture unit basis by using the following function call:

```
glTexEnvi(GL_POINT_SPRITE, GL_COORD_REPLACE, GL_TRUE);
```

Once this function has been called, texture coordinates will be specified for each corner of the point sprite, with (0.0, 0.0) at the top left, and (1.0, 1.0) at the bottom right. These coordinates can be accessed in the fragment shader through the built-in variable, `gl_PointCoord`. `gl_PointCoord` can be used in the fragment shader to sample a texture like any other 2D texture coordinate—by passing it as the second parameter to the `texture()` function:

```
gl_FragColor = texture(texture0, gl_PointCoord);
```

In the above example, `texture0` is the sampler uniform. Although we can now render textured point sprites, they are probably going to be too small to see. To rectify this, we need to set the size of the points. There are two ways of providing the size of the point. The first method is to simply call glPointSize() with the value you require. If you use this approach with a vertex shader enabled, then no distance attenuation is performed (i.e., the point size will not get smaller if it is farther from the camera). The alternative approach is to set the gl_PointSize built-in variable in the vertex shader. In the vertex shader you can calculate your own distance attenuation because you have access to the position of the vertex. By default, you will be unable to set the size of the point in the vertex shader; to allow this you must make the following function call:

```
glEnable(GL_VERTEX_PROGRAM_POINT_SIZE);
```

This will tell OpenGL to use the value set in the vertex shader, rather than the one set by glPointSize(). You can revert to the default behavior by passing the same value to glDisable(). To see an example of point sprites in action, look at the explosion.cpp source file and the particle.vert and particle.frag shaders, which form part of the game source code.

Ogro Invasion!

It's now time to look at the overall design of the mini-game on the CD. The aim of *Ogro Invasion!* is to stop a horde of continually spawning monsters (called Ogros) invading your idyllic island. You have five minutes to kill as many monsters as you can. The game has been designed to be extended; in fact, there are many features obviously missing that are left as an exercise for the reader to implement (see the "On Your Own" section for some suggestions).

Most of the features that make up the game you have seen in previous chapters. We reuse our faithful terrain rendering, alpha tested trees (from Chapter 9), frustum culling (from Chapter 10), and FreeType fonts (from Chapter 11). The explosions and model rendering were the last remaining elements required to make up the whole game. The final thing to understand is the general design of the game. Every visible element (aside from the fonts) is classed as an *entity* and is a subclass of an Entity parent class that has the following definition:

```
class Entity : private Uncopyable {
    private:
        virtual void onPrepare(float dt) = 0;
        virtual void onRender() const = 0;
        virtual void onPostRender() = 0;
```

```
        virtual bool onInitialize() = 0;
        virtual void onShutdown() = 0;
        virtual void onCollision(Entity* collider) = 0;

        bool m_canBeRemoved;

        GameWorld* m_world;
    public:
        Entity(GameWorld* const gameWorld);
        virtual ~Entity();

        void prepare(float dt);
        void render() const;
        void postRender();
        bool initialize();
        void shutdown();
        bool canBeRemoved() const;
        void destroy();

        void collide(Entity* collider);

        virtual Vector3 getPosition() const = 0;
        virtual void setPosition(const Vector3& position) = 0;
        virtual float getYaw() const = 0;
        virtual float getPitch() const = 0;
        virtual void setYaw(const float yaw) = 0;
        virtual void setPitch(const float pitch) = 0;
        virtual Collider* getCollider() = 0;
        virtual EntityType getType() const = 0;

        GameWorld* getWorld() {
            return m_world;
        }
};
```

The important methods to note are the pure virtual functions (the method definitions ending in = 0;). If you aren't familiar with pure virtual functions, they can be briefly described as methods that *must* be overridden by a subclass. For example, one of the subclasses of Entity is the Player. The Player class implements all of the virtual functions. Figure 13.2 shows the class hierarchy of the game; you'll notice that even the terrain is an Entity called Landscape. The

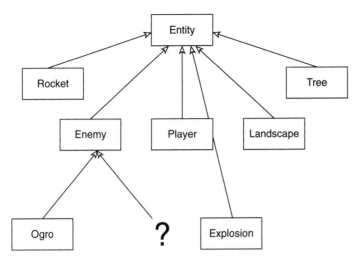

Figure 13.2
The entity hierarchy of *Ogro Invasion!*

`getType()` function can be used on any `Entity` pointer to determine the type of entity it is.

All of the entities in the game are stored in a single list, which is managed by the `GameWorld` class. This class takes care of spawning new entities, keeping track of the number of enemies, deleting dead entities, etc. The entity list is iterated each frame and the following actions are performed:

1. **Entities are prepared.** Each `Entity`'s `onPrepare()` function is called where time-based updates are performed. This is where the model animation occurs for the monsters, and entity movement is calculated.

2. **Collision detection is performed.** Most of the collision detection is determined using simple bounding spheres. If the distance between two entities is less than the radius of their bounding spheres, then a collision occurred.

3. **Dead entities are deleted.** When an entity is no longer in use (for example, a rocket that has been destroyed) its `canBeRemoved` flag is set. These dead entities are removed before rendering.

4. **Mouse movement is calculated.** Each frame the mouse position is recorded and then the cursor is moved back to the middle of the screen. This means each frame we can find the difference the mouse moved from the last frame and use that to update the camera.

5. **Entities are rendered.** This involves calling the onRender() and then the onPostRender() commands. These commands are only called if the entity's bounding sphere is visible (frustum culling).

A Note on Collision Detection

Collision detection is a massive and complex topic that can (and does) have entire books dedicated to it. For this reason, the collision detection that is used in *Ogro Invasion!* is very simplistic. Every entity is given a radius that defines its bounding sphere. Every frame, all entities are compared against all other entities to find the distance between them. If the distance is less than the combined radii of the two entities, then a collision is recorded. If a collision occurs then both entities have their onCollision() function called; the sole parameter to this function is the entity they collided with. This allows for conditional logic, depending on the type of entity that was hit (for example, if a monster collides

Figure 13.3
A screenshot from the game *Ogro Invasion!*

with a rocket, then the monster should be killed in its onCollision() call). The only time sphere-based collision isn't used is when an entity collides with the Landscape; in this case, the entity has its y-axis position changed so that it is positioned above the terrain.

Summary

That's it. Explore the code and extend it, add new features, new bad guys, and better graphics. Either that or just repeatedly try to beat your highest score! Figure 13.3 shows the finished game!

Review Questions

There are no review questions for this chapter.

On Your Own

1. The game has a very plain sky; implement a skybox to give the game more atmosphere.

2. The class hierarchy is designed to allow more than one type of enemy. Using the Ogro class as a basis, add a new, smarter enemy that fights back!

3. Write some code to save the highest score to a text file and alter the Game Over screen to show whether it was beaten.

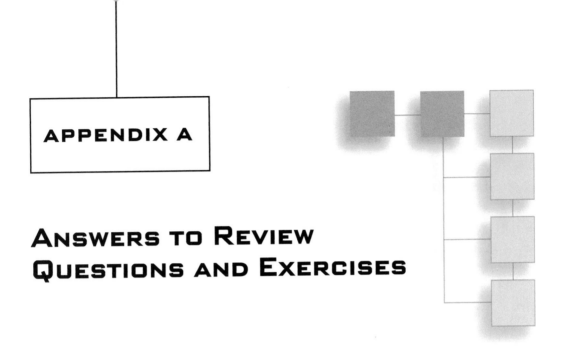

APPENDIX A

ANSWERS TO REVIEW QUESTIONS AND EXERCISES

Chapter 1
Review Questions

1. 1992.

2. OpenGL 3.0.

3. The OpenGL working group, part of the Khronos Group.

On Your Own

1. Change the rendering code to the following:

```
glColor4f(0.0, 0.0, 1.0, 1.0);
glBegin(GL_TRIANGLES);
    glVertex3f(2.0, 2.5, -1.0);
    glVertex3f(-3.5, -2.5, -1.0);
    glVertex3f(2.0, -4.0, -1.0);
glEnd();

glColor4f(1.0, 0.0, 0.0, 1.0);
glBegin(GL_TRIANGLE_FAN);
    glVertex3f(-1.0, 2.0, 0.0);
    glVertex3f(-3.0, -0.5, 0.0);
```

```
                    glVertex3f(-1.5, -3.0, 0.0);
                    glVertex3f(1.0, -2.0, 0.0);
                    glVertex3f(1.0, 1.0, 0.0);
                glEnd();
```

2. Answers may vary.

Chapter 2
Review Questions

1. The rendering context connects OpenGL to a window.

2. On Windows, `wglGetCurrentContext()`.

3. A structure that defines the attributes of the OpenGL context.

4. Sets the color that the color buffer is cleared to when `glClear()` is called.

5. The `DEVMODE` structure.

On Your Own

1. Answers may vary. In `example.cpp`, change the `init()` method to contain the line `glClearColor(1.0f, 1.0f, 1.0f, 1.0f);`, which will change the background color to white. Also add the following to `render()` after the current triangle rendering:

```
glColor4f(1.0f, 0.0f, 0.0f, 1.0f);
glBegin(GL_TRIANGLES);
    glVertex3f(2.0f, 2.5f, -1.0f);
    glVertex3f(-3.5f, -2.5f, -1.0f);
    glVertex3f(2.0f, -4.0f, -1.0f);
glEnd();
```

Chapter 3
Review Questions

1. By calling `glEnable(GL_CULL_FACE);`

2. `glGetString(GL_VERSION);`

3. Counterclockwise.

4. GL_POLYGON_SMOOTH

On Your Own

1. Assuming that m_vertices and m_colors are vectors, then the pyramid data can be specified to OpenGL as:

```
//Create the outer parts of the pyramid
m_vertices.push_back(Vertex(0.0,2.0,0.0));//Top of the pyramid
m_vertices.push_back(Vertex(-1.0,-1.0,-1.0));//its 4 edges
m_vertices.push_back(Vertex(1.0,-1.0,-1.0));
m_vertices.push_back(Vertex(1.0,-1.0,1.0));
m_vertices.push_back(Vertex(-1.0,-1.0,1.0));
m_vertices.push_back(Vertex(-1.0,-1.0,-1.0));

m_vertices.push_back(Vertex(1.0,-1.0,-1.0)); //Bottom
m_vertices.push_back(Vertex(1.0,-1.0,1.0));
m_vertices.push_back(Vertex(-1.0,-1.0,-1.0));
m_vertices.push_back(Vertex(-1.0,-1.0,1.0));

m_colors.push_back(Color(1.0,1.0,1.0));//color for the top
m_colors.push_back(Color(1.0,0.0,1.0));
m_colors.push_back(Color(1.0,1.0,0.0));
m_colors.push_back(Color(0.0,1.0,1.0));
m_colors.push_back(Color(0.0,0.0,1.0));
m_colors.push_back(Color(1.0,0.0,1.0));
m_colors.push_back(Color(1.0,1.0,0.0));
m_colors.push_back(Color(0.0,1.0,1.0));
m_colors.push_back(Color(1.0,0.0,1.0));
m_colors.push_back(Color(0.0,0.0,1.0));

glGenBuffers(1, &m_vertexVBO);
glBindBuffer(GL_ARRAY_BUFFER, m_vertexVBO);
glBufferData(GL_ARRAY_BUFFER, sizeof(GLfloat) * m_vertices.size() * 3,
&m_vertices[0], GL_STATIC_DRAW);

glGenBuffers(1, &m_colorVBO);
glBindBuffer(GL_ARRAY_BUFFER, m_colorVBO);
glBufferData(GL_ARRAY_BUFFER, sizeof(GLfloat) * m_colors.size() * 3,
&m_colors[0], GL_STATIC_DRAW);
```

The pyramid can then be rendered using:

```
//Render the triangle fan for the outer hull of the pyramid
glDrawArrays(GL_TRIANGLE_FAN, 0, 6);
 //Render the bottom of the pyramid -> use the last 4 vertices
glDrawArrays(GL_TRIANGLE_STRIP, 6, 4);
```

Chapter 4
Review Questions

1. glPushMatrix()

2. glTranslatef(10.0f, 5.0f, 0.0f);

3. Any three out of Projection (GL_PROJECTION), Modelview (GL_MODELVIEW), Texture (GL_TEXTURE), and Color (GL_COLOR).

4. glScalef(0.5f, 0.5f, 0.5f);

5. glRotatef()

6. glLoadMatrix()

7. glPopMatrix()

On Your Own

1. Answers will vary. The pyramid rendering code from the last chapter's answer can be adapted for this one.

Chapter 5
Review Questions

1. glGetStringi() returns a list of supported extensions and the first argument should be GL_EXTENSIONS.

2. An ARB prefix means that the extension has been approved by the Architecture Review Board.

3. OpenGL 3.0.

4. To provide the latest cutting-edge functionality and to provide access to features supported by a driver, but not yet supported by the libraries shipped with the compiler.

On Your Own

1. Answers may vary. The following function retrieves the extensions and writes them to a file in OpenGL 3.0:

```
void writeOutExtensions(const string& filename)
{
    //Grab a pointer to the glGetStringi function
    PFNGLGETSTRINGIPROC glGetStringi = NULL;
    glGetStringi = (PFNGLGETSTRINGIPROC)wglGetProcAddress("glGetStringi");

    std::ofstream fileOut(filename.c_str()); //Create an output file
    GLint numExtensions = 0;
    glGetIntegerv(GL_NUM_EXTENSIONS, &numExtensions); //Get the extension
count
    for (int i = 0; i < numExtensions; ++i)
    {    //Print out each extension as a new line in the file
        fileOut << glGetStringi(GL_EXTENSIONS, i) << std::endl;
    }
    fileOut.close(); //Close the file
}
```

Chapter 6
Review Questions

1. The OpenGL Shading Language

2. A shader is a set of code that replaces a certain stage of the rendering pipeline. A shader could perform the logic for vertex processing, for example.

3. With the #version preprocessor directive (e.g., #version 130).

4. A variable that stores data passed from the application, which does not vary on a per-vertex basis.

5. Attributes are specified for each vertex, whereas uniforms can be specified across primitives.

6. `glAttachShader()`

7. `glLinkProgram()`

On Your Own

1. In the fragment shader, change the only line inside the `main()` function to:
`outColor = vec4(1.0, 0.0, 0.0, 1.0);`

Chapter 7
Review Questions

1. A texture object is a structure that holds the attributes related to a specific texture: the texture's state.

2. 128×128, 64×64, 32×32, 16×16, 8×8, 4×4, 2×2, 1×1

3. `GL_REPEAT`

On Your Own

1. Answers will vary.

```
GLuint textureObject;
glGenTextures(1, &textureObject);
glBindTexture(GL_TEXTURE_2D, textureObject);
gluBuild2DMipmaps(GL_TEXTURE_2D, GL_RGBA, 256, 256, GL_RGBA, GL_UNSIGNED_BYTE,
imageData);
```

Chapter 8
Review Questions

1. Light that has reflected from surfaces so much that the source of the light is no longer apparent.

2. Point lights have a position rather than a direction; point lights also apply distance attenuation.

3. Increases the size and intensity of the specular highlight.

On Your Own

1. Answers will vary.

2. Answers will vary.

Chapter 9
Review Questions

1. The discard keyword stops the processing of the current fragment; nothing will be rendered to the framebuffer.

2. Sphere mapping is only effective when viewed from a certain direction. Also, the sphere map usually has to be pre-created, and so will not reflect a dynamic scene.

3. glActiveTexture()

On Your Own

1. Answers will vary.

Chapter 10
Review Questions

1. a = mvp[3] + mvp[0];
   b = mvp[7] + mvp[4];
   c = mvp[11] + mvp[8];
   d = mvp[15] + mvp[12];

2. Divide all four components (a, b, c, and d) by the length of the normal.

3. ax + by + cz + d =0

On Your Own

1. This is a research task.

Chapter 11
Review Questions

1. Texture-mapped fonts suffer from aliasing artifacts and poor layout due to each character being rendered with the same width.

2. The FreeType library provides programmatic access to font information which can be loaded from various different font file types (e.g., TrueType fonts).

3. The font size is set by using the `FT_Set_Char_Size()` function.

On Your Own

1. Answers will vary.

2. Answers will vary.

Chapter 12
Review Questions

1. `glClear()`

2. The `glScissor()` defines a region of the screen that can be updated by rendering commands when scissor testing is enabled.

3. `glDepthMask(GL_FALSE);`

4. `glEnable(GL_STENCIL_TEST);`

On Your Own

1. Answers will vary.

Chapter 13
Review Questions

1. There are no review questions for this chapter.

On Your Own

1. Answers will vary.

2. Answers will vary.

3. Answers will vary.

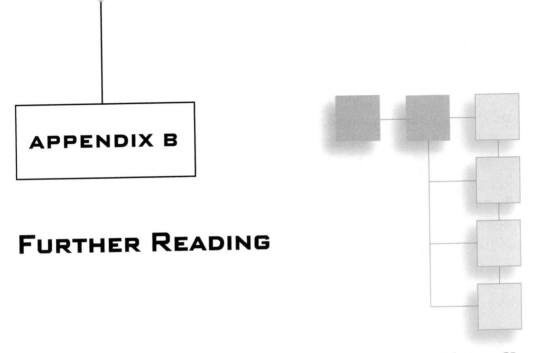

APPENDIX B

FURTHER READING

This book has covered a lot of information on computer graphics with OpenGL. But game development is a very complicated and diverse field so the more good resources you have at your disposal the faster and better a programmer you will be. This appendix provides a list of great websites and books that are worth taking a look at.

Online Resources
OpenGL and Game Development

GameDev.net

http://www.gamedev.net/ GameDev.net was co-founded by the original authors of this book. It is the leading online resource for game development. GameDev.net has an active community with forums and developer journals, thousands of articles, and up-to-date games industry news.

OpenGL

http://www.opengl.org/ The home of OpenGL. The site contains an active forum, regular OpenGL news, and, of course, all the specifications, header files, and extension information you need to develop your OpenGL applications.

Ultimate Game Programming

http://www.ultimategameprogramming.com/   Ultimate game programming is an excellent tutorial website with a large series of tutorials on OpenGL and also tutorials on C++ and DirectX programming.

Flipcode

http://www.flipcode.com/archives/   In its heyday, Flipcode was a large and popular game development site with many excellent articles and tutorials. Unfortunately, the website has been closed down now and no longer receives updates. However, the article archives still remain online and still contain some gems of knowledge.

NeHe

http://nehe.gamedev.net/   NeHe has long been a favorite site for OpenGL beginners. After being founded and selflessly maintained by the dedicated Jeff Molofee for several years, the site was acquired by GameDev.net and is now maintained by Luke Benstead and Carsten Haubold. It's now experiencing a long overdue revamp with new, OpenGL 3.0-based tutorials and regular news updates.

Ozone3D

http://www.ozone3d.net/   Ozone3D is home to an excellent set of GLSL tutorials covering GLSL 1.20.

Lighthouse3D

http://www.lighthouse3d.com/   Lighthouse3D contains a number of OpenGL tutorials on several subjects including GLSL, billboarding, and object selection.

C++ Programming

CPlusPlus.com

http://www.cplusplus.com/   The ultimate online C++ reference site. The site contains information on the standard C and C++ libraries and functions including information on STL containers and algorithms.

Boost.org

http://www.boost.org/ Once you are used to the standard C++ library, Boost should be your next port of call. Boost is a set of peer reviewed, portable libraries, which are designed to work well with the standard C++ libraries. Not only that, but the Boost libraries are the basis for most of the new features to be included in the next C++ standard.

Tools and Libraries

Code::Blocks

http://www.codeblocks.org/ Code::Blocks is a free, open-source IDE released under the GPL license. The Linux examples on the CD were compiled with this IDE and have associated project files.

Microsoft Visual C++ Express Edition

http://www.microsoft.com/express/vc/ Microsoft's free edition of the famous Visual C++ IDE and compiler is available at this URL. If you are developing for Windows, this is a must have.

SDL

http://www.libsdl.org/ As mentioned in the first chapter, SDL is a cross-platform, open-source library, which can simplify creating cross-platform applications with OpenGL. SDL takes care of window creation, event handling, threading, joystick input, and audio. This is definitely worth checking out if you want your applications to work on more than one platform. At the time of writing, SDL 1.2 is the current stable release, while SDL 1.3 is under development. SDL 1.3 will contain support for OpenGL 3.0 context creation.

FreeType

http://www.freetype.org/ FreeType has already been featured in the font chapter. You can always find the latest version on this website.

Books
C++ Programming
Effective C++ Third Edition
Scott Meyers, Addison-Wesley, 2005

Effective STL
Scott Meyers, Addison-Wesley, 2006

C++ Coding Standards
Herb Sutter and Andrei Alexandrescu, Addison-Wesley, 2005

OpenGL and 3D Math
More OpenGL Game Programming
Dave Astle, Thomson Course Technology PTR, 2006

Mathematics for 3D Game Programming & Computer Graphics
Eric Lengyel, Charles River Media, 2004

OpenGL Shading Language, Second Edition
Randi J. Rost, Addison Wesley, 2006

APPENDIX C

WHAT'S ON THE CD

The CD that accompanies this book includes many resources to be used along-side the text.

Source Code

Of course, the most important item on the CD is the source code! The CD contains two source folders: one for the up-to-date OpenGL 3.0 code, and another that contains OpenGL 2.1 versions of the same applications. Inside each of these folders, the applications are organized by chapter. When browsing the source code, take note of the following:

- Applications before Chapter 5 are identical for both versions of OpenGL.

- The differences between the two code versions are minor. The most common difference is the GLSL code, which is written in GLSL 1.20 for those cards that do not yet support GLSL 1.30. The only chapter in which the C++ source code is different is Chapter 5, which makes use of `glGetStringi()` for the OpenGL 3.0 version and `glGetString()` for the OpenGL 2.1 version.

- The Visual C++ project files are for Windows. The Code::Blocks project files are for Linux.

- The game in Chapter 13 will fall back to OpenGL 2.1 if OpenGL 3.0 is not supported.

GLee

The GLee OpenGL extension library is included on the CD. The version included supports OpenGL 3.0. The latest GLee can be found on Ben Woodhouse's website at: http://elf-stone.com/glee.php.

SDL 1.2

The current stable release of the SDL library is included on the CD. Although it does not include the ability to create an OpenGL 3.0 context (which is slated to be added in version 1.3), it is still a very powerful library for creating cross-platform games.

FreeType

The FreeType library is an amazingly powerful open-source font library. As you saw in Chapter 11, the ability to load fonts directly from the font file is really useful. The latest version of FreeType 2 is included on the CD. The latest Free-Type libraries can be found at http://www.freetype.org/.

Code::Blocks

The open-source Code::Blocks IDE is included on the CD with installers for the following operating systems:

- Windows (with the mingw compiler)
- Ubuntu Linux
- Mac OSX

The latest stable version of Code::Blocks at the time of writing is 8.02. For the latest version, see the Code::Blocks website at http://www.codeblocks.org/.

INDEX

You're a teen with a great imagination...

Written specifically for teens in a language you understand, on topics you're interested in! Each book in the *For Teens* series features step-by-step instructions to help you conquer the tools and techniques presented. Hands-on projects help you put your new skills into action. And the accompanying CD-ROM or web downloads provide tutorials, instructional videos, software programs, and more!

...unleash your creativity with the series!

Computer Programming for Teens
ISBN: 1-59863-446-1 • $29.99

Web Comics for Teens
ISBN: 1-59863-467-4 • $29.99

Game Programming for Teens
Third Edition
ISBN: 1-59863-518-2 • $29.99

Game Creation for Teens
ISBN: 1-59863-500-X • $29.99

Torque for Teens
ISBN: 1-59863-409-7 • $29.99

Web Design for Teens
ISBN: 1-59200-607-8 • $19.99

Microsoft Visual Basic
Game Programming for Teens
Second Edition
ISBN: 1-59863-390-2 • $29.99

Game Art for Teens
Second Edition
ISBN: 1-59200-959-X • $34.99

License Agreement/Notice of Limited Warranty

By opening the sealed disc container in this book, you agree to the following terms and conditions. If, upon reading the following license agreement and notice of limited warranty, you cannot agree to the terms and conditions set forth, return the unused book with unopened disc to the place where you purchased it for a refund.

License

The enclosed software is copyrighted by the copyright holder(s) indicated on the software disc. You are licensed to copy the software onto a single computer for use by a single user and to a backup disc. You may not reproduce, make copies, or distribute copies or rent or lease the software in whole or in part, except with written permission of the copyright holder(s). You may transfer the enclosed disc only together with this license, and only if you destroy all other copies of the software and the transferee agrees to the terms of the license. You may not decompile, reverse assemble, or reverse engineer the software.

Notice of Limited Warranty

The enclosed disc is warranted by Course Technology to be free of physical defects in materials and workmanship for a period of sixty (60) days from end user's purchase of the book/disc combination. During the sixty-day term of the limited warranty, Course Technology will provide a replacement disc upon the return of a defective disc.

Limited Liability

THE SOLE REMEDY FOR BREACH OF THIS LIMITED WARRANTY SHALL CONSIST ENTIRELY OF REPLACEMENT OF THE DEFECTIVE DISC. IN NO EVENT SHALL COURSE TECHNOLOGY OR THE AUTHOR BE LIABLE FOR ANY OTHER DAMAGES, INCLUDING LOSS OR CORRUPTION OF DATA, CHANGES IN THE FUNCTIONAL CHARACTERISTICS OF THE HARDWARE OR OPERATING SYSTEM, DELETERIOUS INTERACTION WITH OTHER SOFTWARE, OR ANY OTHER SPECIAL, INCIDENTAL, OR CONSEQUENTIAL DAMAGES THAT MAY ARISE, EVEN IF COURSE TECHNOLOGY AND/OR THE AUTHOR HAS PREVIOUSLY BEEN NOTIFIED THAT THE POSSIBILITY OF SUCH DAMAGES EXISTS.

Disclaimer of Warranties

COURSE TECHNOLOGY AND THE AUTHOR SPECIFICALLY DISCLAIM ANY AND ALL OTHER WARRANTIES, EITHER EXPRESS OR IMPLIED, INCLUDING WARRANTIES OF MERCHANTABILITY, SUITABILITY TO A PARTICULAR TASK OR PURPOSE, OR FREEDOM FROM ERRORS. SOME STATES DO NOT ALLOW FOR EXCLUSION OF IMPLIED WARRANTIES OR LIMITATION OF INCIDENTAL OR CONSEQUENTIAL DAMAGES, SO THESE LIMITATIONS MIGHT NOT APPLY TO YOU.

Other

This Agreement is governed by the laws of the State of Massachusetts without regard to choice of law principles. The United Convention of Contracts for the International Sale of Goods is specifically disclaimed. This Agreement constitutes the entire agreement between you and Course Technology regarding use of the software.